STUDIES IN THE EARLY HISTORY OF BRITAIN

General Editor: Nicholas Brooks

———

# The Mildrith Legend:
## A Study in Early Medieval Hagiography in England

D. W. ROLLASON

# The Mildrith Legend

*A Study in
Early Medieval Hagiography
in England*

LEICESTER

UNIVERSITY PRESS

1982

First published in 1982 by Leicester University Press
First published in 1982 in the United States of America
by Humanities Press, Inc., Atlantic Highlands, N.J. 07716
and also distributed by them in North America

*The publication of this book has been assisted
by a grant from the Twenty-Seven Foundation*

Designed by Douglas Martin
Set in 'Monophoto' Ehrhardt
Printed in Great Britain by BAS Printers Limited
Over Wallop, Hampshire
Bound by The Pitman Press, Bath

*British Library Cataloguing in Publication Data*
Rollason, D. W.
The Mildrith legend. —(Studies in the early history of Britain)
1. Mildred, *Saint*—Legends—History and criticism
I. Title    II. Series
398.2′2    BX4700.M/
ISBN 0-7185-1201-4

For Mum and Dad

# Contents

# *Illustrations*

# Abbreviations

*Note* Places of publication are given only for works published outside the United Kingdom. In abbreviating less frequently cited periodicals the commonly accepted usage of *Soc.* for Society, *J.* for *Journal*, *Trans.* for *Transactions* etc. has been followed. Other abbreviations are listed below.

| | |
|---|---|
| *AB* | *Analecta Bollandiana* |
| *Arch. Cant.* | *Archaeologia Cantiana* |
| *ASC* | *Two of the Saxon Chronicles Parallel*, ed. Charles Plummer and John Earle, revised Dorothy Whitelock (2 vols., 1952) |
| *ASE* | *Anglo-Saxon England* |
| *ASS* | *Acta Sanctorum*, ed. J. Bollandus, G. Henschenius et al. (Antwerp, Brussels, Tongerloo and Paris, 1643—) |
| BAR | British Archaeological Reports, British Series |
| *BHL* | *Bibliotheca Hagiographica Latina Antiquae et Mediae Aetatis*, ed. Society of Bollandists (2 vols., Brussels, 1898–1901) |
| BL | British Library |
| *CS* | *Cartularium Saxonicum*, ed. Walter de Gray Birch (3 vols., 1885–93) |
| *DHE* | *Die Heiligen Englands*, ed. Felix Liebermann (Hanover, 1889) |
| *DNB* | *Dictionary of National Biography* |
| *EH* | *Bede's Ecclesiastical History of the English People*, ed. and trans. B. Colgrave and R. A. B. Mynors (1969) |
| *EHR* | *English Historical Review* |
| *Fl. Wig.* | *Florentii Wigorniensis Monachi Chronicon ex Chronicis*, ed. B. Thorpe (2 vols., 1848–9) |
| *HP* | Marvin L. Colker, 'A hagiographic polemic', *Mediaeval Studies*, XXXIX (1977), 60–108 |
| *KCD* | *Codex Diplomaticus Aevi Saxonici*, ed. J. M. Kemble, (6 vols., 1839–48) |
| *Leechdoms* | *Leechdoms, Wortcunning and Starcraft of Early England*, ed. O. Cockayne (RS, 3 vols., 1864–6) |
| *NLA* | *Nova Legenda Anglie*, ed. C. Horstmann (2 vols., 1901) |
| *PL* | *Patrologiae Cursus Completus . . . Series (Latina) Prima*, ed. J. P. Migne (221 vols., Paris, 1844–64) |
| RS | Rolls Series |
| *SO* | *Symeonis Monachi Opera Omnia*, ed. T. Arnold (RS, 2 vols., 1882–5) |
| *TRHS* | *Transactions of the Royal Historical Society* |
| *TT* | *Textus translationis et institutionis monasterii beatae Mildrethae cum miraculorum attestatione* (*BHL* 5961 and 5964) |

# *Foreword*

The aim of the *Studies in the Early History of Britain* is to promote works of the highest scholarship which open up virgin fields of study or which surmount the barriers of traditional academic disciplines. As interest in the origins of our society and culture grows whilst scholarship yet becomes ever more specialized inter-disciplinary studies are needed more urgently, not only by scholars but also by students and by laymen. The series will therefore include research monographs, works of synthesis and also collaborative studies of important themes by several scholars whose training and expertise has lain in different fields. Our knowledge of the early Middle Ages will always be limited and frag-mentary, and progress will only be made if the work of the historian embraces that of the philologist, the archaeologist, the geographer, the numismatist, the art historian and the liturgicist – to name only the most obvious. The need to cross and to remove academic frontiers also explains the extension of the geographical range from that of the previous *Studies in Early English History* to include the whole island of Britain. The change would have been welcomed by the editor of the earlier series, the late Professor H. P. R. Finberg, whose pioneering work helped to inspire, or to provoke, the interest of a new generation of early medievalists in the relations of Britons and Saxons. The approach of the new series is therefore deliberately wide-ranging and will seek to avoid being unduly insular. Early medieval Britain can only be understood in the context of contemporary developments in Ireland and on the Continent.

Dr Rollason's pioneering study of the many texts concerned with St Mildrith, her cult and her background, reveals the sort of riches that have long lain untapped in the superficially difficult field of medieval hagiography. Paradoxically, by concentrating on a single hagiographical tradition, he has thrown light very widely on the religious, the social and the political development not only of Kent, but also of Essex, of East Anglia and of Mercia. At the heart of his work lies the meticulous study of the different versions of the legend, and it was therefore right to encourage him to publish here the most important versions that have hitherto been unprinted. In this way the reader can see the raw materials from which an exciting edifice has been built, and others may be encouraged to emulate Dr Rollason's approach so that hagiography is no longer a neglected field of British medieval studies.

Nicholas Brooks
University of St Andrews

# *Preface*

This book is based on my thesis of the same title, which the University of Birmingham accepted for the degree of Doctor of Philosophy in December 1978. I owe the idea of publishing that thesis as a book to the general editor of this series, Dr Nicholas Brooks, who also gave me much appreciated guidance and encouragement in executing the necessary revision.

My interest in the Mildrith Legend arose out of a general interest in considering the extent to which English medieval hagiographical writings can be utilized as historical sources. I was given the opportunity to pursue this interest as a research student at the University of Birmingham, where I worked under the enthusiastic and exacting supervision of Dr Wendy Davies. It was she who suggested that I should restrict my attention to a small group of hagiographical texts so that I might be better able to solve the purely textual problems typical of such sources before attempting more general interpretations. Her help and encouragement in carrying out this project and the example of scholarly rigour which she set were of inestimable value to me.

Of the many other past and present members of the University of Birmingham who helped and stimulated me, I should mention particularly Dr Patrick Sims-Williams, who guided me at the outset and was generous with his knowledge and expertise throughout; Professor R. H. C. Davis, whose support and criticism were always highly valued; and Professor Geoffrey Shepherd, whose patience and humour with my dogmatic views left me a wiser man.

I should like to thank the staff of the University Library, Birmingham, the Bodleian Library, Oxford, the British Library and Lambeth Palace Library, London, and the University Library, Durham, for their courtesy and assistance and for supplying microfilm and photographs of manuscripts in their care. For permission to publish the texts which appear in Appendices B and C, I am grateful to the Keepers of Western Manuscripts at the Bodleian Library and the British Library.

In the final stages of my work, Dr Michael Lapidge and Dr Michael Winterbottom did much to improve the quality of Appendices B and C; I am very grateful for their much-needed help, although I must emphasize that they are in no way responsible for any errors which remain. Mrs Mary Holcroft Veitch added greatly to the ease of my work by producing an immaculate typescript from my deplorably tatty manuscript and to her too I am very grateful.

My greatest debt, however, is to my family. My wife has contributed more to my work than she realizes – in inspiration, enthusiasm and fearless criticism. My father has been a stern guardian of my English style and has brought to the problems of medieval hagiography an understanding sharpened by a strenuous career in international telecommunications. My mother's support has never wavered; and her example of energetic determination has in large measure made it possible for me to write this book at all.

David Rollason
Department of History, University of Durham
December 1980

# Introduction

This book is a study of a group of texts, chiefly hagiographical in character, which concern the eighth-century abbess of Minster-in-Thanet, St Mildrith, and the Kentish, East Anglian and Midland saints related to her. Its purpose is to examine the extent to which such hagiographical texts were related to the political and social contexts in which they were written and read; and to explore the ways in which they can yield information about the attitudes of their authors and audience, not only to the supernatural but also to the everyday world in which they lived. Since such a study necessarily involves assumptions about the function, audience and characteristics of medieval hagiography, it is important to consider these briefly at the outset.

We should note first of all that hagiography was usually written in connection with the promotion and functioning of the cult of the saint or saints who formed its subject. In order to be successful, a shrine needed written accounts of its saint's holy life, posthumous miracles and, in some cases, the 'invention' of his or her relics and their translation to the church in which they were enshrined. Such accounts furnished material for Latin readings in the liturgy, for private devotional reading for the monks or clerics of the community, for sermons preached to pilgrims and visitors to the shrine and for the vernacular homily on the saint's life which often formed part of the mass.[1] Thus Alcuin remarked that his works on St Willibrord consisted of three texts, one in prose for reading in church, one in verse for private reading and one suitable for preaching to the people.[2] A shrine might therefore require: several versions of the saint's *vita*; a *translatio* describing how the church came to be in possession of the relics and how they were known to be genuinely those of the saint; a collection of *miracula* describing the wonders already worked through the agency of the relics; and one or more sets of *lectiones* drawn from the other texts and suitable in length for liturgical reading. The large number of surviving medieval texts of all these types is in itself an indication of the importance set on the cult of saints and on providing the literary apparatus to serve it. Devotion to the saint was intensified if people knew of the history of his or her life and relics. They wanted in particular to be reassured that the relics they were venerating were really what they were claimed to be, that they derived from a genuine saint and that they had a history of effective miracle-working. This was not restricted to the upper classes; for Gregory of Tours described how the shrine of St Patroclus was neglected by the people of the district because no passion of the martyr was extant.[3] For, he added, peasants venerate more devoutly those whose passions can be read.

The saint's shrine was not only highly articulate; it was also potentially very influential and by its nature it tended to attract a large and varied audience for the hagiography. For, in the Middle Ages, the relics of a saint often gave the church in which they lay an importance which extended beyond the walls of that church and deep into the surrounding society.[4] Their ecclesiastical guardians viewed them with pride and reverence. They were a source of prestige and revenue; and their presence was believed to ensure the saint's protection of the church and its interests. They were thought to possess thaumaturgic powers and all types of people from kings to peasants came to the shrine in search of miraculous cures for illnesses and physical or mental disabilities. Some shrines had wide spheres of influence while the catchment areas of others were more restricted.[5] A visit to a shrine was regarded as an act of piety in itself: King Robert the Pious, for example, felt it necessary to tour the shrines of southern France before his death.[6] Gatherings of pilgrims were especially great on the feast-day of the saint whose shrine it was and pilgrimages would be organized. It is difficult now to appreciate how great was the sheer religious attraction of a saint's relics for the laity as well as for the religious. Pilgrims to the shrine of St Foy at Conques, for example, were so numerous and so insistent that they could not be excluded from the church even at night and they interrupted the monastic offices with their 'rustic songs'. At Fleury-sur-Loire, saints' relics had to be set up under a marquee outside the church to allow women, who were not admitted to the church, to approach them.[7]

Pilgrimages to the shrine and attendance at its services were not the only ways in which the cult and legend of the saint impinged on people's lives. In some circumstances, the legend reached a still greater audience because the church encouraged wandering *jongleurs* to incorporate it into their songs.[8] And the saint's relics themselves acquired a wider importance through their use for judicial purposes in the trial by ordeal, in the manumission of slaves and as objects on which oaths were sworn – as, it was claimed, Harold Godwinson had sworn allegiance to William of Normandy on relics.[9] In addition, a saint's relics were frequently taken from the shrine and carried in procession through the surrounding towns and countryside; and they attracted veneration and were thought to work wonders wherever they went. Such processions were undertaken not only at certain ecclesiastical festivals, notably on Rogation-days, but also when they were thought necessary to counter some special peril or to solve some particular problem. To transfer the relics physically to the actual site of the difficulty or danger was conceived to be the most effective means of deploying their power. Once they were set down on church lands, for example, they acted as a powerful deterrent to any layman intending to claim the lands for himself. Carried through a disease-ridden area they could restore health; solemnly deposited at the meeting-place of a council they lent authority to the decisions.[10] In Anglo-Saxon England, the homilies of the Pseudo-Wulfstan advised the use of relics to ward off war, famine, pestilence and cattle-plague and to prevent harvest failure.[11] In each case the relics were to be carried among the people and in each case it was thought that they would influence the course of their lives.

In view of these observations about medieval shrines and the role of hagiography in connection with them, it is arguable that the audience for hagiography was more varied and the scope for disseminating ideas by means of hagiographical writing was greater than for any other type of medieval writing. Yet hagiographical texts appear at first glance to be unsatisfactory sources for the student of history. There are two reasons for this. Firstly, although some hagiographers, notably those writing shortly after the death of their subjects, were preoccupied with the circumstantial details of the saints' lives, many were either ignorant of these details or were not concerned to record them. Secondly, all hagiographers were to a greater or lesser extent concerned to present their subjects as the archetype of sanctity and as related to earlier saints who shared in turn the same powers and virtues as biblical heroes. Sanctity was conceived as a common essence, the workings of the Holy Spirit among men. Hagiographers therefore stressed those aspects of the lives and miracles of saints which were similar to the lives and miracles of earlier saints (from which indeed they often borrowed extensively) and ultimately to those described in the Bible.[12] For this reason Bede, for example, often chose to emphasize those miracle-stories concerning Anglo-Saxon saints which could be related to analogous stories told by Gregory the Great of the Italian fathers; for it was not the originality of English saints but their links with Christian sanctity in general which Bede wished to stress.[13] He described, for example, how St Cuthbert extinguished a phantom fire created by the devil and how in this the saint was imitating St Benedict of Nursia, to whom Gregory assigned a comparable miracle in the *Dialogues*. Bede also described how, on another occasion, Cuthbert diverted the spread of a real fire; and the writer was anxious to draw the parallel with a similar miracle performed by Marcellinus of Ancona, which Gregory had also described. For Bede, the point of Cuthbert's miracles was that they had been performed by his saintly predecessors and that 'thus in two miracles he imitated the miracles of two of the fathers'. Cuthbert's miracles were important to his account just because they were common to the achievements of 'perfect men who served God faithfully'.[14]

Constrained by this need to relate his subject to earlier saints, the hagiographer often produced a *vita* which was based on a conventional schema and dominated by commonplaces concerning, for example, the various stages of the saint's life and his or her consecration, virtuous practices, struggles with the devil, admonitory death-bed discourse and posthumous miracles.[15] The same tendency for commonplaces to predominate is evident also in other types of hagiographical writings such as the accounts of translations of saints' relics and the collections specifically of posthumous miracles. Common in the *translationes* are such literary motifs as the spirit of a dead saint inducing slumber in the guards to facilitate the translation of his or her relics, choosing a proposed resting-place by making the relics too heavy to move, the fragrance (often associated with the incorruptibility of the body) which arose from an opened saint's tomb and the miraculous means by which those who resisted a desired translation were thwarted.[16] The posthumous *miracula* are potentially more circumstantial in composition but they too are often heavily overlaid by literary form and their subjects are presented as the archetypal lepers, blind persons and sick children, who lend themselves to biblical reminiscence.

These features of medieval hagiography, however, should not blind us to the very considerable scope which the hagiographer had in his writing to express his own attitudes and to reflect those of his audience. In the first place, while presenting his saint as the type of sanctity, he was still at liberty to emphasize different aspects of that type. His work thus reflected his own and his audience's concept of sanctity – what sorts of person were most likely to be regarded as saints and in what ways their sanctity was manifested. The concept of sanctity was not uniform but varied from place to place and from period to period. The hero of Merovingian hagiography was often a bishop who, in a society dominated by bishops rather than by monks, was presented as fulfilling the active duties of a pastoral ecclesiastic while at the same time possessing also the ascetic virtues of the heroes of the Egyptian desert.[17] In Carolingian Aquitaine, on the other hand, the ideal of sanctity was predominantly monastic and even the minority of saints who were bishops, hermits or laymen were presented as aspiring to monastic virtues.[18] In the Low Countries in the tenth and eleventh centuries, it was again the monasteries which dominated the scene and monastic founders and monastic virtues were the predominant subject of the hagiography.[19] Cistercian hagiography of the diocese of Liège in the thirteenth century, to quote a final example, was characterized by an emphasis on the progress of mysticism in the lives of the saints.[20] Hagiography can thus provide evidence for changes in the priorities and attitudes of medieval people, which may be of wider significance.

Not only attitudes to sanctity found expression in hagiography; more mundane concerns also figured prominently. For example, the extent of its audience made the hagiographer's work an excellent vehicle for the propagation of materialistic claims advanced by the church in which the relics lay. Claims to lands allegedly alienated by laymen were a frequent preoccupation and their inclusion in the hagiography gave them an awesome solemnity and perpetuity. Embedded in the saint's *vita* and read regularly to the people in the solemn atmosphere of the church on the feast-day, the hagiographer's account of how the lands in question had originally been given to the saint under miraculous circumstances formed powerful propaganda against the offending layman.[21] The desire to defend his church's lands, and also in some cases the relics themselves, often involved the hagiographer in historical research and interpretation of the sources available to him; and his writing tended to lose its hagiographical character and to assume more of the nature of a local history. The *Historia de Sancto Cuthberto* is an example of this.[22] In these circumstances, the hagiography provides an insight into a community's attitude to its endowment.

The attitudes expressed in hagiography could be of wider implication, especially when the church which possessed the saint's relics occupied a politically influential position. Tenth-century German saints' lives sometimes exhibit strong political overtones and Ludwig Zoepf remarked that it is often difficult to decide where politics ends and edification begins.[23] Moreover, writers often introduced apparently extraneous material into their work, the inclusion of which may have been random, as Antonia Gransden is inclined to believe, or it may have

been motivated by deliberate purposes.[24] The eleventh-century sections
of the Miracles of St Benedict at Fleury-sur-Loire, for example, contain
many passages devoted to the history of the late Carolingian and early
Capetian kings, the latter being generally presented in a very favourable
light. Since Fleury occupied a position of great political importance in the
Capetian kingdom of France, it seems likely that the writers of the
Miracles inserted this historical material with the deliberate aim of
promoting the prestige of the Capetian kings.[25]

   For all these reasons, medieval hagiography must clearly be regarded
as potentially an important source for the study of mentality and attitudes
– of the hagiographer, of the community which possessed the saint's
relics and of the pilgrims to the shrine, who formed the outside audience
for the hagiography. It is this which chiefly justifies a close examination of
the hitherto relatively neglected texts of the Mildrith Legend.

# [1]

## The Content of the
## Mildrith Legend

The Mildrith Legend consists of a number of related accounts of
Kentish, East Anglian and Midland saints and royal persons. One of
these accounts is devoted to the life and sanctity of St Mildrith. The
legend is found in a number of versions which, although they have much
common ground, differ significantly in their contents.[1] In some versions,
Mildrith is the most prominent figure, in others she has much less
importance and from some she is completely absent. If, however, the
various elements from all the versions are assembled, they present
collectively a legend which deals first with the Kentish royal house,
beginning with the baptism of King Æthelberht I by St Augustine. It
then relates that Æthelberht's children by his Frankish queen, Bertha,
were Æthelburg and Eadbald and that the former went to Northumbria
with her chaplain, Paulinus, to be the queen of King Edwin. After the
latter's death, she returned to her brother Eadbald, then king of Kent.
According to some versions, she brought back treasures to the church of
Canterbury and Paulinus returned with her and was made bishop of
Rochester; other versions, however, do not mention this but describe
instead how she accepted land from Eadbald and founded a monastery at
Lyminge in Kent. Eadbald's queen, Ymme, was also a Frankish princess
and she bore him a daughter, Eanswith, who founded a monastery at
Folkestone in Kent, and two sons, Eorcenberht, his successor on the
throne, and Eormenred, on whose status the versions differ but who was
either a joint king or merely a prince. Eormenred's queen was called
Oslafa; she bore him two sons, Æthelred and Æthelberht, and seems to
have borne him three daughters, Eormengith, Domne Eafe and
Eormenburg.[2] Domne Eafe married King Merewalh of the Magonsætan
and gave birth to three daughters: St Mildrith herself, St Mildburg, the
foundress of Much Wenlock in Shropshire, and St Mildgith, who was
buried in Northumbria; and one son, Merefin, who died in childhood.
Domne Eafe and Merewalh later separated for religious reasons.

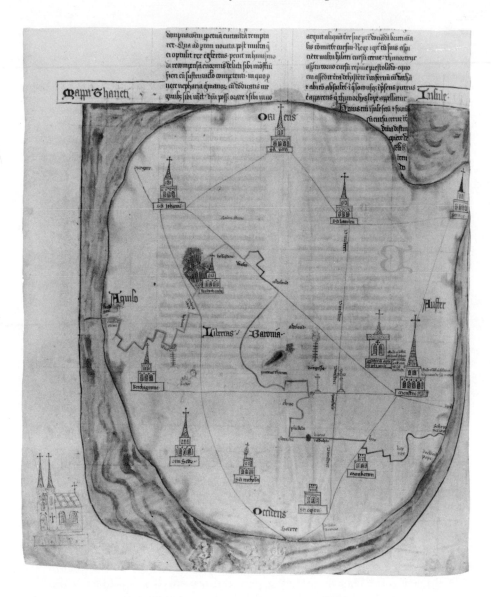

Cambridge, Trinity Hall MS 1, f.28b. This early fifteenth-century map of Thanet illustrates the course said to have been taken by Domne Eafe's hind when it designated the land to be granted to Minster-in-Thanet. The hind itself appears on the left side of the map; its course is represented by the line which twists and turns from where it stands at *Westgate* (Westgate-on-Sea) to *schrreves pope* (Sheriff's Court); and the two churches of Minster-in-Thanet appear on the right of the map, opposite the hind. (For further information on the map, see D. W. Rollason, 'The date of the parish-boundary of Minster-in-Thanet, Kent', *Archaeologia Cantiana*, XCV (1979), 7–17).

Meanwhile, Eorcenberht begot four children by his queen, Seaxburg: two sons, Egbert and Hlothhere, who succeeded to the throne in turn, and two daughters, Eormenhild and Eorcengota.

The legend then describes the killing of Eormenred's sons, Æthelred and Æthelberht. When their father died, they were entrusted to his brother, Eorcenberht, who was then king of Kent, but, on Eorcenberht's death, they became the responsibility of his son, Egbert, who had succeeded him. According to some versions, Egbert's servant, Thunor, persuaded his master that his princely cousins were a threat to his throne and should be done away with. According to other versions, Egbert himself took the initiative and ordered them to be assassinated. Thunor accordingly killed them and buried their bodies under the throne in the king's hall at Eastry in Kent, where a miraculous column of light revealed their whereabouts. According to some versions, this prompted Egbert to interrogate Thunor; according to others, the king spontaneously admitted his own guilt.

These killings were the prelude to the foundation of the abbey of Minster-in-Thanet. According to the most developed versions, Egbert assembled his councillors to discuss what action he should take. On their advice, he summoned Domne Eafe and offered her whatever compensation she might choose for the killing of her brothers. She chose to have as much land on the Isle of Thanet as her tame hind would run round in one circuit and accordingly accompanied the king and his court to the isle, which was at that time completely detached from the mainland. As they all followed the hind's course, Thunor, who resented the proposed grant to Domne Eafe, tried to dissuade the king from continuing the proceedings. He was at once swallowed by the earth and the site, covered with a pile of stones, came to be called *Thunores hleaw*, which means Thunor's mound. The hind then finished its course and, on the land thus designated, Domne Eafe founded the monastery of Minster-in-Thanet and became its abbess.

From the story of this foundation, the legend at last passes to Mildrith herself. Domne Eafe is said to have brought her to Minster-in-Thanet and then to have sent her abroad to the monastery of Chelles near Paris to receive a monastic education. The fullest versions describe how she was received there by an abbess called Wilcoma and how this abbess was related to a man of power and influence, whom she tried to persuade Mildrith to marry. When she refused, Wilcoma placed her in a heated oven but the intended victim was miraculously saved. When, in exasperation, Wilcoma beat her severely, Mildrith preserved some of her

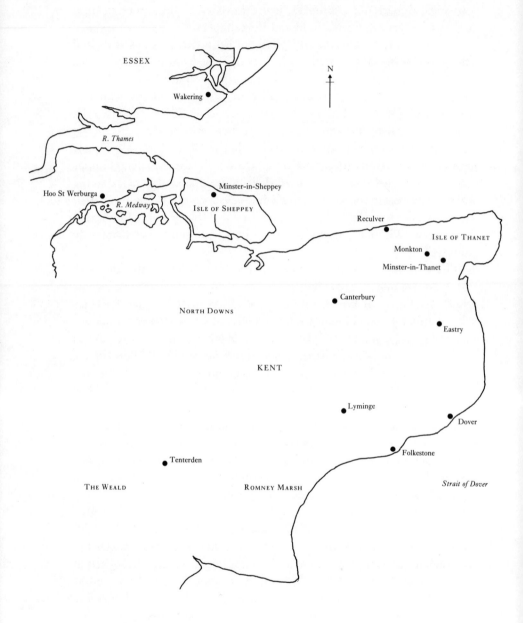

2. Places associated with the Mildrith Legend in South-East England.

own hair torn out in the course of this treatment, placed it in a psalter and sent it to her mother as a signal for help. Domne Eafe at once despatched rescuers who were forced to remove Mildrith from the monastery clandestinely. They succeeded in their mission despite Mildrith's insistence on returning to her cell in the face of great danger to recover some relics which she had inadvertently left there. The saint and her rescuers were hotly pursued and were able to escape only because the tide miraculously favoured them and their pursuers turned their own arms against themselves. The rescue party safely reached Thanet, where Mildrith's footprints as she disembarked were preserved on a rock which subsequently acquired healing powers. Mildrith was consecrated in company with 70 virgins and became the second abbess of Minster-in-Thanet. She was favoured with divine and angelic visitations and was eventually buried in the abbey church, which was dedicated to St Mary. After some years, her successor, Eadburg, found her body undecayed and translated it to a second church, which she had built, dedicated to SS Peter and Paul.

Some versions of the legend add further information about the kingdom of Kent. This concerns the apostasy of Eadbald, from which he was saved by Archbishop Laurentius whose proposed flight from Kent was thwarted by St Peter who visited and scourged him; the foundation of Minster-in-Sheppey by Seaxburg with assistance from her son, King Hlothhere; the career of King Eorcenberht's daughter, Eorcengota, at the Frankish monastery of Faremoûtier-en-Brie; the foundation of the monastery of St Martin's, Dover, by King Wihtred under the guidance of St Martin himself; the burial of Wihtred at St Augustine's Abbey; and, in the case of a version prefixed to the Worcester Chronicle, the succession of the Kentish kings down to the end of the kingdom.[3] Some versions provide further information about other Anglo-Saxon kingdoms. This concerns the daughters of King Anna of the East Angles – Æthelthryth who married two husbands but remained a virgin, Wihtburg and Seaxburg, the wife of King Eorcenberht of Kent; the marriage of Seaxburg's daughter, Eormenhild, to King Wulfhere of Mercia and the birth of their daughter, Werburg; and the daughters of King Penda of Mercia, Cyneburg and Cyneswith, and their relative, Tibba. A version of the legend in the prologue to the life of St Mildburg has a lengthy account of the conversion of Merewalh which presumably belongs to West Midland tradition. This version and another version in the prologue to the life of St Werburg are accompanied by narratives which belong to the hagiography of SS Mildburg and Werburg respectively rather than to the Mildrith Legend.[4]

The versions of the legend differ from each other in content, emphasis or both. In the texts in which they have been preserved, they also differ from each other in wording and, in some cases, in the language in which they are written. All the versions nevertheless seem to belong to a single literary tradition. This conclusion is based on two observations. Firstly, despite their overall differences, the texts of the various versions show, in many cases, verbal or stylistic resemblances to each other, some of which will be discussed in due course. Secondly, the broad outline of events and their sequence is more or less consistent in the various versions. Although they vary, as we have remarked, in the events which they describe and the emphasis which they place on them, it is notable that their narratives have actual discrepancies on only a handful of points, most of which have been noted in the account of the legend given above.

# [2]
## *The Diffusion of the*
## *Mildrith Legend*

The previous chapter considered the probability of the various versions of the Mildrith Legend being affiliated to a single literary tradition. The aim of the present chapter is to study those versions in detail in order to build up a picture of the diffusion of the legend in early medieval England. Only by investigating as far as possible the periods and locations in which versions of the legend were written, revised or read, can it be placed in context and exploited as a source for the study of medieval attitudes and mentality. This investigation is complicated by two factors. Firstly, the texts which embody the various versions have, in common with much English medieval hagiography, received little study; several have never even been printed. Secondly, the extant versions often show clear signs of having been based on earlier versions which are now lost. Their histories must be unravelled if the history of the legend's diffusion is to be fully understood.

### (a) The *Historia Regum* Text

The earliest version of which there is evidence no longer survives in its original form but it is represented by the *Passio sanctorum Ethelberti atque Ethelredi regiae stirpis puerorum*.[1] This text will be referred to as the *Historia Regum* Text because it now forms the first item of the *Historia Regum*, which is a miscellany of historical material covering the period up to the mid-twelfth century.[2] In origin, however, it must have been an independent text since, unlike every other section of the *Historia Regum*, it has a rubric of its own and since the compiler specifically notes that he is *inserting* this *vita et passionis triumphus* at the beginning of his history.[3] The text itself was written, as will be discussed later, at the abbey of Ramsey in Huntingdonshire in the late tenth or early eleventh century.[4] But it seems to have been based on an earlier version of the Mildrith

Legend, composed in the second quarter of the eighth century, for it describes the resting-place of Mildrith's body as being at Minster-in-Thanet in the church dedicated to the Virgin Mary.[5] Mildrith remained buried in that church for only the period between her death, which occurred after 732,[6] and her translation to the church of SS Peter and Paul, also at Minster-in-Thanet. This translation cannot have occurred later than 748, since the charter, *CS* 177, which refers to it, had certainly been written by that time.[7] This document also mentions that Abbess Eadburg, Mildrith's successor, built the church and effected the translation. The eleventh-century hagiographer Goscelin, who had access to the early records of Minster-in-Thanet, corroborated this account when he described in his *Vita Mildrethae* the construction of the new church and the translation of Mildrith's remains in more detail.[8] Further corroboration is afforded by those Old English texts which embody versions of the Mildrith Legend. While these do not specifically mention the two churches and their dedications, they do state that Eadburg 'raised the church in which her [Mildrith's] body now rests'.[9] Another feature of the *Historia Regum* Text which suggests that a version of earlier date lay behind it is the occurrence of *Easterige*, an early form of the place-name Eastry, which is similar to forms of the name found in early ninth-century charters but not in documents of later date, in which the medial *e* or *o* has disappeared, giving *Eastrige* or, in Domesday Book, simply *Estrei* or *Estre*.[10]

This earlier version seems to have been composed at a certain *monasterium Wacrinense* which is referred to by the *Historia Regum* Text and was apparently located at one or other of the adjacent villages of Great or Little Wakering in Essex.[11] Firstly, the *Historia Regum* Text is very complimentary to this otherwise virtually unknown religious house. It refers to the monastery as 'very famous'; and it describes how the relics of Æthelberht and Æthelred were translated thither in words which were clearly designed to increase the monastery's prestige. The decision to effect this translation is said to have been made 'by the very soundest counsel' and only after attempts to move the princes' relics firstly to Christ Church, Canterbury, and then to St Augustine's Abbey, Canterbury, had failed because they became too heavy to move, signifying that the martyrs were unwilling for their remains to rest in either of these abbeys. When they were finally translated to Wakering, they became light and easy to move and were enshrined before the high altar with great jubilation.[12] Secondly, this account of the translation is followed in the *Historia Regum* Text by a passage which is of special interest to Wakering. It describes how a sheep-stealer was miraculously struck dead there through the intercession of the martyred princes.[13]

It is not certain that this Wakering version was itself composed in the second quarter of the eighth century. It may have been written later than that and have been based on a version of eighth-century date which the Wakering community possessed but lacked the information to bring up to date. On the other hand, the *Historia Regum* Text asserts that the remains of the martyred princes were translated to Wakering soon after their murder in the late seventh century.[14] Two other sources afford some corroboration of this account since they mention that the relics in question were at Wakering by the tenth century. They are: first, the *Passio Beatorum Martyrum Ethelredi atque Ethelbricti* (*BHL* 2641–2) which contains a version of the Mildrith Legend and which will be referred to as the Bodley 285 Text because it is found only in Oxford, Bodleian Library, Bodley MS 285; and, second, the Ramsey Chronicle.[15] Since the Wakering villages are near the Essex coast, facing Kent, and since Eastry was probably accessible by sea in the early Middle Ages, the translation would have been an easy one to carry out by sea.[16] If it did take place in the late seventh century, it would have been natural for the Wakering community to have produced its own version of the Mildrith Legend for use in connection with the princes' cult soon after that. There is therefore a strong presumption that the Wakering version was itself composed in the second quarter of the eighth century. It may well have been based on a version which came from Kent with the princes' relics.

Those relics did not remain permanently at Wakering. According to the Bodley 285 Text, they were translated at some time in the period 978–92 to the abbey of Ramsey. The fact that this translation took place is confirmed by the Ramsey Chronicle and the *Secgan be þam Godes sanctum*, a list of saints' resting-places which gives Ramsey as that of the princes' relics.[17] Neither text gives a date but, since the *Secgan* had reached its present form by 1031, its information confirms to some extent the date given by the Bodley 285 Text.[18] It seems likely that the Wakering version of the Mildrith Legend came to Ramsey with the princes' relics. At any rate, it was at Ramsey that Byrhtferth, a writer active at that abbey in the late tenth and early eleventh centuries, wrote the *Historia Regum* Text, apparently founding it on that Wakering version.[19] A preoccupation with stylistic considerations was typical of medieval hagiographers; and Byrhtferth and his colleagues no doubt considered the Wakering version to be in need of re-writing in order to bring it into line with the literary fashion of their own age. Byrhtferth was a natural choice for such a task since he was skilled in the use of obscure vocabulary and convoluted phraseology, stylistic features which were much appreciated in late Anglo-Saxon England.[20]

The *Historia Regum* Text seems to have been incorporated into an earlier historical miscellany which was itself incorporated in the twelfth century into the *Historia Regum*. This miscellany was probably assembled shortly after Byrhtferth wrote the *Historia Regum* Text. The last date occurring in any of the texts of which it is composed is 975; and it is characterized throughout by a literary style similar to Byrhtferth's own.[21] It was probably compiled at Ramsey, not only because of the inclusion of Byrhtferth's work but also because some northern annals in a later section of the miscellany are closely akin to those found in the Ramsey *Computus* manuscript, Oxford, St John's College, MS 17.[22]

### (b) The Bodley 285 Text

The Ramsey monks seem, however, to have been dissatisfied with Byrhtferth's work, possibly because it contained no account of how the princes' relics had come to Ramsey. This deficiency was supplied by another version of the Mildrith Legend, represented by the Bodley 285 Text, which is sub-divided by rubrics into a *prologus* or *genealogia*, a *relatio* or *passio*, and what is in effect a *translatio*.[23] These three sections do not form a unified whole and are not all of the same provenance. The *translatio* awkwardly combines material concerning Wakering with accounts of the princes' translation to Ramsey, where it appears to have been written. The account of the translation displays precise knowledge of that monastery and lays emphasis on the quality of monastic observance there; and one of the accounts concerning Wakering is the miracle-story of the sheep-stealer's death in almost precisely the same words as in the *Historia Regum* Text, from which it was presumably culled. This too points to Ramsey since the *Historia Regum* Text, having been written at Ramsey, was in all probability available there for the writer of the *translatio* to use.[24] The *genealogia* and *passio* were clearly written independently of the *translatio* for they do not resemble it in style. Moreover, they are more coherent in composition and they have no direct link with the narrative of the *translatio* – the *passio* ends abruptly with the consecration of Mildrith and the *translatio* begins equally abruptly with the translation of the princes' relics to Ramsey. The *genealogia* and *passio* do resemble each other in style and their narratives are closely linked. In fact, they comprise a truncated version of the Mildrith Legend, taking it no further than Mildrith's consecration, whereas other texts of comparable fullness continue up to her death and Eadburg's succession as abbess.

It is important to emphasize that the *genealogia* and *passio* of the Bodley 285 Text are not based on the *Historia Regum* Text. They show no knowledge of the circumstances surrounding the princes' translation to Wakering, which is a special feature of the *Historia Regum* Text, nor do they reflect in any way the eulogies of the martyrs which are so characteristic of it. The *genealogia* and *passio* of the Bodley 285 Text also differ from the *Historia Regum* Text in their narrative of the murders: they assert, for example, that King Egbert's council merely advised him on what action to take after the discovery of the bodies, whereas the *Historia Regum* Text credits this council with having arranged the disinterment; and they give no reason for Egbert's awakening on the fatal night, whereas the *Historia Regum* Text attributes this to the cries of his household.[25] This leads to the conclusion that the Ramsey monks obtained a version of the Mildrith Legend which differed from the one they already possessed. They truncated this newly obtained version, producing the extant *genealogia* and *passio* of the Bodley 285 Text; and to this they added the *translatio* of their own.

One phrase in the *genealogia* of the Bodley 285 Text suggests strongly that the version thus treated was originally written in the middle years of the eleventh century at St Augustine's Abbey, Canterbury. The phrase in question gives a description of Mildrith's resting-place at that abbey as 'before the High Altar, between the *cancelli*'.[26] The significance of this lies in the fact that Mildrith's remains occupied that position for only a short period, namely from 1035 (immediately after she was translated to Canterbury from Minster-in-Thanet)[27] to the time of Abbot Wulfric (1047–59), who moved her relics into the north *porticus* in the course of his attempt to reconstruct the abbey church of St Augustine's.[28] In view of this, only a version composed at St Augustine's Abbey in that period is likely to have given so precise a description of what was in fact a temporary resting-place for Mildrith's remains. It would have been appropriate for such a version to have laid emphasis on Mildrith herself, given the presence of her relics at St Augustine's Abbey. This presumably explains why Mildrith is so prominent in the *passio* of the Bodley 285 Text, even though the Bodley 285 Text as a whole is meant to be devoted to the martyred princes. It is not clear exactly when this St Augustine's Abbey version reached Ramsey or exactly when it was modified there to form the Bodley 285 Text. All that can be said is that it arrived at Ramsey and received its modifications there between the mid-eleventh century, when it was composed, and the thirteenth century, when Bodley MS 285 was written.[29]


(c)  The *Vita Mildrethae*, the Latin *þa halgan* and *KCD* 900

For a considerable period from the late tenth century onwards, the abbey of Ramsey was an important centre for the study and propagation of the Mildrith Legend. It was surpassed, however, by Canterbury, which was, in the years following Mildrith's translation to the city in 1035, the scene of considerable literary activity connected with the legend. The earliest version of the legend produced there seems to have been that which, as has already been noted, was composed in the mid-eleventh century and is now represented by the *genealogia* and *passio* of the Bodley 285 Text. This version was succeeded in date by the most elaborate and longest of the Canterbury versions, the *Vita Deo dilectae virginis Mildrethae* (*BHL* 5960). In its earliest manuscripts, London, British Library, Cotton MS Otho A.viii, which dates from the eleventh century, and Cotton MS Vespasian B.xx, Harley MS 105 and Harley MS 3908, which date from the early twelfth century,[30] this text is followed by the *Textus translationis et institutionis monasterii beatae Mildrethae cum miraculorum attestatione*, an account of the history of Minster-in-Thanet after Mildrith's death, the translation of Mildrith's relics to St Augustine's Abbey and the miracles supposed to have been worked there by her intercession. It can be dated to the period 1087–91 since it does not refer to the translation of Mildrith's relics in 1091 to the chapel of the Holy Innocents in the then newly constructed abbey church, yet it mentions the death of Abbot Scotland which occurred in 1087.[31] The author of the *Textus translationis Mildrethae* specifically refers to his having composed the *Vita Mildrethae* also and it is likely that he executed both works at about the same time.[32] The writer in question was certainly the Flemish hagiographer, Goscelin, who was at that time a monk of St Augustine's Abbey. This attribution to him is based on a line of argument which is extended but conclusive. A contemporary note in the eleventh- or twelfth-century manuscript, Cambridge, Corpus Christi College, MS 312, attributes the *Historia maior sancti Augustini* (*BHL* 777) to Goscelin, and, at the end of this work, Goscelin expressed his intention of supplementing this biography of Augustine with a collection of posthumous miracles which were in fact written and are extant under the title, *Historia maior de miraculis sancti Augustini* (*BHL* 779). In this composition Goscelin alludes to the *Textus translationis Mildrethae* as his own work and thus claims also the *Vita Mildrethae*. [33]

St Augustine's Abbey was in addition responsible for producing two shorter versions of the Mildrith Legend. The first is preserved in a twelfth-century cartulary of the abbey, London, British Library, Cotton MS Vitellius A.ii. It consists of a Latin translation and adaptation of an Old English text of the Mildrith Legend, *Her cyð ymbe þa halgan þe on Angelcynne restað*;[34] and it was produced after 1035, since it mentions Mildrith's translation to Canterbury, but before 1091, since it locates King Wihtred's remains in the church of St Mary at St Augustine's Abbey, whence they were translated in that year to the crypt of Abbot Scotland's new abbey church.[35] The attribution of this version to St Augustine's Abbey is confirmed by its account of how Mildrith's relics were translated to that house by divine will and at the saint's own command 'as to a more worthy place, the mausoleum of St Augustine and his successors'.[36] The second of these shorter versions from St Augustine's Abbey is in the form of a charter, *KCD* 900, which gives a résumé of the Mildrith Legend's account of the killing of the princes and the foundation of Minster-in-Thanet. It purports to be the record of a confirmation by King Edward the Confessor of the rights of St Augustine's Abbey over Minster-in-Thanet. In fact, however, it is almost certainly a forgery which was made at St Augustine's Abbey in the late eleventh century.[37] It therefore belongs to the same period of interest in the legend at the abbey as do the *Vita Mildrethae* and the Latin *þa halgan*.

### (d) The Gotha Text

Interest in the Mildrith Legend in eleventh-century Canterbury was not limited to St Augustine's Abbey. According to Goscelin's *Libellus contra inanes sanctae virginis Mildrethae usurpatores*, the canons of St Gregory's Priory, which had been founded by Archbishop Lanfranc outside the walls of the city in 1084 and 1085, began to claim from about 1087 or 1088 onwards that their church possessed the relics of both St Mildrith and her successor, St Eadburg.[38] They believed that both these saints had been buried at Lyminge in Kent rather than at Minster-in-Thanet and that Archbishop Lanfranc had had their remains translated from there to St Gregory's Priory in 1085.[39] The monks of St Augustine's

Abbey were not concerned by the claim that St Eadburg's relics had come to St Gregory's Priory. They were, however, furious at the claim that St Mildrith's relics, of which they considered themselves the sole possessors, had also been obtained by that house. Goscelin's *Contra usurpatores* chronicled the controversy which ensued and to which it was itself a contribution. It appears that the canons of St Gregory's Priory wrote or commissioned two successive texts in support of their claim to possess the relics of St Mildrith and St Eadburg. The first of these, according to Goscelin, was characterized by the erroneous assertion that the Eadburg whose relics were claimed to be at St Gregory's Priory was not only Mildrith's successor but also a daughter of King Æthelberht I and thus her great-great-aunt.[40] The second text, by Goscelin's account, explained that St Mildrith and St Eadburg had come to be buried at Lyminge rather than at Minster-in-Thanet because the community of Minster-in-Thanet had fled to Lyminge to escape attacks by the Vikings.[41]

Goscelin's descriptions of these texts from St Gregory's Priory make it possible to conclude that both of them have been preserved in amalgamated form as the *Vita sanctorum Æthelredi et Æthelberti martirum et sanctarum virginum Miltrudis et Edburgis*. This text will be referred to as the Gotha Text because it is to be found in unabridged form only in Gotha, Forschungsbibliothek, MS I.81, fos. 185v–188v.[42] It contains both the claim that Eadburg was a daughter of Æthelberht I, which Goscelin attributed to the first of St Gregory's Priory's texts, and the claim that the community of Minster-in-Thanet fled to Lyminge, which, according to Goscelin, was found in the second of them. Moreover, Goscelin quoted lengthy passages from both of the texts in the course of rebutting their arguments and all these passages are found in the Gotha Text.[43] At what stage the two texts of St Gregory's Priory were amalgamated to form the Gotha Text is less clear. The amalgamation could have been carried out by the compiler of Gotha I.81, which is a collection of English saints' lives;[44] or it could have been done by the canons of St Gregory's Priory, who were still defending their claims in the early fifteenth century and so would have found it useful over a long period.[45]

In addition to expressing the claims of St Gregory's Priory to possess the relics of St Mildrith and St Eadburg, the Gotha Text is also a version of the Mildrith Legend, omitting the sections concerning the immediate descendants of King Æthelberht I, but including accounts of the murder of the princes, the foundation of Minster-in-Thanet, the career of Mildrith and the treatment of her relics by Eadburg. Although it is clear that this version must represent the one known at St Gregory's Priory, it is more difficult to determine from what source the canons of that house obtained it. For they are unlikely to have derived it from the other eleventh-century Canterbury versions of comparable fullness, namely those produced at St Augustine's Abbey and represented by the Bodley 285 Text and the *Vita Mildrethae*, because there are marked differences between these texts and the Gotha Text. Even if the Gotha Text's assertion that Eadburg was Mildrith's great-great-aunt is put down to confusion at St Gregory's Priory or at some other stage in the history of this version, many differences still remain. The Gotha Text spells the names of Mildrith and Eadburg, *Miltrudis* and *Eadburgis*; the Bodley 285 Text and the *Vita Mildrethae* spell them *Mildretha* and *Eadburga*. The Gotha Text places the blame for the killing of the princes squarely on King Egbert; the Bodley 285 Text and the *Vita Mildrethae* are equally emphatic that it was Thunor's. The Gotha Text gives the assessment of the land on Thanet granted to Domne Eafe as 80 units; the Bodley 285 Text gives it as 40, the *Vita Mildrethae* as 48. The Gotha Text identifies Domne Eafe with Eormenburg; in the Bodley 285 Text and the *Vita Mildrethae*, these are the names of different persons. Finally, the accounts of visions received by St Mildrith differ in detail in the Gotha Text and the *Vitae Mildrethae* (they are not found in the Bodley 285 Text, probably as a result of its having been truncated).[46] The Gotha Text does agree with the shorter St Augustine's Abbey version, the Latin *þa halgan*, on the question of the identity of Domne Eafe and Eormenburg; but apart from this it differs from it in the same ways as the longer versions do; and the Latin *þa halgan* lacks the accounts of visions received by Mildrith.[47] Similarly, the Gotha Text's attribution of blame primarily to Egbert is found in the St Augustine's Abbey charter, *KCD* 900. But, in view of its extreme brevity, the version in this document is unlikely to have provided the canons of St Gregory's Prory with a model for their version.

It must be emphasized that, with the exception of the spelling of the names of Mildrith and Eadburg, the assertion that Eadburg was a daughter of King Æthelberht I and the account of the flight of the community of Minster-in-Thanet to Lyminge, all the features of the Gotha Text are found in other versions of the Mildrith Legend, although, as has been noted, they mostly occur in different forms in the versions known at St Augustine's Abbey.[48] It seems therefore that the canons of St Gregory's Priory did not simply invent their version or even embroider a much briefer version. They obtained it from somewhere.

The most likely source would seem to be Lyminge. There is no reason to doubt that Archbishop Lanfranc translated relics of saints from Lyminge to St Gregory's Priory, a natural enough move since he had endowed the priory with the estates of Lyminge;[49] and a version of the Mildrith Legend may well have been given to St Gregory's Priory at the same time. It is true that there is no evidence that Mildrith's relics were ever at Lyminge so the assertion made by the canons of St Gregory's that they were among the relics translated by Lanfranc to their house is implausible. Two sources, CS 317 (dated to 804) and the Old English version of the Mildrith Legend, þa halgan, mention that St Eadburg's relics were at Lyminge but are silent about the alleged presence of Mildrith's relics there.[50] Their silence is probably fatal to the canons' claim to possess the relics of the latter saint although what they do say tends to support the canons' claim to possess Eadburg's relics. The presence of Eadburg's relics at Lyminge until 1085 makes it likely that the Lyminge community would have possessed a version of the Mildrith Legend for use in her cult. There is in addition evidence of literary activity having taken place at Lyminge in connection with the legend. The abbreviated version of the Gotha Text in Nova Legenda Anglie is followed by accounts of miracles, some of which seem to have pertained to Lyminge, before it ceased to be a religious house, and may well have been composed there.[51] One refers to the 'monastery of St Eadburg', presumably a reference to Lyminge, as if it still existed; another which describes how a priest took refuge from the Danes at St Eadburg's shrine, must also refer to the period before the destruction of the monastery at Lyminge. The foundation of that monastery is described in the Old English version of the legend, þa halgan, which suggests that Lyminge may also have been involved in producing some version of the legend.[52]

Although Lyminge was probably the immediate source of the version known at St Gregory's Priory, the ultimate source may well have been Minster-in-Thanet. The presence of the relics of an abbess of Minster-in-Thanet, Eadburg, at Lyminge suggests that there must at some time have been close contact between the two monasteries. The existence of such contact was also the essential proposition of the canons' account of how the community of Minster-in-Thanet had fled to Lyminge in the face of Viking attacks. This account contained inconsistencies which Goscelin was quick to point out; but in outline it seems to have been correct.[53] In the late eighth and early ninth centuries, one abbess, Selethryth, appears to have governed Minster-in-Thanet and Lyminge simultaneously. In his Textus translationis Mildrethae, Goscelin described her as abbess of Minster-in-Thanet in the time of King Cuthred (798–807), Archbishop Æthelheard (793–805) and Archbishop Wulfred (805–32).[54] In precisely the same period, she appeared as abbess of Lyminge in CS 317, a charter drawn up in 804. Another charter of 786 (CS 248) describes her as an abbess but does not specify the religious house or houses which she governed. It was, however, preserved at Christ Church, Canterbury, and so probably referred to Lyminge, the archive of which came into Christ Church's possession.[55] The same is true of the latest document to mention her as living, CS 1336, which was drawn up in 805. By 824, she was dead, for in that year CS 378 referred to her as such. Selethryth is a rare name so the possibility that two separate persons bearing it were contemporary abbesses of Minster-in-Thanet and Lyminge is remote.[56]

It cannot be established how Selethryth came to be abbess of both monasteries. Viking attacks, which were already affecting Kent at the beginning of the ninth century and may have begun to do so earlier,[57] could have led to the creation of this double office. Goscelin says that Selethryth did much to restore the monastery of Minster-in-Thanet which had presumably suffered in part at least from the depredations of the Vikings. Selethryth as abbess of Lyminge was equally preoccupied with Viking attacks: CS 317 records a grant made to her of land in Canterbury to serve as a refuge from the Vikings for her community.[58] Whatever the reason, the existence of close contact between the two houses provides a context for the diffusion of the Mildrith Legend from Minster-in-Thanet to Lyminge.

### (e) The *Vita Mildburgae*

So far we have been considering religious houses which produced or modified versions of the Mildrith Legend and which claimed to have acquired by way of translations the relics of saints figuring in that legend. Two other religious houses, Much Wenlock in Shropshire and Hanbury in Staffordshire, also produced or modified versions of the legend. They, however, claimed to be the original resting-places of saints figuring in it. Much Wenlock claimed to be the resting-place of Mildrith's sister, St Mildburg, and Hanbury claimed to be the resting-place of Mildrith's cousin, St Werburg. The version associated with Much Wenlock is contained in the prologue to the *Vita beatae ac Deo dilectae virginis Mildburgae* and is there associated with material concerning the conversion, deeds and burial of King Merewalh of the Magonsætan.[59] This text was obviously written in its present form at Much Wenlock, the monastery founded by St Mildburg, for its author refers to himself and his colleagues as *nobis eius (sc. Mildburgae) domesticis*.[60] It must have been composed after 963, since it refers to the sepulture of Cyneburg, Cyneswith and Tibba at Peterborough, whither they were translated in that year;[61] and before 1101, since it does not mention the 'invention' of Mildburg's relics at Much Wenlock in that year.[62] Within that period, it most probably belongs to the years after 1080 × 1081 when the house was refounded as a Cluniac priory. It had previously been undistinguished, although it escaped destruction by the Danes.[63]

### (f)  The *Vita Werburgae*

The version of the legend associated with Hanbury consists only of the genealogical sections of the Mildrith Legend and is incorporated in the prologue to the *Vita sanctae Werburgae virginis* (*BHL* 8855).[64] This states that Werburg was originally buried at Hanbury but that her remains were at Chester at the time of writing. A translation from Hanbury to Chester is also mentioned by the Old English text of the Mildrith Legend, *þa halgan*;[65] it must have taken place between 907, when the city of Chester, previously ruined, was reconstructed, and 958, in which year a community of St Werburg which almost certainly possessed the saint's relics was resident at Chester.[66] The present text must of course be later than the translation – indeed it must be later than 963 since it mentions the presence of the relics of Cyneswith, Cyneburg and Tibba at Peterborough, where they arrived in that year;[67] and it was probably written at Chester for use in connection with Werburg's cult there. Apart from this, the circumstances of its composition cannot be established.

It seems likely, however, that the present *vita* is a superficial adaptation of a more ancient Hanbury *vita*. The main evidence for this is a passage which is clearly intended to enhance the prestige of Hanbury by describing how the people of that monastery received divine aid in their successful attempt to secure Werburg's body from *Triccengeham*, the actual place of her death, despite the vigorous resistance of people there.[68] Moreover, the present *vita* not only offers no explanation of how Werburg's relics came to be at Chester; it also asserts that her body, which had remained at Hanbury in an incorrupt state, dissolved away of its own accord when the Danes came so that it should not fall into the hands of unbelievers.[69] Such an account of the dissolution of the saint's remains cannot have been a very satisfactory basis for the subsequent claim to possess the relics made at Chester; it is much more likely to have been composed at Hanbury before there was any question of a translation to Chester, but after the Danish invasions of the ninth century. The present *vita* thus provides evidence for the incorporation of a section of the Mildrith Legend into a *vita* of Werburg, composed at Hanbury in the late ninth or early tenth centuries.

## (g) The *Genealogia Regum Cantuariorum*

The versions examined so far have been associated to a greater or lesser extent with relics of saints figuring in the Mildrith Legend; so it seems likely that they were composed, revised or adapted to satisfy the needs of liturgical cults centred on those relics. Two important texts of the legend, however, are connected with centres which neither claimed to possess relics of Mildrith Legend saints nor, so far as is known, offered liturgical cults to them. These texts are the *Genealogia regum Cantuariorum*, associated with Worcester, and *Her cyð ymbe þa halgan þe on Angelcynne restað*, associated with Winchester.

The first of these is an account of the history of early Kent, beginning with the coming of Hengest and Horsa, and incorporating accounts of the descent of the Kentish royal family and the murder of the princes, which is part of the Mildrith Legend.[70] The text is one of a series of histories which deal in turn with Kent, East Anglia, Essex, Mercia, Northumbria and Wessex and which are found only amongst the miscellaneous material prefixed to the Worcester Chronicle in all its manuscripts.[71] In view of their close association with the Worcester Chronicle, these histories were almost certainly produced at Worcester, not earlier than 1100, since this is the date of the last event mentioned in them, and before the early-to-middle years of the twelfth century, when their oldest manuscript, Oxford, Corpus Christi College, MS 157, was written.[72] They have generally been regarded as contemporary with the chronicle and by the same author. But the date and authorship of the chronicle are themselves disputed by many authorities;[73] and the true relationship between the histories and the chronicle is open to doubt. All that can be said is that there was at Worcester by the mid-twelfth century a version of the Mildrith Legend which was the object of purely historical interest and was used in the compilation of the *Genealogia regum Cantuariorum*.

## (h)  *þa halgan*

*Her cyð ymbe þa halgan þe on Angelcynne restað* is a much fuller version of the Mildrith Legend than that contained in the *Genealogia regum Cantuariorum*.[74] It seems to have been written down in London, BL Stowe MS 944, the *Liber Vitae* of New Minster, Winchester, in or soon after 1031.[75] It may of course have been known in Winchester from an earlier date but there is no evidence of this. The version which it represents must have originated in Kent, since it uses the sulung, a distinctively Kentish unit of land-assessment, and before 974, in view of the respective contents of sections 21 and 25 of the printed text.[76] Section 25 gives the resting-place of Eormenhild as Ely and mentions that she rests there with her mother Seaxburg and her aunt Æthelthryth; but it makes no reference to Æthelthryth's sister Wihtburg whose remains were translated to Ely from East Dereham in 974.[77] Section 25 would hardly have failed to mention her presence at Ely had it been written after that translation. Section 21 on the other hand, which does mention that Wihtburg rests with her sister Æthelthryth at Ely, must therefore be a later interpolation in the original version.[78] A further indication of date is provided by Section 24 which mentions Werburg's translation from Hanbury to Chester. This suggests that the original version was compiled after this event, which occurred, as has been noted, in the period 907 to 958.[79] It is possible, however, that section 24 was altered to show Werburg's translation to Chester after the compilation of the version as a whole. This would have been an appropriate modification for the Winchester scribe who inserted *þa halgan* into Stowe 944 to have made. For it seems likely that Werburg's translation to Chester was connected with Æthelflaed's reconstruction of that town, which was itself an aspect of the consolidation of the power of Wessex and its allies in the northern Midlands.[80] If section 24 has been modified in this way, the compilation of the version of the Mildrith Legend represented by *þa halgan* can be dated no more precisely than to the period between the latest event mentioned in it, the death of King Wihtred in 725, and the translation of Wihtburg to Ely in 974.

## (i)  Hugh Candidus's Text

A Latin version of the Mildrith Legend similar but not identical to *þa halgan* was incorporated by the Peterborough writer, Hugh Candidus, into the chronicle which he wrote in the second half of the twelfth century.[81] Since it gives Werburg's resting-place as Chester, this version must in its present form have been composed after her translation to that town in the period 907 to 958.[82] Its presence at Peterborough may possibly have been associated with the translation to the abbey in 963 of the relics of St Cyneburg and St Cyneswith, daughters of King Penda, and their relative, St Tibba, all of whom are mentioned in it.[83] They are, however, mentioned only briefly and any such connection between their cult and this Peterborough version of the Mildrith Legend was forgotten by the time of Hugh Candidus. He treated it as a general guide to English saints and it may, at Peterborough, always have been regarded as such.[84]

(j) S. Mildryð
and
(k) The Lambeth Fragment

Two other versions of the Mildrith Legend, both in Old English, are extant. Neither is complete and for neither is there sufficient evidence for its date or provenance to be determined with any confidence. The versions in question are found respectively in London, British Library, Cotton MS Caligula A.xiv, fos. 121v–124v (entitled and hereafter referred to as S. Mildryð), and London, Lambeth Palace, MS 427, f.211 (hereafter referred to as the Lambeth Fragment).[85] The former recounts the Mildrith Legend up to the destruction of Thunor, at which point it breaks off in mid-sentence. The latter begins with Mildrith's posthumous miracles and Eadburg's succession as abbess; and it finishes with an account of Minster-in-Sheppey. Oswald Cockayne, who published these fragments, regarded them as parts of the same text; but there is no evidence for this and their script, although similar, is not identical. It is more justifiable to regard them as fragments of different texts. Cockayne was also wrong to regard f.210 of Caligula A.xiv as part of the same version of the Mildrith Legend. The Old English fragment on this leaf contains an account of an unnamed girl's consecration as a nun by her mother and her humility and piety; but it bears no relationship to any other version of the Mildrith Legend and the sense does not run on between it and either the Lambeth Fragment or S. Mildryð.

Of S. Mildryð, it can be said that it is written in a mid-eleventh century script; and it is headed with the date of Mildrith's feast, which suggests that it was used in a devotional context. It may have served as a homily since Ælfric's homily on St Martin appears on the back of the leaf. *S. Mildryð's* script appears to be similar to that which N. R. Ker assigns to Exeter, so the fragment may be evidence of interest in the Mildrith Legend in the West, possibly to be associated with the appearance of the feasts of Mildrith and other Mildrith Legend saints in a range of tenth- and eleventh-century kalendars from that part of the country.[86]

The Lambeth Fragment is written in a later eleventh-century Exeter script and preserved in a manuscript from Llanthony near Gloucester, so it probably fits into the same pattern, although there are no specific indications that it was used devotionally.[87] In its case, however, there is evidence that it, or something like it, was known at Ely; for it bears a close relationship to the Latin *Vita beatae Sexburgae reginae* (*BHL* 7693) which occupies fos. 108–20 of London, British Library, Cotton MS Caligula A.viii. Fos.59–191 of this manuscript were written in the twelfth century and belonged to Ely.[88] The *Vita Sexburgae* was no doubt written at Ely to promote the cult of Seaxburg, whose relics were enshrined there. It clearly belongs to the post-Conquest period; for, although the latest event mentioned is a Danish ravaging of Sheppey, presumably that which occurred in the ninth century, the author referred to Old English writings, which he cited as sources, as *ancient*.[89] There can be little doubt that the Old English text from which he drew his information about Minster-in-Sheppey was the version of the Mildrith Legend contained in the Lambeth Fragment. The accounts of Minster-in-Sheppey and St Seaxburg are very similar in the Lambeth Fragment and the *Vita Sexburgae*. The chief difference between them is that the Lambeth Fragment states that Seaxburg was regent on behalf of her son Hlothhere and subsequently bought from him the land on which Minster-in-Sheppey was founded, whereas the *Vita Sexburgae* describes the same incident but substitutes the name of Seaxburg's other son, Egbert, for that of Hlothhere.[90] Given the sequence of the Kentish kings in the late seventh century, the *Vita Sexburgae* is likely to have been correct in naming Egbert. Its author, if his source was the version contained in the Lambeth Fragment, may have had sufficient knowledge of his own to correct it in this respect.

When and where the versions of the Mildrith Legend represented by the two Old English fragments were originally composed remains obscure. It is tempting to regard the one embodied in the Lambeth Fragment as in origin a product of Minster-in-Sheppey. It includes many traditions about that monastery – how Seaxburg and her daughter became nuns at Milton in Kent, how Seaxburg founded Minster-in-Sheppey, how the Isle of Sheppey was dependent on Milton, and how Seaxburg endowed Minster-in-Sheppey and obtained a blessing for it from Rome. As to date, the Lambeth Fragment's version cannot be later than the second half of the eleventh century (to which date Lambeth 427 is assigned); and it must be later than the Viking invasions of the ninth century – otherwise the account of Seaxburg receiving an angelic prophecy concerning the ravages of a heathen people would have no point.[91] *S. Mildryð* probably antedates 1035 since it gives the resting-place of Mildrith's relics as Minster-in-Thanet rather than St Augustine's Abbey, Canterbury, to which monastery she was translated in that year.[92] The version may have been known in Canterbury since *S. Mildryð* is very similar, given the difference in their language, to the Bodley 285 Text, which embodies a version written at St Augustine's Abbey, Canterbury, after Mildrith's translation.[93] The texts differ in some details, notably the names of Eormenred's daughters and the size of the land-grant on Thanet, but the overall similarity of style and content is striking. *S. Mildryð*'s version is plainly related to the St Augustine's Abbey version. It may even represent a Minister-in-Thanet version which came to the abbey in company with Mildrith's relics in 1035. This suggestion cannot be substantiated, but it should be noted that it was not unknown for hagiographical texts to be preserved in the shrines of saints.[94]

# [3]
## The Genesis of the Mildrith Legend

There is, as was noted in the previous chapter, evidence that versions of the Mildrith Legend were widely written, revised, modified and presumably read in early medieval England and that, in view of the evidence with regard to the Wakering version, the legend was in existence in the second quarter of the eighth century.[1] There is, however, no direct evidence to show where and when the legend originated. Such evidence as we have is derived from the general form and content of the legend. Although it is circumstantial, it points very clearly to the conclusion that the legend originated in Kent. The legend's knowledge of the Kentish royal house is considerable and it gives details of its history which are otherwise unknown, such as the name of Eadbald's queen, Ymme, and the existence of his second son, Eormenred, and his wife and children, whom it names. The dynasties of other kingdoms are alluded to strictly in connection with the Kentish royal house. Thus Anna, king of the East Angles, is mentioned principally as the father of Seaxburg who married King Eorcenberht of Kent; King Merewalh of the Magonsætan is mentioned as the husband of Eormenred's daughter, Domne Eafe; and Wulfhere, king of the Mercians, as the husband of Eorcenberht's daughter, Eormenhild. Kentish monasteries also occupy a prominent place in the legend. The histories of Minster-in-Thanet and Minster-in-Sheppey are found in some detail, although neither house figures in other early sources. The references to the foundation of monasteries at Folkestone and Lyminge are likewise peculiar to the legend; and þa halgan gives an account of the foundation of St Martin's, Dover, which is otherwise unknown and which probably formed part of the general tradition of the legend since the *Genealogia regum Cantuariorum* alludes to it.[2] It describes how St Martin showed King Wihtred in a vision the site at Dover where the latter was to found the monastery. In the twelfth century, Gervase of Canterbury gave a quite different account of Dover priory's origins, involving a vision of St Martin which Wihtred received on the battlefield and which caused him to make the foundation.[3] The legend's version seems to represent an earlier tradition, unknown to Gervase. As for monasteries outside Kent, their appearances in the legend are always in connection with Kentish matters. Hanbury is mentioned as the resting-place of St Werburg, grand-daughter of King Eorcenberht of Kent, Much Wenlock as the resting-place of St Mildburg, grand-daughter of his brother Eormenred, and Ely as the resting-place of Seaxburg, his wife, and Eormenhild, his daughter. Although the career of the celebrated Æthelthryth and her resting-place at Ely is sometimes described in more detail, it is conceived in relation to the links between the Kentish and East Anglian royal families and in relation to Ely itself which became the mausoleum of the Kentish brides, Seaxburg and her daughter, Eormenhild. The tradition of Seaxburg's role as abbess of Ely is not mentioned although it is found in Bede's *Ecclesiastical History* and in the *Vita Sexburgae*.[4] Non-Kentish monasteries are generally treated in a more cursory fashion than their Kentish counterparts and no mention at all is made, for example, of Wihtburg's resting-place at East Dereham, although her eventual resting-place at Ely does form an interpolation in *þa halgan*.[5] In the case of Mildgith's resting-place, no monastery is named and the site is vaguely located 'in Northumbria'.

The evidence afforded by the content of the legend points in particular to Minster-in-Thanet as the centre principally involved in its development. The story of the foundation and first abbesses of Minster-in-Thanet forms a very important element in the legend, constituting in many versions the most developed section of the narrative. There is no doubt that that monastery was in existence in the late seventh century since its series of apparently authentic charters begins at that time. The earliest of these to have survived in complete form are *CS* 35, *CS* 40, *CS* 41 and *CS* 42.[6] All date from 690 or thereabouts and all record grants of land, some on Thanet and some on the mainland, to an abbess called *Æbba*, who must be identified with the Domne (i.e. Lady) Eafe, the first abbess of Minster-in-Thanet in the legend's account.[7] There seems once to have existed a still earlier charter recording a grant to this person, which was preserved only in a summarized form (*CS* 44) by the fifteenth-century historian, Thomas of Elmham, and which recorded a grant made to Domne Eafe by King Hlothhere, apparently in 678.[8] There is therefore no difficulty in regarding Minster-in-Thanet as the chief home of a legend which had evolved by the second quarter of the eighth century, by which time the Wakering version had been produced.

Indeed, there is no obstacle to regarding King Egbert as Minster-in-Thanet's founder and so accepting the broad historical outline, excluding the legendary details, of the legend. Whilst it is true that no charter of his for Minster-in-Thanet is extant, it should be emphasized that there are no surviving charters of any kind from his reign. The use of charters may not have been general then and indeed may have scarcely begun if it is correct to attribute the introduction of charters into England to Archbishop Theodore, who took office only five years before Egbert's death.[9] Any grant made by Egbert for Minster-in-Thanet's foundation may well have been oral; and the charters recording grants of land on Thanet to Minster in the later seventh century may represent additions to the original grant or confirmations of it.

The early charters of Minster-in-Thanet show that, from an early date in its history, it was a veritable focus of royal interest and generosity. As we have seen, *CS* 44 records a grant of land by King Hlothhere; *CS* 35, 40, 41 and 42 record similar grants by his successors, Oswine and Swæfheard; *CS* 86 and 96 record further grants made in the 690s by King Wihtred and *CS* 141 records a grant made in 724 by his son, Æthelberht. Finally, *CS* 846 records a grant made three years later by King Eadberht. Other early charters record royal grants of privileges for Minster: a general grant by King Wihtred (*CS* 88) and grants and confirmations of toll-remissions from King Eadberht (*CS* 189) and from the Mercian overlords of the Kentish kings, Æthelbald (*CS* 149, 150 and 177) and Offa (*CS* 188). This impressive series of charters suggests that Minster-in-Thanet was the object of a more extensive and more continuous series of early land-grants than any other early Kentish monastery not excepting St Augustine's Abbey, Canterbury. The vicissitudes of preservation of documents may of course have distorted the picture, but Minster-in-Thanet had no especially good opportunity to preserve its early charters and St Augustine's Abbey certainly had a less troubled history in the period of Danish attacks.[10] The Kentish kings and their Mercian overlords clearly regarded Minster-in-Thanet as a very important monastery indeed during the late seventh and much of the eighth centuries and their generosity and interest must have placed it in a good position to play a major role in the development and diffusion of the Mildrith Legend.

Minster-in-Thanet may also have been well equipped from a cultural and scholarly viewpoint. Boniface, the 'apostle of Germany', corresponded with an abbess called Eadburg who was active in the first half of the eighth century and may have been Mildrith's successor as abbess of

Minster-in-Thanet. Boniface's correspondent was clearly head of a very learned and literary house and had a pupil called Leobgytha who had learned 'poetical tradition' under Eadburg's directon. If it is correct to identify her with the Eadburg of Minster-in-Thanet, that house was evidently well able to produce texts of the Mildrith Legend in the early eighth century.[11]

In addition, Minster-in-Thanet was the resting-place of Mildrith's relics before their translation to Canterbury in 1035. It naturally formed the focus of her cult and had the greatest need of a written legend which devoted attention to her and her monastery's foundation. The translation of her relics to the church of SS Peter and Paul by her immediate successor probably marked the inception of her cult for, at that period, elevations and translations of bodies were often regarded as formal canonizations of those to whom those bodies had belonged.[12] This was especially so when the body in question exuded a sweet fragrance and more particularly when it was found undecayed: both these phenomena were observed, according to Goscelin's *Vita Mildrethae*, when Eadburg opened Mildrith's grave in order to translate her to the new church.[13] Mildrith was clearly an important saint for Minster-in-Thanet and her popularity had not faded when Abbot Ælfstan arrived to translate her relics to Canterbury and met such fierce resistance from the Thanet people.[14] Her popularity had apparently extended to secondary relics associated with her, such as a nail of the Cross which she is said to have brought back from Gaul, and a rock which, according to Goscelin, had preserved her footprints as she alighted from the ship on her return to Thanet and which had by his time become the object of a thaumaturgic cult and been enclosed in a chapel.[15] Interest in Mildrith's cult may also have spread to one of Minster-in-Thanet's appurtenances for there is a church dedicated to her at Tenterden, the name of which settlement means swine-pasture of the men of Thanet.[16] It evidently belonged to Minster-in-Thanet since it appears in the thirteenth-century *Black Book* of St Augustine's Abbey as part of the manor of Minster which that abbey held.[17] This abbey acquired the estates of Minster-in-Thanet at about the time of Mildrith's translation to Canterbury in 1035. Since it seems unlikely that the church of Tenterden should have been dedicated to Mildrith after both it and Minster had been acquired by St Augustine's Abbey and the direct link of dependence between them thus broken, the dedication was probably first made when Minster-in-Thanet was a flourishing and independent concern, for Tenterden was one of those pasture-estates in the Weald which were an essential part of the economy of agricultural centres located in eastern Kent.[18]

Although it may have been the primary centre of the legend's genesis, Minster-in-Thanet need not have been the only one. Minster-in-Sheppey probably contributed the traditions concerning its own history and that of its foundress, St Seaxburg, which are found in the Lambeth Fragment and *þa halgan*.[19] It may have played a more general role in the forming of the legend. Rather surprisingly, there is no indication that Canterbury played any part in the legend's development before Mildrith's translation to St Augustine's Abbey in 1035. With the exception of the *Genealogia regum Cantuariorum*, whose historically-minded compiler was probably responsible for adding the information about the foundation of St Augustine's Abbey to the legend,[20] none of the texts mentions the two Canterbury abbeys in connection with Æthelberht's piety. The *Historia Regum* Text denigrates them by implying that the martyred princes had no wish to rest in either of them.[21] St Augustine's Abbey appears in *þa halgan* in connection with Wihtred's burial in the south *porticus* of St Mary's Church, built as part of the abbey complex by King Eadbald. This relates, however, more to the odour of sanctity surrounding the Kentish dynasty than to the abbey's glorification; and the information about Eadbald need not even have been derived from a St Augustine's Abbey source since it is given by Bede.[22] The abbey is referred to in a complimentary fashion only in connection with Mildrith's translation there, as in the Latin *þa halgan*'s mention of this.[23] Of the other early Kentish monasteries, Reculver and Hoo do not feature in the legend. Dover and Folkestone make brief appearances, the former only in *þa halgan* and the *Genealogia regum Cantuariorum*.[24] Lyminge too is represented briefly and only in certain texts; but in this case, as has been noted, there probably was some literary activity there.[25]

The argument which has been advanced that the genesis of the Mildrith Legend occurred in seventh- or eighth-century Kent, chiefly at Minster-in-Thanet, would be seriously weakened if it could be shown that the legend contains anachronisms or other statements about the historical context of the narrative which would have seemed improbable to an audience of that period. This is not in fact the case and, where the legend's information about Kent can be checked against independent sources, it inspires confidence. Its account of the descent of the Kentish kings from Æthelberht through Eadbald to Eorcenberht is confirmed by Bede. Its assertion that Eorcenberht had a brother called Eormenred is not ruled out by the testimony of Bede or any other writer and the name is a plausible one for a scion of the Kentish royal house in view of its alliterative relationship to Eorcenberht and Eormenburg.[26] Eormenred's existence finds some confirmation in *CS* 40, a charter recording a grant (or a confirmation of an earlier grant) made by Oswine, king of Kent, for the benefit of Domne Eafe in c. 690, in which Eormenred is referred to as the former possessor of land on Thanet. This person may well be the legend's Eormenred, especially as his name is thus linked with the history of Minster-in-Thanet.[27] Most versions of the legend, including the *Historia Regum* Text assign no office to him, but *S. Mildryð* refers to him as a king. The *Genealogia regum Cantuariorum* describes him as a kinglet (*regulus*).[28] This too is plausible: he may well have shared the kingship with Eorcenberht as Hlothhere is known to have done with Eadric, and Wihtred with Æthelberht II. Indeed, Kent may have been divided into two sub-kingdoms for at least part of its history.[29] The bulk of the evidence for this comes from tenth-century charters and from entries in the Anglo-Saxon Chronicle s.a. 999 and 1009. A king called Sigiræd, however, describing himself as king of half of Kent (*rex dimidiae partis provinciae Cantuariorum*), appears in the late eighth-century charter *CS* 194; and the foundation of a second bishopric at Rochester in western Kent in 604 may indicate that the subdivision was as old as that.[30]

We have already seen that the legend's placing of the foundation of Minster-in-Thanet in the reign of Egbert is compatible with the early charters of that house. Those charters also endorse the sequence of early abbesses given by the legend, since they record grants first to Domne Eafe (*CS* 35, 40, 41, 42, 44, 86 and 96), then to Mildrith (*CS* 88, 141, 149, 150 and 846) and then to Eadburg (*CS* 177).[31] All the charters recording grants to Domne Eafe refer to her as Æbba or Eaba; there is no trace of the *domne* (*domina*) found in the texts of the legend. While the charters corroborate the legend's account, they are sufficiently different from it in this significant detail to make it unlikely that they are derived from it or it from them.

It is, however, much more difficult to find any corroboration for the legend's account of the killing of Eormenred's sons. The charter *KCD* 900, which records the killing, is an eleventh-century fabrication based on the Mildrith Legend itself; the entry in the Canterbury version of the Anglo-Saxon Chronicle s.a. 640, mentioning the killings, is an interpolation in red ink and was probably added in Canterbury as a result of resurgence in interest in Mildrith in that city in the eleventh century.[32] But a passage in William of Malmesbury's *De Gestis Regum* does seem to provide some independent corroboration. According to this, Egbert's misfortunes and Hlothhere's death were due to Egbert's responsibility for the killing of the princes and Hlothhere's derision of their status as martyrs.[33] This idea is not found in any of the texts of the Mildrith Legend; and it is evident that William was not at this point even referring to such a text since he remarked subsequently that Egbert granted part of Thanet to the princes' *mother*: all versions of the legend make Domne Eafe the princes' sister.[34] The late date of the compilation and the fact that William implies that he is drawing on rumour makes this evidence very difficult to evaluate. The story could either be an ancient tradition or an historical speculation made when interest in the Old English past was strong in the early twelfth century.

There is, however, one scrap of very indirect early evidence which may support the veracity of the Mildrith Legend's account of the killings. Bede states in connection with his assessment of the reign of King Æthelred of Mercia that in the year 676 that king devastated Kent in an especially savage manner 'without respect for religion or fear of God'. The incident seems to have been an isolated raid rather than part of any consistent campaign of Mercian aggression against Kent in some attempt to establish a hegemony over that kingdom.[35] Bede's emphasis on its especial ferocity might nevertheless suggest that it was not a mere booty-raid but had some more specific motive. According to the Mildrith Legend, Æthelred was related by marriage to the murdered princes since his brother Merewalh had married their sister Domne Eafe. This relationship between Domne Eafe's family and the Mercian royal house was specifically acknowledged in the next century when King Æthelbald of Mercia made a grant to Minster-in-Thanet 'for love of my blood-relationship to the venerable abbess Mildrith' (*CS* 177). Despite Egbert's propitiatory gesture in bestowing lands on Domne Eafe, Æthelred may have felt some further retribution on behalf of his family to be required and the 676 raid may have been the form it took.[36]

One difficulty does arise from the Mildrith Legend's account, namely the problem of Eormenred's daughters. The *Historia Regum* Text, the Gotha Text, *S. Mildryð* and the Old English and latin *þa halgan* assert that Domne Eafe, who was one of those daughters, had an alias, Eormenburg.[37] This seems to be incorrect. *CS* 99, an apparently authentic document of the late seventh century,[38] is attested by Æbba (the Latin form of Domne Eafe) and Eormenburg, who were presumably Eormenred's daughters. It is clear that they were separate persons. Such a confusion, however, could have arisen at an early date. Moreover, other versions of the legend, apart from the Lambeth Fragment which does not mention Domne Eafe, agree with *CS* 99 in presenting Domne Eafe and Eormenburg as separate persons.[39]

# [4]
# The Mildrith Legend and the
# Independent Kingdom of Kent

.The previous chapter showed that the context in which the Mildrith Legend originated was the independent kingdom of Kent in the seventh and eighth centuries. All versions of the legend seem to reflect a deep concern to demonstrate the prestige and sanctity of that kingdom's royal house from the time of its first Christian king, Æthelberht I; in fact this concern is one of the dominant factors in the legend.

No real hagiographies of St Mildrith seem to have been written until the eleventh-century Canterbury versions represented by the Gotha Text, the Bodley 285 Text and the *Vita Mildrethae*.[1] The earlier versions must have devoted much less attention to Mildrith; for the *Historia Regum* Text, while describing her career, pays no attention to her virtues and ascribes no miracles to her, although it does refer to her having received comfort directly from Christ and having been visited by an angel.[2] The references to her in the other extant versions are equally brief and give the impression that the legend's account of Mildrith before the eleventh century was, by hagiographical standards, very restrained. The explanation seems to be that the perspective of the legend, especially in its pre-eleventh-century phase, transcended Mildrith herself and embraced all the saints who were descended from King Æthelberht I or were linked to his line by marriage or other affinity. These numbered no less than 19 and the legend often reads like a spectacular celebration of the saintly virtue associated with the Kentish royal house. The legend carefully assigns to all these saints places in the family tree of the Kentish kings, explaining their relationships to persons who themselves had no claim to sanctity. This gives the legend a markedly genealogical character which, although not unique in medieval hagiographical texts, is especially striking in this case, showing that it must have been regarded by the legend's compilers as of especial importance. The writer who compiled the miscellany which included the *Historia Regum* Text was so impressed by that text's bearing on the Kentish royal house that he referred to it as a *genealogia regum Cantuariorum* and added an introductory paragraph consisting of a repetition of its genealogical material, together with the genealogy of Æthelberht I which he took, with acknowledgment, from Bede.[3] The reaction of the rubricator who labelled the first section of the Bodley 285 Text a *genealogia* was evidently similar;[4] and so was that of the Worcester writer who adapted a version of the legend to form his *Genealogia regum Cantuariorum*, expanding it to form a comprehensive account of the Kentish kings down to the end of their history and presenting it in conjunction with a genealogical table.[5]

Certain versions of the legend have sections so genealogical in tone as to sound very much as if the legend's compilers were actually drawing on written royal genealogies. This is most marked in the Old English texts, which have entries of which the following excerpt from *þa halgan* is typical:

> Ðonne waes Ecgbriht cyningc and Loðhere cyningc
> and sancta Eormenhild and sancta Ercengota – waeron
> Ercenbrihtes bearn and Sexburge, his cwene. Þonne waes
> sancte Eormenburge oðer nama Domne Eve; heo waes
> forgifen Merwale, Pendan sunu cynges; and þar hi
> begeaton sancte Mildburge and sancte Mildryþe and
> sancte Mildgiðe and sancte Merefynn.[6]

The *Historia Regum* Text contains comparable passages such as:

> Huic vero in regiminis sumministratione succedit
> filius Eadbaldus . . . de quo procreantur bini regalis
> stirpis filii, Eormenredus et Erconbyrhtus.[7]

Similar sections of genealogy are found in most of the Latin texts although these are heavily overlaid with hagiographical elaboration in the Bodley 285 Text, the *Vita Mildrethae* and the *Vita Mildburgae*. Two further examples may be taken from the *Vita Werburgae* and the version in Hugh Candidus's chronicle respectively:

> Eadbaldus quoque ex alterius regis Francorum filia
> Emma Eormredum atque Ergombertum principes sanctamque
> virginem Answytham . . . propagavit. Eormredo autem
> ex inclyta conjuge Oslava nati sunt Æthelredus,
> atque Æthelbrichtus . . . quatuor quoque sibi filiae . . .[8]

> Sancta vero Sexburga regina Erconbrihti construxit
> monasterium [sancte Marie] in Scepe ege eumque cum
> Lothero filio honorifice ditavit. Ipsaque sancta

Sexburga et sancta Etheldritha et beata Wihtburga
filie erant Anne regis Orientalium Anglorum. Desponsata
est vero beata Etheldritha Egfrido regi Northanhumbrorum . . .
Filia autem Sexburge Ermenilda desponsata erat Wlfero
regi, et ex eis nata est sancta Wereburga.[9]

Royal genealogies were being constructed in Kent at about the time of
the Mildrith Legend's inception. A Kentish genealogy embedded in the
*Historia Britonum* follows the royal family backwards in time from King
Egbert; and another in the so-called 'Anglian' collection starts from
Æthelberht II, the successor of Wihtred who is the last king mentioned in
*þa halgan*.[10] Genealogies such as these, however, seem unlikly to have
influenced the legend. They are terser and briefer than the legend's
genealogical sections. The first example has the form, *Aedilberht filius
Irminrici, cuius pater Octa*, and the second, *Æðelberht Uihtreding,
Uihtred Ecgberhting*. Moreover, they deal solely with the male line
whereas any genealogy underlying the Mildrith Legend must have taken
in many other members of the royal house. Although most surviving
Anglo-Saxon genealogies resemble the two Kentish examples, other
types of genealogy, more expansive in content and different in arrangement, did exist in pre-Conquest England.[11] The genealogy of King
Æthelwulf of Wessex, for example, contains an account of his ancestor
King Ine;[12] and the genealogy of King Edgar's sons in London, British
Library, Cotton MS Tiberius B.v, Part I, f.23r, also contains more
information than the terse genealogies cited above.[13] It cannot be proved
that expansive genealogies of this or some other type were available to the
Mildrith Legend's compilers; but it is possible. Léopold Genicot has
noted the general tendency for genealogies to become increasingly
discursive.[14] Such a process may already have been taking place in the
kingdom of Kent.

If the Mildrith Legend was based on genealogies which had developed
in this way, it represented an evolution in the purpose of genealogies.
Whereas Anglo-Saxon genealogies generally tended to emphasize the
connection of royal lines with pre-Christian warlords and pagan gods, the
legend's genealogical interest began with the Christian history of the
Kentish royal line and stressed its fecundity in saintly offspring. In the
legend, we may be seeing the Church's alternative to the conventional,
dangerously pagan, genealogy.

The legend's genealogical information is sufficiently detailed for us to
draw up the following table solely on the basis of its various versions:

It is at once apparent that the legend's picture of the saintly descendants of Æthelberht embraced not only the Kentish dynasty itself but also the dynasties of the East Angles, the Mercians and the Magonsætan, into which members of the Kentish royal family had married. The width of this perspective is emphasized by the legend's practice of specifying the resting-place of the remains of almost every saint mentioned. This is such a consistent practice in one Old English version of the legend, *þa halgan*, that it was apparently regarded as chiefly a resting-place list and had been combined by the early eleventh century with the *Secgan be þam godes sanctum*, a text which is purely and simply a list of saints' resting-places.[15] Like the saints themselves, the resting-places mentioned in the legend embrace Kent, where St Mildrith rested at Minster-in-Thanet, St Eanswith at Folkestone and SS Æthelburg and Eadburg at Lyminge; Mercia, where St Werburg rested at Hanbury and SS Cyneburg, Cyneswith and Tibba at Peterborough; the kingdom of the Magonsætan, where St Mildburg rested at Much Wenlock; Essex, where SS Æthelred and Æthelberht rested at Wakering; the kingdom of the East Angles, where SS Seaxburg, Æthelthryth, Eormenhild and, from 974, Wihtburg rested at Ely; and Northumbria, in which kingdom Mildgith's resting-place was said to lie.

All this not only redounded to the glory of Kentish royal sanctity; it also stressed the political influence of the Kentish kings in the seventh and eighth centuries. Bede confirms the marriage of Seaxburg to King Eorcenberht; he explains the connection between Kent and Northumbria in terms of Æthelburg's marriage to King Edwin, itself mentioned by some versions of the legend; and he states that King Æthelberht I's sister, Ricula, married a king of the East Saxons and that Æthelberht supervised that people's conversion, so establishing a liaison between the kingdoms which must have facilitated the removal of the princes' relics to Wakering.[16] The connection between Kent and Essex persisted at least into the late seventh century when King Swæfheard of Kent claimed to be the son of King Sebbi of Essex.[17] The marriage-alliances between the Kentish royal house and the royal houses of the Mercians and the Magonsætan are mentioned only in the legend itself; but the relationship with Mercia finds some confirmation in King Æthelbald of Mercia's reference in *CS* 177 to his consanguinity with Mildrith.

The Mildrith Legend is also concerned with the participation of the Kentish royal house in the foundation and endowment of abbeys, chiefly in Kent. Minster-in-Thanet's foundation-history figures most prominently, as we have noted, although it is accorded less importance in the

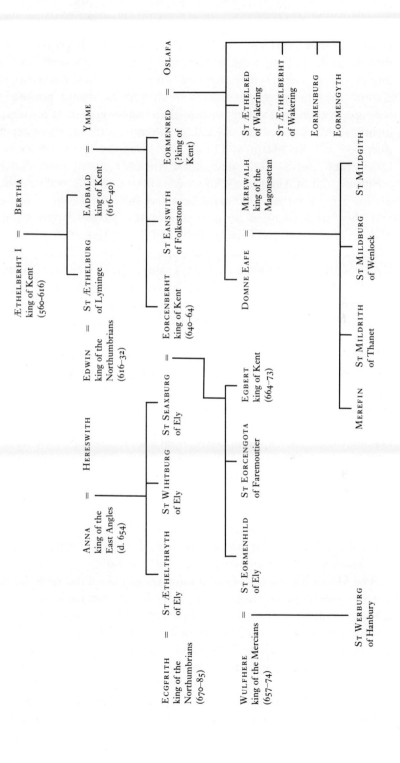

ÆTHELBERHT I = BERTHA
king of Kent
(560–616)

EADBALD = YMME
king of Kent
(616–40)

ST ÆTHELBURG
of Lyminge

EDWIN = ST ÆTHELBURG
king of the
Northumbrians
(616–32)

EORMENRED = OSLAFA
(?king of
Kent)

EORCENBERHT
king of Kent
(640–64)

ST EANSWITH
of Folkestone

MEREWALH = DOMNE EAFE
king of the
Magonsaetan

ST ÆTHELRED
of Wakering

ST ÆTHELBERHT
of Wakering

EORMENBURG

EORMENGYTH

ANNA = HERESWITH
king of the
East Angles
(d. 654)

ST WIHTBURG
of Ely

ST SEAXBURG
of Ely

EGBERT
king of Kent
(664–73)

ST EORCENGOTA
of Faremoutier

EGCFRITH = ST ÆTHELTHRYTH
king of the
Northumbrians
(670–85)

of Ely

WULFHERE = ST EORMENHILD
king of the Mercians
(657–74)

of Ely

ST WERBURG
of Hanbury

MEREFIN

ST MILDRITH
of Thanet

ST MILDBURG
of Wenlock

ST MILDGITH

*Historia Regum* Text and the *Vita Mildburgae* which do not link it directly to the killing of the princes, an incident which seems to have interested the compilers of these versions simply because it concerned the Kentish royal house and its sanctity.[18] Minster-in-Thanet, however, is only one of six Kentish abbeys which the various versions of the legend mention in varying degrees of detail.[19] The early histories of Minster-in-Sheppey and St Martin's, Dover, are given by some versions in considerable detail; Folkestone and Lyminge received more cursory mentions; and St Augustine's Abbey is mentioned briefly as the resting-place of King Wihtred. All these abbeys were alike in one respect, namely that they were founded by members of the Kentish royal family: Minster-in-Thanet by Domne Eafe and King Egbert; Minster-in-Sheppey by King Eorcenberht's queen, Seaxburg; Folkestone by Eanswith, daughter of King Eadbald; Lyminge by Æthelburg, daughter of King Æthelberht; St Martin's, Dover, by King Wihtred; and St Augustine's Abbey, Canterbury, by King Æthelberht.[20] Of the Kentish monasteries, in the foundation of which there had been royal participation, the legend omits Christ Church, Canterbury, which King Æthelberht I helped to found,[21] Reculver, which King Egbert endowed,[22] and Hoo, which appears in a list of royal monasteries in *CS* 91, a document fabricated in the early ninth century.[23] The history of Hoo is obscure. If it is correctly identified with the *Hogh* of the Peterborough foundation-charters, and if those charters are based on authentic material, it appears to have been founded by King Caedwalla of Wessex, presumably at the time of his intervention in Kent in 686–7, and to have been granted to Peterborough Abbey shortly afterwards.[24] This connection with a Mercian abbey may explain why its dedication, which is given by the *Textus Roffensis*, was to St Werburg, the Mercian princess.[25] Since Werburg was also a relative of Mildrith, that dedication raises the possibility that Hoo was connected with the Mildrith Legend even though it figures in none of the extant versions.

The Mildrith Legend's concern for royal Kentish abbeys emphasizes again its preoccupation with the prestige and sanctity of the Kentish royal house, a preoccupation which is naturally attributable to its origins in the royally founded abbey of Minster-in-Thanet and at other monasteries also of royal foundation. This milieu seems to have influenced the compilers of the legend in their choice of the saints to whom they gave prominence. The legend's saints are not only of royal blood; they are also predominantly the abbesses of royally founded monasteries. The only exceptions are St Augustine, who is included because he baptized King

Æthelberht, and SS Æthelberht and Æthelred. But the last two were relatively neglected by the legend, for only the *Historia Regum* Text mentions their resting-place at Wakering and treats them as genuinely saintly.[26] There is no indication that they were venerated in Kent, their relics having been enshrined in Essex. In Kent, it was princess-abbesses of royally founded abbeys who were regarded as the real saints.

The close relationship between the Kentish abbeys and the Kentish royal house has already been noted. The first abbesses of Minster-in-Thanet, Minster-in-Sheppey, Folkestone and Lyminge were royal princesses, as also was the second abbess of Minster-in-Thanet, Mildrith.[27] The relationship was long-lived. Surviving charters show many of those houses receiving grants from the Kentish kings and their Mercian overlords over a long period. Minster-in-Thanet's charters are amongst the most numerous.[28] Another group of extant charters record grants to Lyminge by the Kentish kings, Wihtred, Æthelberht II, Eadberht and Egbert II, and by King Coenwulf of Mercia.[29] St Augustine's Abbey preserved many apparently authentic charters from various Kentish kings from Hlothhere onwards, although the charters allegedly granted to it by Æthelberht I are eleventh-century forgeries.[30] Reculver is known to have received grants from the Kentish kings, Hlothhere, Eardwulf and Ealhmund.[31]

The abbeys may have been involved in some way with the royal governmental system of the kingdom of Kent and it was not unknown for Anglo-Saxon monasteries to fulfil political functions. Winchcombe, for example, served as an archive for one branch of the Mercian royal house.[32] In the case of the Kentish abbeys, the question hinges around the relationship between them and the units of royal administration known as *regiones* in documents from the independent kingdom and probably appearing in modified form as the lathes of Domesday Book. Centred on royal vills and supervised by royal reeves, the *regiones* served originally for the collection of the royal *feorm* or food-rent.[33] A comparison of their distribution with that of the royal Kentish monasteries suggests that connections between the two existed in at least some cases. Thanet was probably a *regio*, inhabited by a named group, the *Tenet-ware*, possessing a royal haven at Sarre and assessed at 80 sulungs, an assessment characteristic of the Kentish *regiones*.[34] If the Isle was a *regio*, Minster-in-Thanet may well have been its centre or at least have played some part in its administration. Another *regio* was probably that of Lyminge, which appears in modified form in Domesday Book as Limowart Lathe. The *-ge* ending of the place-name is significant since it means district or province.[35] Lyminge was the site of a royal council in 689 so it may itself have been the administrative centre of the *regio*; it is, however, possible that Lympne, site of the Roman shore-fort and meeting-place of the Kentish council, was the secular centre, Lyminge its ecclesiastical counterpart.[36] In either case, the monastery of Lyminge may have been important in the royal government of the *regio*. The monastery of Hoo may have stood at the centre of a *regio*, for a *regio* of Hoo appears in a charter of 738 (*CS* 159). Its people, the *Howara*, were apparently an important group, responsible for maintaining two piers of Rochester bridge.[37] It has been suggested that in the eleventh century it incorporated the hundreds of Rochester and Chatham and so had an assessment in Domesday Book of almost 80 sulungs.[38] Folkestone commanded an area assessed at 40 sulungs in Domesday Book and this too may have represented a *regio* which had been lost.[39]

The Mildrith Legend itself seems to reflect such a connection between the royal monasteries and the royal *regiones* since, although chiefly concerned with the former and their saints, it shows particular awareness of the postulated royal *regiones* of Eastry and Thanet. As for Eastry, the Mildrith Legend's account of the burial of the princes under the king's throne in the royal hall is the only evidence that Eastry was a royal vill. It confirms the evidence of the *ge* ending of the early form of the place-name, the ninth-century charter reference to a reeve of Eastry, and the appearance of the lathe of Eastry in Domesday Book, that Eastry was the centre of a *regio*.[40] The case of Thanet is more problematic. Those early versions of the Mildrith Legend which refer to the size of the grant of land there made to Domne Eafe give it as 80 sulungs.[41] This figure can have had no connection with Minster-in-Thanet's estates as these were claimed by St Augustine's Abbey in the eleventh century, for they were then assessed at 48 sulungs.[42] Eighty sulungs seems rather to have been the assessment of the whole isle. It was also a typical assessment of an early *regio*.[43] It is possible that the legend's compilers were aware of this and were hinting at a connection between that *regio* and the abbey of Minster-in-Thanet rather than referring literally to the latter's estates.

It is possible that some of the Kentish royal monasteries were important to the Kentish kings because they were responsible for the ecclesiastical and pastoral organization of wide areas in the period before the development of parish churches.[44] Dover, Folkestone, Lyminge and St Augustine's Abbey were certainly playing a modified form of this role in the eleventh century when they were listed as mother-churches – the first three in the *Domesday Monachorum* of Christ Church, Canterbury, and the fourth in the 'White Book' of St Augustine's Abbey, Canterbury.[45] Whether they and other royal monasteries had wide pastoral functions in the period of the independent kingdom is more difficult to say.[46] They may all have had the capability of acting in this way since even the nunneries are likely to have been double-monasteries, incorporating communities of clerics who could have undertaken pastoral duties.[47]

We have already seen how the legend was propagated through English kingdoms other than Kent, where it originated. Wakering in the kingdom of the East Saxons had the version underlying the *Historia Regum* Text. In the kingdom of the East Angles, a version of the legend similar to that of the Lambeth Fragment was available to later medieval writers at Ely and may have been there from an early date. Mercia had the *Vita Werburgae*, written at Hanbury. The kingdom of the Magonsætan had the *Vita Mildburgae*, produced at Much Wenlock.[48] We cannot be sure that these versions were known at the time of Kent's political influence over these kingdoms but it is tempting to believe that the dissemination of the legend was in fact a manifestation of that political influence; one might almost say the result of a campaign of political propaganda by Kent.

For all its preoccupation with the prestige, sanctity, generosity to the church and influence of the Kentish royal house, the Mildrith Legend was ambivalent. Royal monasteries may have been concerned with the affairs of kings, but they also owed allegiance to the church, whose interests did not always accord with those of the crown. This may explain the legend's emphasis on the killing of the princes, an episode hardly flattering to the royal house since King Egbert was clearly guilty whether he ordered the murders or merely failed to prevent his servant, Thunor, from carrying them out.[49] The church was in a position to coerce, if it wished, any of Egbert's successors who might be unco-operative with the story of his guilt, shown in sharp contrast to the sanctity of those for whose deaths he had been responsible.

The church may have had another interest in the affair, namely its desire to reduce the incidence of damaging feuds. In order to fulfil this, the church sought to encourage an injured kin to accept a *wergild*, or compensation, for the killing of one of its members rather than to pursue a feud against the killer and his kin.[50] This policy was vigorously pursued by Archbishop Theodore, who reduced the penance required for a homicide in cases where the killer had offered to pay a *wergild*;[51] and who settled a feud between King Ecgfrith of Northumbria and the Mercians by arranging for the latter to pay the king a *wergild* for the death of his brother, Ælfwine, in a battle between the Northumbrians and the Mercians in 679.[52] The Mildrith Legend seems to be in line with this policy; for most versions of it emphasize that King Egbert's grant of land on Thanet for the foundation of Minster-in-Thanet was a *wergild* in compensation for the killing of the princes. The Old English versions use the word *wergild* itself; and the Latin *þa halgan*, the Bodley 285 Text and the *Vita Mildrethae* render this *precium*.[53] *Wergilds* were normally assessed in shillings but there is no reason why they should not have been assessed and paid in hides or in sulungs.[54] The figure of 80 sulungs given by the earlier versions for the size of the land-grant on Thanet may have had a further significance here; for it may have been an appropriate figure for the *wergild* of two members of the highest class of early Anglo-Saxon society.[55] Two incidents in the *Liber Eliensis* suggest that 40 hides, which seem at some periods to have been equivalent to sulungs,[56] may have been the land associated with one such person. In the first of these, we hear how the brother of Wulfric, abbot of Ely (1044 × 5–66), was rejected as a suitor by the daughter of a 'very powerful man' because he did not possess 40 hides and so could not be numbered 'amongst the nobles' (*proceres*); in the second, we are told that Alderman Æthelstan of East Anglia had, according to his sons, exchanged his patrimony for an estate of 40 hides.[57] The source of these accounts is of twelfth-century date but it may embody earlier material. It raises the possiblity that the figure of 80 sulungs may have had a precise significance in the context of the murdered princes' *wergild*. There would of course have been no objection in an Anglo-Saxon audience's mind to Egbert having paid the *wergild* on Thunor's behalf; for the responsibility of a master to pay a *wergild* on behalf of his servant is laid down in the seventh-century Kentish laws of Hlothhere and Eadric.[58]

If the church wished to promote the payment of *wergilds*, it must have desired still more that those *wergilds* should take the form of lavish endowments to monasteries such as that made for the foundation of Minster-in-Thanet. The same notion seems to appear in Bede's account of the foundation of the monastery of Gilling in Northumbria, which occurred in similar circumstances. In that case, King Oswiu of Bernicia (641–70) founded the monastery after his servant had murdered King Oswine of Deira in 651. The foundation was made at the request of Eanfled, a relative of the victim, and the first abbot was another relative, Trumhere, who is said to have held that post because of his relationship to Oswine. Bede specifically says that Gilling's foundation was 'to atone for this crime' and, as Henry Mayr-Harting has noted, it was 'in effect an act of compensation in a blood-feud'.[59]

In the case of Minster-in-Thanet, a further element seems to have been introduced into the church's approach since the feud which Egbert's *wergild* was thought to have avoided was probably regarded as a feud with God – a feud such as that between God and Grendel which is referred to in *Beowulf*.[60] The Mildrith Legend stresses that the killing of the princes was carried out secretly and that Thunor attempted to conceal the bodies from human eyes – 'and he supposed that they never would reappear', as *S. Mildryð* puts it.[61] This would have struck an Anglo-Saxon audience as being a *morðweorc*, a killing done not openly but in secret and so beyond the protection of the kin and giving rise neither to feud nor to composition. But this killing was not kept secret from God, who revealed the princes' corpses by means of a miraculous column of divine light which stood over them; and it was of an offence offered to God that Egbert knew himself to have been guilty when he saw it. A monastic foundation, the legend seems to be saying, is a suitable *wergild* to avoid what must otherwise have been the most terrible of all feuds.

# [5]
## The Mildrith Legend in
## Tenth- and Eleventh-Century
## England

The Mildrith Legend's role as an instrument for the aggrandisement –
and criticism – of the royal house of King Æthelberht I and his
descendants must have been relatively transitory. That house, which
could trace its descent back to the founders of the Kentish kingdom, came
to an end in or soon after 762. Kings who were apparently unrelated to it
then began to reign in Kent, but their power was short-lived. During the
late eighth century, the kingdom of Kent fell under the dominance of
King Offa of Mercia. In 825, even the nominal independence which it
enjoyed under Mercian overlordship was lost when King Egbert of
Wessex expelled Baldred, the last occupant of the Kentish throne, and
absorbed Kent into his own kingdom.[1] The royal abbeys of Kent seem to
have declined sharply in importance from about that time onwards,
probably as a result of Viking attacks. Leofruna, said to have been the last
abbess of Minster-in-Thanet, was captured in Canterbury by the Danes
in 1011,[2] and her church had been reduced to parochial status by the time
of Mildrith's translation to Canterbury in 1035.[3] Reculver was granted to
Christ Church, Canterbury, in 949 (*CS* 880). Hoo does not appear again
after being mentioned in *CS* 91, a document fabricated in the early ninth
century;[4] Folkestone, Dover and Lyminge are not heard of after being
mentioned in a document of 844 (*CS* 445). Although some form of
regular life may have continued at some or all of these places, they lost the
importance which they had possessed in the time of the Kentish
kingdom. Only the Canterbury abbeys of Christ Church and St
Augustine's maintained and improved their positions.[5] The territorial
organization which had been established by the Kentish kings must also
have been terminated or greatly modified soon after the demise of the
kingdom; the administrative functions of the royal *regiones* were then
taken over by the West Saxon hundreds.[6]

The ending of Kent's independence, royal house and ecclesiastical and administrative organization did not destroy the appeal of the Mildrith Legend and it continued to attract interest, as the surviving versions of it show. One reason for this was that it projected attitudes to the Kentish royal house which were equally applicable in other contexts. The legend's account of the killing of the princes carried wider implications for the murders of royal persons in general, especially as the church came to express its condemnation of such crimes in very strong terms. The legatine councils held in England in 786 promulgated a canon declaring that a king was the 'Lord's anointed' and that those who murdered such a one and those who merely consented to this crime were to be consigned to eternal anathema, associated with Judas Iscariot and burned hereafter in the eternal fires.[7] The murder of princes was not specifically condemned; but the legates laid down in the same canon that kings should be legitimately conceived and the implication must have been that princes of the blood, although not yet anointed, were in effect potential kings, whose murder should be regarded with comparable horror.

This canon no doubt represents an ecclesiastical attitude which had existed for some time and may have been formed already at the time of the killing of Æthelberht and Æthelred in the seventh century. It is, however, the clearest statement of the attitude known in an English context; and its publication may have encouraged continued interest in the Mildrith Legend's account of the princes' deaths. This canon may indeed have paved the way for the revival of their cult which was to follow the translation of their relics from Wakering to Ramsey at some time in the period 978–92 and of which the *Historia Regum* Text was the literary expression. After the two legatine councils of 786, the church seems to have intensified its campaign against murders of kings and princes by encouraging interest in and veneration of the victims of such murders as a practical means of pressing home its condemnation of crimes of this sort. Although the history of the cults of murdered kings and princes is obscure, there are signs that they may have been especially numerous in the period after the 786 councils. According to the early annals in the *Historia Regum*, King Ælfwald of Northumbria, who was present at one of these councils, was himself venerated as a saint after his murder in 798.[8] The same source hints that King Eardwulf of Northumbria was considered to be saintly as a result of his having been miraculously revived after his execution in 790 (Alcuin's letters tend to confirm the existence of this belief).[9] The annals also recount the murder in 800 of the Northumbrian prince Ealhmund, whose cult at Derby in Mercia is known from other sources.[10] Mercia was equally prolific in such saints in the late eighth and the ninth centuries. The killing of King Æthelberht of the East Angles at Hereford in 794 resulted in his veneration as a saint.[11] Although his cult is not actually attested until the mid-eleventh century, it may possibly have developed in an earlier period. The cult of Kenelm, said to have been a Mercian child-king murdered on his sister's orders in 821, grew up at Winchcombe in Gloucestershire: it is not attested until the late tenth century[12] but it too may possibly have developed earlier. St Wigstan was said to have been the grandson of King Wiglaf of Mercia and to have been murdered in 849 and 850; in his case there is positive evidence to show that his cult was practised in the ninth century at Repton in Leicestershire.[13]

This tradition of murdered royal saints was very much alive in and around the late tenth century, when the Kentish princes were translated to Ramsey. The cult of Kenelm was flourishing at Winchcombe, a house connected with Ramsey through common interest in the tenth-century movement for monastic reform;[14] and the cult of Wigstan was revived in King Cnut's reign when the saint's relics were translated from Repton to Evesham, another house revitalized by the monastic reformers.[15] Most important of all was the cult of King Edward the Martyr, who was murdered in 978 or 979 by the retainers of his half-brother, Æthelred, who consequently became king.[16] If it is true that a law ordering the observance of Edward's feast throughout England belongs to the reign of Cnut, Edward's cult probably reached its zenith at that time.[17] But he was already widely venerated as a saint in King Æthelred's reign: the *Vita Oswaldi*, written at Ramsey between 995 and 1005, contains a description of his murder and treats him as a saint;[18] his extant *passio*, although written in its present form in the late eleventh century, is probably based on a text composed before 1001;[19] and King Æthelred himself referred to Edward as a saint and mentioned his miracles in a charter of 1001 (*KCD* 706) recording a grant of land at Bradford-on-Avon to Shaftesbury Abbey for the construction of a refuge for Edward's relics.

The Mildrith Legend's account of the murder of Æthelberht and Æthelred clearly had a particular connotation in an age preoccupied with royal murders. It may also have had a specific relevance to the cult of Edward the Martyr. The earliest account of the latter's death, given by the *Vita Oswaldi*, was written at Ramsey itself, probably by Byrhtferth who also wrote the *Historia Regum* Text.[20] It suggests clear parallels between Edward's killing and that of the princes. Both were carried out by the agents of those who stood to gain most by their deaths. Moreover, both the Mildrith Legend and the *Vita Oswaldi* emphasized the notion of *wergilds* payable to avert a feud waged by God to avenge the killings. In the case of the princes, the Mildrith Legend seems to have represented Egbert as appeasing God by endowing Minster-in-Thanet as a *wergild*.[21] In the case of Edward, the *Vita Oswaldi* describes how Ealdorman Ælfhere of Mercia, whom the writer apparently regarded as implicated in Edward's murder, translated Edward's remains with great honour to Shaftesbury, and presents this as, in D. J. V. Fisher's words, 'an attempt at expiation by the guilty party' – a form of *wergild*. It was, however, insufficient. God had not forgotten or overlooked the killing, as the guilty ones had hoped, continues the *Vita Oswaldi*, but demanded the blood of the killers for the blood of his soldier, Edward. One of the killers went blind as a result of God's feud and the others were deprived of the possibility of penitence and thus of the hope of escaping being consigned to hell after their deaths.[22] The revival of the Kentish princes' cult and of the Mildrith Legend may therefore have carried a pointed message to the effect that no adequate atonement had been made for Edward's killing and contrasting this with the munificent *wergild* paid by Egbert in expiation of the killing of Æthelberht and Æthelred.

Propaganda of this sort need not have been the work of the church alone. Enemies of the killers or of the interests they represented also had much to gain from promoting the royal victim's cults, thus highlighting the guilt of the killers, discrediting those who were implicated with them and damaging the reputation of their families. Such may have been King Cnut's motive, if he was indeed involved in promoting the cult of Edward, whose murder had allowed Æthelred to come to the throne. The cult and its attendant legend must have damaged the reputation of Æthelred, whom Cnut had overthrown by conquest and whose exiled sons represented a possible future threat to Cnut's hold on England.[23]

During Æthelred's lifetime, Edward's cult may have had other political significance in the context of the opposition between Æthelwine, ealdorman of East Anglia, and Ælfhere, ealdorman of Mercia. The reason for Æthelwine's opposition to Ælfhere was ostensibly that Æthelwine was supporting monasticism whereas Ælfhere was actively opposing it; but this religious conflict probably concealed a political divergence.[24] There is no evidence that Æthelwine directly promoted Edward's cult, but he seems to have been closely involved with the translation to Ramsey of the relics of Æthelred and Æthelberht.

Ramsey was his own foundation; he was lord of Wakering where the princes' relics lay; and it is he who was said to have given permission for the translation.[25] By encouraging this translation and thus fostering interest in the Mildrith Legend, he may have intended to keep alive interest in Edward's death and to evoke again the guilt of his killers. More specifically his action could be regarded as an attack on Ælfhere, who died only in 983 and so may have been alive at the time of the translation.[26] The contrast between the generosity of King Egbert, who paid so munificent a *wergild*, and Ealdorman Ælfhere, who was so parsimonious in his atonement and merely translated Edward's relics, was no doubt particularly significant to Æthelwine, who claimed to be a patron of monasticism and would therefore have applauded the form as well as the scale of Egbert's payment. The form of the implied attack on Ælfhere would have been appropriate in view of Ælfhere's avowed opposition to monasticism.[27]

The Mildrith Legend's emphasis on the sanctity of the Kentish royal house was another reason for continued interest in it. The version of the legend, *þa halgan*, was transcribed in or around 1031 in the *Liber Vitae* of New Minster, Winchester.[28] The text is immediately followed by the *Secgan be þam godes sanctum þe on Engla lande ærost reston*, a list of the resting-places of English saints, which covered most of England apart from Kent and probably reached its present form in early eleventh-century Winchester, although it appears to be a compilation based on earlier lists of more limited geographical scope. *Þa halgan* seems to have been joined to it because, since it mentions the resting-places of a number of saints, most of which are in Kent and many of which are not found in the *Secgan*, it supplemented it and filled a gap in its coverage. Whoever placed *þa halgan* next to the *Secgan* in the *Liber Vitae* was probably responsible for placing over the former the title *Her cyð ymbe þa halgan þe on Angelcynne ærost restað* since that is a correct description not of *þa halgan* itself but of *þa halgan* and the *Secgan* combined. *Þa halgan* thus became part of a survey of the sanctity of Anglo-Saxon England which included, in the *Secgan*, the ancient saints of Mercia and Northumbria and the saints of the new monasteries of the tenth-century reform movement; and, in *þa halgan*, a record of the ancient sanctity of the Kentish royal house and of its scions in other kingdoms.[29]

For an England unified by the efforts of the West Saxon kings, it was appropriate for such a survey to be drawn up at Winchester, the city which had become its capital. It is significant that it seems to have been done in the reign of King Cnut who, as a foreign king of England, no doubt felt the need for ecclesiastical support. 'From the beginning of his reign', noted Sir Frank Stenton, 'he set himself to win the respect of the English church.'[30] It cannot be shown that Cnut was directly involved with the survey of saints' resting-places, although the atmosphere of his reign may have been propitious for its compilation. It is clear, however, that he took an especial interest in the translations of English saints: he is said to have granted permission for St Mildrith to be translated from Minster-in-Thanet to Canterbury and St Ælfheah, the murdered archbishop, from London to Canterbury, and to have taken the initiative in the translation of St Wigstan from Repton to Evesham.[31] It is possible that Cnut intervened in these translations in observance of a canon promulgated in 813 by the Council of Mainz. This said that no translation could be effected without the advice of the bishop or the prince;[32] but more probably his prime aim was to show himself a worthy heir to the traditions of English dynasties which had fostered and venerated saints and so, although a Dane, achieve popular acceptance as king of the English. The Evesham *Passio et miracula sancti Wistani* emphasizes that he arranged Wigstan's translation when he learned of that martyr's alleged blood-relationship to King Coenred of Mercia.[33] The Mildrith Legend's stress on the royal saints of Kent would have had an especial appeal for Cnut. He would also have welcomed the opportunity of favouring St Augustine's Abbey, the house where the remains of the Kentish kings were interred, by allowing Mildrith's relics to be translated to it.

So it can be seen that the Mildrith Legend described events and circumstances which were relevant to the political and social environment of Anglo-Saxon England and this no doubt was one reason for continued interest in the legend. Another was the continued observance of the cults of the saints of the legend, especially by the religious communities which possessed their relics and therefore had need of documentary histories of these objects of veneration. This was true of Much Wenlock which possessed the relics of St Mildburg, of Chester which laid claim to those of St Werburg, of Ramsey which had obtained those of SS Æthelred and Æthelberht, and of St Augustine's Abbey, Canterbury, to which Mildrith's relics were translated in 1035.

St Augustine's Abbey was most prolific in producing versions of the legend and also produced texts concerning the history of Mildrith's relics. The chronology of this literary activity at St Augustine's Abbey is significant. The earliest version produced there belongs to the middle years of the eleventh century and is the Latin version now represented by the Bodley 285 Text: it may well have been written shortly after Mildrith's translation to provide material for her cult and it was possibly based on a text from Minster-in-Thanet.[34] There was then a pause followed by an extraordinary burst of activity towards the end of the eleventh century. The translation and modification of *þa halgan* was undertaken at St Augustine's Abbey at that time; so also was the fabrication of *KCD* 900, a charter containing a partial account of the legend. In addition, Goscelin's *Vita Mildrethae*, the lengthiest of all the extant versions, belongs to the period 1087–91 and was apparently written in conjunction with his *Textus translationis . . . Mildrethae*, an account of Mildrith's monastery, translation and miracles. Shortly afterwards there appeared the same author's *Contra usurpatores*, a defence of St Augustine's Abbey's claim to possess Mildrith's relics.[35]

The last of these texts had to be written to counter the rival claim made by St Gregory's Priory; but no such explanation is immediately apparent of the other late eleventh-century texts produced at St Augustine's Abbey at that time and on such a large scale. Possibly they were connected with the scepticism of certain late eleventh-century churchmen towards the genuineness of Anglo-Saxon saints. Archbishop Lanfranc is said to have expressed his doubts on this subject to Anselm in 1079.[36] He was on that occasion referring specifically to the cult of the murdered Archbishop Ælfheah and he was convinced by Anselm's arguments on behalf of the alleged martyr. His opposition to English cults was more general, as Eadmer implies. He advised Walter, the first Norman abbot of Evesham, to subject the relics of his church to the test of fire, which was certainly carried out in the case of the relics of St Wigstan.[37] This scepticism did not necessarily reflect a division of opinion between Normans and English. On the one hand, Anselm, a member of the Norman abbey of Bec, was a devotee of SS Ælfheah and Dunstan;[38] on the other, the veneration of English saints in Canterbury seems to have been giving way to the continental devotions introduced *via* the church of Winchester long before the arrival of Norman churchmen; and Lanfranc seems to have been encouraging rather than instigating change.[39] Nevertheless there was a division of opinion and it is likely that St Augustine's Abbey, the burial-place of the kings of Kent and of the early archbishops and the resting-place of Mildrith, was anxious to espouse the cause of Old English sanctity and to defend its own saints.

The best way of achieving these aims was to promote writings about the Anglo-Saxon saints. It seems that the lack of a carefully written account of St Ælfheah encouraged Lanfranc's scepticism. Once persuaded of the martyr's genuineness, however, he ordered an account to be written in prose for reading and another to be set to music for singing in church.[40] The community of St Augustine's may well have wished to head off comparable scepticism about St Mildrith when they turned to Goscelin to provide them with elaborate literary works concerning her. Their choice could not have been better calculated to impress men such as Lanfranc whose critical faculties had been sharpened by long exposure to the burgeoning scholarship of continental Europe, for Goscelin was himself a representative of that movement. Originally a monk of St Bertin, he had come to England in the early 1060s to join the household of the Lotharingian bishop, Herman of Ramsbury. Like his compatriot, Folcard of St Bertin, he was in great demand as a hagiographer and, although the full scope of his literary output is still disputed, he certainly wrote lives for Wilton, Sherborne, Barking, Ely and Ramsey before finally settling at St Augustine's.[41] His contemporary at Canterbury, Reginald, described him as a 'rhetor and grammarian, a dear friend of the muses'.[42] In the twelfth century, William of Malmesbury praised his 'distinguished skill in letters and in singing', rated him second only to Bede as a hagiographer of English saints and, significantly, emphasized that he had re-written *vitae* of ancient saints which had been ignorantly edited or lost through hostility.[43]

In the case of his works on Mildrith, Goscelin's methods can be examined in some detail. In his prologue to the *Vita Mildrethae*, he tells us that he was basing his account on an earlier version of Mildrith's life and miracles.[44] This was almost certainly the mid-eleventh-century Latin version, now preserved in truncated form in the Bodley 285 Text. What is left of this version's narrative is strikingly similar to that of the *Vita Mildrethae*. Both name Theodore as the archbishop involved in King Egbert's *witan* (other texts either do not name an archbishop or name him as Deusdedit).[45] Both contain identical details of Mildrith's stay in Gaul which are found in no other text. These include her purchase of a nail of the Cross; the name of Abbess Wilcoma of Chelles, where she stayed; this person's attempts to detain her; and her miraculous escape in company with her mother's legates; all appear, detail for detail, arranged in almost identical narrative order in the two versions.[46]

The mid-eleventh-century version's literary style seems to have been the chief objection to it. If its style is faithfully reflected in the Bodley 285 Text, it did indeed tend to be tortuous and to make use of the hermeneutic vocabulary beloved of later pre-Conquest Anglo-Latin writers.[47] At any rate, Goscelin regarded it as insufficiently decorous: in it, he observed, Mildrith's glories were like 'the sun behind a cloud, gold in the earth, a jewel besmeared with mud, a nut in its shell, wheat encased in chaff'.[48] What was needed was to raise Mildrith's *vita* to new levels of stylistic clarity. In place of the tortuousness of the Bodley 285 Text, Goscelin substituted a melliflyous flow of words, delighting in simile and heightening the spiritual significance of the events described by means of scriptural and classical references. In the following passages, the mid-eleventh-century writer has striven after an involved style and has resorted to bombastic phraseology. Goscelin has clarified the Latin and has added a touch of grandeur: the three daughters of Domne Eafe are likened to a trifoliate lily and reflect both the Song of Songs and classical poetry. In Goscelin's picture, their brother Merefin is like a yellow flower among lilies.

Bodley 285 Text[49]

Porro tradita est
Domneva Meruueale filio
Pendan Merciorum regis in
consortium legitimae
copulationis, qui Domini
annuente clementia ibi
amoene prolis posteritatem
adepti sunt: formosas videlicet
filias sic pulchro vocitamine
dictas: beata Mildburga ac
egregia Mildritha et inclita
Mildgith, ornatu virgineo
cunctae excellenter comptae,
sanctumque Merefin qui dum
adhuc infantiles gereret
annos, ex hac molestia
corporis corruptibilis ad
mansura gaudia celestis
regni subvectus est.

*Vita Mildrethae*[50]

Gloriosa autem Domneva tres
pretiosissimas Sanctae Trinitatis
gemmas, tres sanctissimas
Christo sponsas, Mildburgam,
Mildritham et Mildgitham
florificavit, et hoc quasi
trifolium lilium pro sceptro
tulit. Nomina simillima, par
formarum gloria, aequalis gratia,
mens et amor et sanctitas trium
erat unica. Hinc Mildburga ut
fides, inde Mildgitha ut spes,
media choruscat Mildritha ut
caritas. Nam et in Cantico
Canticorum, *Media caritate
constrata sunt*, et ut aliquid
hic de poetarum fabulis adiungamus,
*Tres erant pariles gratiae sorores . . .*
Quartam quoque sobolem virginum
fratrem Merefin dictum quasi
croceum florem in medio liliorum
produxit, quem Christus parvulum
suscipiens paradisi floribus
addidit.

Goscelin was a scholar as well as a stylist and this too was important in presenting Mildrith's claim to sanctity in the context of late eleventh-century England. In the *Vita Mildrethae*, his scholarship showed itself in the scriptural and classical allusions and in the inclusion of passages and information culled from Bede and presumably intended to add an air of authenticity to Mildrith's history.[51] The scope for scholarly research was greater when it came to proving that St Augustine's Abbey's relics really were those of Mildrith and that their translation to the abbey had been in line with the saint's own wishes. This was the purpose of the *Textus translationis . . . Mildrethae*, in which Goscelin adopted a truly historical approach.[52] He carefully traced the history of Minster-in-Thanet after the death of Eadburg, naming its abbesses and assessing their achievements. He then reconstructed the whole affair of the translation of Mildrith to St Augustine's, explaining the negotiations which made it possible, naming the persons involved and adding an elaborate account of the date of the translation, in which he made a meticulous, although unsuccessful, attempt to achieve accuracy.[53] His scholarly method is also apparent in the miracle-stories, in which the persons involved are often named and the circumstances described in some detail. Goscelin occasionally went so far as to acknowledge his sources: he asserted, for example, that his account of Abbess Selethryth was based on 'annals, privileges of the fathers and the charters of her monastery', and that his account of a Canterbury anchoress's youthful experiences of Mildrith's powers is in fact the verbatim report which she gave to the prior of St Augustine's in the presence of witnesses.[54]

Nowhere was the desire for objective demonstration of a saint's genuineness more apparent than in the controversy which arose between the community of St Augustine's Abbey and that of St Gregory's Priory, Canterbury, when the latter began to claim in about 1088 that it had received from Lyminge in 1085 not only the relics of a certain St Eadburg but also those of St Mildrith herself. Goscelin's *Contra usurpatores*, a reply to two successive books written by or for the canons of St Gregory's in support of their claim, is an exercise in historical argument (and polemic) which could not have been entirely unworthy of Edward Gibbon.[55] The St Gregory's canons' first book had claimed that their St Eadburg was Mildrith's successor as abbess of Minster-in-Thanet. It then fell into error by identifying this person with the foundress of Lyminge, who was in fact called Æthelburg and could not have been Mildrith's successor since, being a daughter of King Æthelberht I, she was her great-great-aunt. Goscelin pounced on this blunder. While accepting the tradition that a daughter of Æthelberht had founded

Lyminge, he stated correctly that she was called not Eadburg but Æthelburg. He was prepared to accept that local people at Lyminge might have confused the name, transmuting it to Eadburg; but he pointed out that any daughter of Æthelberht I, whatever her name, must have lived in the early seventh century and could not be identified with Mildrith's successor who flourished in the middle of the eighth century. There was thus a century and a half between Æthelberht's daughter, the foundress of Lyminge, and Mildrith's successor, Eadburg. Goscelin concluded that if the St Gregory's Eadburg had no connection with Minster-in-Thanet, she could have had no connection with Mildrith either. He was prepared to allow the canons to believe that their St Eadburg was Mildrith's successor – although he emphasized that the name was a common one – as long as they did not make use of this identification to lay claim to the relics of Mildrith also.[56]

The canons' second book seems to have shifted the emphasis of the case, perhaps in response to Goscelin's attack. It dropped the question of Eadburg's relationship to Æthelberht I, although Goscelin was not prepared to let the canons forget their original claim, and it gave a lengthier account of how the relics of Eadburg and Mildrith came to be at Lyminge. The canons do not seem to have known the evidence which demonstrates a connection between Minster-in-Thanet and Lyminge in the time of Abbess Selethryth;[57] and they had little real information to work on. They took refuge in obscurity, claiming that Mildrith and Eadburg had fled from Minster-in-Thanet to find refuge at Lyminge in the face of Danish raids, but failing to suggest a date or period for this flight and failing even to make it clear whether it was the saints themselves who had fled as living persons or whether it was the saints' relics which had been taken by later members of the community fleeing from the Danes.[58] Goscelin dealt savagely with this muddle. He made capital out of the way in which the canons' book was more precise about Eadburg's arrival at Lyminge than about Mildrith's. Had Mildrith's relics remained at Minster-in-Thanet, he asked, when Eadburg and all the nuns fled? If so, who was left to translate Mildrith? What was the location of a certain ruined church to which the canons' writer referred vaguely as the repository of the two saints' relics? Why should Lyminge have been regarded as a refuge anyway since it was just as vulnerable to the Danes as Minster-in-Thanet?[59]

In addition to this historical disputation, Goscelin drew attention to other forms of evidence supporting his case. It seems that the monks of St Augustine's had found Thanet islanders who remembered in detail the circumstances of Ælfstan's translation of Mildrith to Canterbury in 1035, although Goscelin admitted that some felt such evidence to be weak compared with historical documentation.[60] The St Augustine's monks were alarmed by hearing that the tomb at Lyminge had actually been marked *Miltrudis* when it was excavated. The abbot of St Augustine's managed to approach the Lyminge parishioner who had exhumed the relics and interrogated him to the abbot's complete satisfaction. It seemed that the tomb had been unnamed and that the label *Miltrudis* had been an invention of the St Gregory's canons.[61] The canons too resorted to the judicial objectivity of their time by employing the ordeal by water. They consecrated a cauldron of water, took a boy, bound his arms around his knees, threw him into the cauldron and conjured the water to accept him if St Mildrith were really at St Gregory's. In Goscelin's account, the boy floated and was nearly drowned by the efforts of the canons to sink him.[62]

By contrast, the testimony of miracles occupied only a subsidiary place in the controversy. It appears from the arrangement of the *Contra usurpatores* that Goscelin's attack on the first St Gregory's book was accompanied only by reiterations of miracles which he had described in the *Textus translationis . . . Mildrethae* as having occurred at St Augustine's Abbey and which he therefore regarded as proof that that house genuinely possessed the relics: nothing new was felt to be necessary and Goscelin's appeal to miracles is rather half-heartedly appended to his historical arguments.[63] When he attacked the second St Gregory's book, his historical arguments were weaker and his appendix of miracles, although similarly slipped in after the historical material, contains several additions. These were of a specialized character and consisted of various visions and signs by which Mildrith affirmed her presence at St Augustine's Abbey.[64]

Stylistic excellence and scholarly acumen were evidently valued by the monks of St Augustine's in their efforts to establish and promote Mildrith's sanctity. They treasured Goscelin's writings about the saint, gathering them together in the early twelfth century in two imposing volumes with illuminated initials, London, British Library, Cotton MS Vespasian Bxx and Harley MS 105, and in a smaller manuscript devoted solely to Mildrith, London, British Library, Harley MS 3908.[65]

In addition to his defence of their claim to St Mildrith's relics, Goscelin's work may have been important to them for two further reasons. Firstly, it could be adapted for use in the liturgy, which occupied an important place in Anglo-Norman monasticism with its albeit distant links with the Cluniac reform.[66] Harley MS 3908 contains a mass for Mildrith's feast and a *Historia de sancta Mildretha*, which is a much abbreviated version of the *Vita Mildrethae* and the *Textus translationis . . . Mildrethae* set to music for liturgical use. All three manuscripts contain a set of eight lections based on the *Vita Mildrethae* and intended for reading in church. London, British Library, Harley MS 652, a manuscript of early twelfth-century date, contains on fos. 209v–210r summaries of the *Textus translationis . . . Mildrethae* which were for the same purpose.

Secondly, Goscelin's writings at St Augustine's Abbey were executed in a period which was difficult not only for the reputation of English saints but for the abbey itself. Æthelsige, the last Anglo-Saxon abbot, had fled abroad at the time of the Conquest to elude the new Norman masters, who clearly suspected him of being involved in English resistance.[67] Although Scotland, the first Norman abbot, succeeded in governing the house peacefully, trouble flared up after his death in 1087 when Archbishop Lanfranc imposed on the abbey a new abbot, Wido, a Norman and a monk of Christ Church. Resentment was bitter and Lanfranc had considerable difficulty in controlling the monks, one of whom admitted that he had conspired to kill the new abbot. After the archbishop's death in 1089, the monks allied with the townspeople to eject Wido; and he was only reinstated after the infliction of savage punishments and the dispersal of the recalcitrant monks, who were replaced by a contingent from Christ Church.[68] The reasons for this dispute are obscure. David Knowles regarded it as 'racial and personal'; but hostility was no doubt also aroused by Lanfranc's disregard for the monks' claim to the right of free election of their abbot.[69] At any rate, Goscelin was writing the *Vita Mildrethae* and the *Textus translationis . . . Mildrethae* at the time of this dispute. These works may well have been viewed as a gesture of conciliation made by Wido and his Norman colleagues towards the ancient traditions of St Augustine's Abbey. As Goscelin came forward to give Mildrith literary respectability, so in 1091 Wido arranged the splendid translation of the relics of the early archbishops and of Abbot Adrian and of Mildrith herself into the new Norman abbey-church.[70]

Goscelin's writings on Mildrith also reveal a narrowing of attitudes towards the saint and her legend. The broader preoccupations of the legend which we have examined in earlier chapters are not emphasized. For Goscelin and the monks of St Augustine's Abbey in the late eleventh century, Mildrith was primarily one of the chief tutelary saints of their community. By visions, miracles and cures, she showed her favour towards it; and she attracted for it the support of all sorts of people – the common masses, whose support the canons of St Gregory's Priory threatened to alienate by preaching to them that Mildrith's relics were at their house,[71] and the powerful, such as William I, who was said to have been sufficiently impressed by Mildrith's powers to confirm the abbey's right of sanctuary, and Queen Emma, who, it was claimed, attributed her restoration to favour to Mildrith's intercession.[72]

The St Augustine's monks were also preoccupied with Mildrith's role as an object of liturgical celebration. Goscelin describes how, at the time of her translation, Abbot Ælfstan and his party were unable to open her tomb at Minster-in-Thanet to take out her relics until the abbot promised that her feast should be celebrated at St Augustine's on the same scale as the feasts of the most important saints and that a mass should be said daily over her relics there.[73] In the *Textus translationis . . . Mildrethae*, Goscelin went out of his way to emphasize that this promise was being kept, that the feast of Mildrith's translation was also being observed and that, on one occasion at least, the celebration of the mass on Mildrith's feast-day had been a propitious time to seek the saint's intercession in effecting a miraculous cure.[74] It was the lavish liturgical celebration of Mildrith's feast by the canons of St Gregory's Priory which first induced the abbot of St Augustine's to take action to restrain them from making their claim to her relics.[75]

Goscelin emphasized further that St Augustine's Abbey had acquired the erstwhile lands of Mildrith's church at the same time as it had acquired her relics. He described in some detail how Abbot Ælfstan's acquisition of half the former lands of Minster-in-Thanet had spurred him on (aided by a vision of Mildrith) to obtain the saint's relics and the remainder of her lands; and how King Cnut had granted to him those lands and the relics.[76] The Mildrith Legend's account of the selection of Minster-in-Thanet's endowment by the agency of Domne Eafe's hind thus came to have a purely parochial importance for the St Augustine's monks: it described how their own estates on Thanet had been delineated since they were thought to be identical with the early estates of Minster there. In their translation and modification of *þa halgan*, the monks modified the Old English version's figure of 80 sulungs for Minster's original endowment to 48 sulungs: this was the actual assessment of the St Augustine's estate on Thanet in Domesday Book so the modification emphasized the identity of this with the land delineated by Domne Eafe's hind.[77] The importance of the Latin *þa halgan* for the abbey's land-claims was further emphasized by its inclusion in a St Augustine's cartulary, London, British Library, Cotton MS Vitellius A.ii. The association between the legend and the abbey's lands on Thanet found further expression in *KCD* 900, the fabricated charter purporting to be a document recording that King Edward the Confessor confirmed the abbey's possession of Mildrith's relics and her lands and rehearsing those aspects of the legend relating to Minster-in-Thanet's foundation.[78] That association was still strong in the early fifteenth century when Thomas of Elmham produced a map of Thanet to illustrate the legend, showing the course of Domne Eafe's hind as the boundary of the St Augustine's estates (see fig. 1).[79]

Goscelin's account shows that, once St Augustine's Abbey had gained possession of Minster-in-Thanet's estates, it was anxious to foster and emphasize the links between itself and the isle, not least because, having established a grange at Minster-in-Thanet, it was concerned to gain the allegiance of the people.[80] To this end, Goscelin explained in the *Textus translationis . . . Mildrethae* that, when Abbot Ælfstan and his companions had removed Mildrith's remains from her tomb at Minster-in-Thanet, they had been careful to leave some of the dust of her flesh to console the islanders in their grief and anger at the loss of the main relics of the saint.[81] Goscelin pointed out in addition that Mildrith demonstrated her continued presence on Thanet by frequent miracles and visions, some of which he described, often alternating these accounts with descriptions of miracles worked at Canterbury through Mildrith's intercession.[82] Furthermore, Goscelin described how Wulfric, abbot of St Augustine's, habitually celebrated Mildrith's feast at Minster-in-Thanet, presumably as a gesture of conciliation towards the islanders, who are said to have flocked to attend the celebration.[83] Finally, Goscelin emphasized Mildrith's continued spiritual presence on Thanet after her translation to Canterbury by describing the rock at Ebbsfleet which preserved Mildrith's footprints and which was in his time the centre of a thaumaturgic cult.[84]

The tendency in eleventh-century Canterbury for the Mildrith Legend to lose its wider connotations and to become merely the legend of a particular saint and the justification of a particular religious house's claims is thrown into sharp relief by the controversy between St Augustine's Abbey and St Gregory's Priory over which of them possessed Mildrith's relics. The dispute was in itself a parochial, self-interested squabble between an old-established monastery and a new house seeking to associate itself with ancient sanctity. It was started by the canons of St Gregory's, who claimed in about 1088 that the unidentified body which they had received from Lyminge three years before was that of Mildrith. They made their claim first of all by celebrating Mildrith's feast lavishly, then by preaching it to the people, then by writing or commissioning literary accounts to justify it. The claim was not endorsed by their founder and the instigator of the translations from Lyminge, Archbishop Lanfranc, for he attempted, at the request of the abbot of St Augustine's, to restrain the canons of St Gregory's from making it.[85] It arose in fact from the narrow, sectional interest represented by the canons themselves. From being a legend of the Kentish royal house in the seventh and eighth centuries, relevant in later Anglo-Saxon England to the problem of royal murders on the one hand and to the saintly ethos of a unified country on the other, the Mildrith Legend had come to be bound up with the petty jealousies of two squabbling religious houses in post-Conquest Canterbury.

# Conclusion

This book has been concerned in essence with the study of attitudes and in particular with the way in which these governed the interaction of cults, legend and society. The cults were subsidiary to the legend in this respect; for in themselves they were merely expressions of the pious, penitential and thaumaturgic aspects of medieval religion. They persisted, as did that of Mildrith at Minster-in-Thanet, at times when the relevance of the legend had faded away. What brought them to special significance was the link between the legends on which they were based and the attitudes and aspirations of particular groups of people at particular moments in time. Those groups often wrote new hagiographical texts or refurbished those which had lain dormant in libraries or perhaps even in the shrines of the saints. Far from being primarily a devotional genre out of touch with life beyond the monastery's or church's walls, hagiography appears as intimately concerned with wider attitudes and aspirations, a living genre which in some cases may have as much claim to have been in touch with the society in which it was written or read as medieval historical writing itself. The cults too appear as intimately connected with that society, although in a subsidiary role.

This study has been deliberately restricted to one legend and to one closely related group of cults, dominated by that of St Mildrith. Such a narrowly focused examination has shown itself to have several advantages. Firstly, it has made the textual problems of the legend reasonably manageable so that it has been possible, with varying degrees of certainty, to establish the dates, provenances, development and interrelationships of the legend's texts. Secondly, it has facilitated the detection of significant variations between texts written or re-written at different times and places. These variations have not, in the case of the Mildrith Legend, been very great nor have they principally involved the narrative of the legend. More commonly they have been in emphasis, presentation, literary style and in the liturgical, historiographical and other functions which often correspond to these. Such variations can be of great importance but are often only revealed by close scrutiny. Thirdly, this study's narrow approach has made possible close examination of the historical contexts in which the texts were written or read; and it is this close examination which has provided the clues to the attitudes revealed in the texts and thus to their significance.

The same narrowly focused approach could probably be applied to many other legends, although some would clearly be more rewarding than others. Two factors should probably be considered in selecting legends for close study. Firstly, the existence of a rich and varied textual tradition makes it likely that a legend can be successfully related to several contexts and that its corresponding changes in content, emphasis and presentation can be understood. The legends of Cuthbert, Æthelthryth, Edmund and Guthlac seem especially promising cases but no doubt many more would be equally rewarding.[1] The same type of approach could probably also be applied to certain *miracula*, especially those which are composite works, consisting of material written at different periods. Secondly, the potential interest is further heightened when the legend to be examined can definitely be associated with one or more centres which are known to have possessed considerable influence. Legends associated with kings may likewise be valuable subjects for study because of their political associations. The choice of legend should nevertheless not be determined primarily by these considerations of association with influential centres or persons; for the attitudes of those not on the forefront of the historical stage are equally worthy of study.

The advantages of a narrowly focused approach, however, should not blind us to the necessity for broader examination of hagiography and of the attitudes which it can reveal. Firstly, it would be desirable for the purely textual problems of the hagiographical texts to be unravelled with reference to a wider range of examples. In the long run, the same precision which the narrowly focused approach permits can be profitably applied to more extensive bodies of material. In this way, some appreciation could be developed of the composition of hagiographical manuscripts as a whole, the entire productions of specific centres such as Canterbury, the characteristics of traditions of hagiographical writing and the *œuvres* of particular hagiographers such as Goscelin and Folcard. It is especially necessary that the liturgical material, particularly the kalendars which influence one another extensively, should be examined in this way. Such broad but rigorous textual studies would in themselves be of considerable historical as well as literary interest;[2] but they would also have the effect of providing a firmer basis for studies of the type pursued in this book, which has been forced in the present state of scholarship to devote so much space to textual discussion. A firmer basis would also permit more effective investigations of the changes in literary form in hagiography and of the developments in the ideal of sanctity, some studies of which in continental contexts have proved profitable where textual studies of the hagiography were already sufficiently advanced.[3]

A final note should perhaps be added to place these studies in relationship to an allied approach, that of the study of the interaction of saint and society during the saint's lifetime. It so happens that the texts examined in this book either do not consider a saint's life in any detail or were written too long after the saint's death for them to be valuable for such an approach. We have therefore examined only the interaction between legend, posthumous cult and society. In some cases where the material permits us to perceive it, however, there clearly was considerable interaction between the living holy man or woman and the society in which he or she flourished. Such a situation presents analogous opportunities for the study of attitudes. Some of these have been explored by Peter Brown in the Mediterranean context and Henry Mayr-Harting has followed his example in connection with the English hermit, Wulfric of Haselbury.[4] The *vitae* of such figures as Robert of Knaresborough, Godric of Finchale and Bartholomew of Farne would probably be equally rewarding subjects.[5] Where the living holy man or woman as well as the posthumous cult can be perceived, therefore, a further dimension can be added to the study of the hagiography.

The present study has been a tentative attempt to examine the significance of a particular legend on the basis of detailed textual studies. Its results are, it is hoped, interesting in themselves. But it is also hoped that some contribution has been made to defining methods and approaches by means of which the large body of extant hagiographical texts can be made more accessible to historical study and can contribute to our understanding of the past.

# Summaries of the Texts

This appendix contains summaries of the extant texts of the Mildrith Legend, arranged in the following order, which corresponds to that in which the texts are discussed in Chapter 2. Full references are given in that chapter.

(a)  The *Historia Regum* Text
(b)  The Bodley 285 Text
(c)  The *Vita Mildrethae*
(d)  The Gotha Text
(e)  The *Vita Mildburgae: genealogia*
(f)  The *Vita Werburgae: genealogia*
(g)  The *Genealogia Regum Cantuariorum*
(h)  *Þa halgan*
(i)  Hugh Candidus's Text
(j)  *S. Mildryð*
(k)  The Lambeth Fragment

## (a) The *Historia Regum* Text

Rubrics

1.  Descent and baptism of Æthelberht.
2.  Accession of his son Eadbald, whose sons were Eormenred and Eorcenberht.
3.  Accession of Eorcenberht, who abolished idols and instituted a Lenten fast.
4.  Eorcenberht's son was Egbert. Eormenred's sons were Æthelberht and Æthelred, whose *passio* will now be inserted into this history.
5.  Baptism, benevolence and death of Æthelberht.
6.  His son Eadbald succeeded him and begot two sons, Eormenred

and Eorcenberht, of whom the younger was made king by his father.

7.  Eorcenberht's son Egbert ruled after his death.

8.  Eormenred lived on powerless; he had two sons, Æthelberht and Æthelred, who enjoyed saintly baptism and pure lives.

9.  They were orphaned while young and entrusted to King Egbert.

10. Thunor, the king's principal councillor and favourite, resented their saintly lives and sought to have them killed.

11. He slandered them to the courtiers and told the king that they were a threat to himself and his children and should be exiled or killed.

12. Egbert's resistance to this proposal weakened and Thunor killed the princes in his absence.

13. He buried them under the king's throne without any burial rites.

14. At night a column of light stood over the palace and disturbed many.

15. Awakened by their cries, Egbert rose and saw the column of light coming from the throne when he went to attend Matins.

16. He interrogated Thunor, who confessed and indicated where the bodies were.

17. The king called his council, which included Archbishop Deusdedit, and the bodies were exhumed.

18. These things happened in the royal vill of Eastry.

19. After it had proved impossible to move the bodies to Christ Church or St Augustine's, Canterbury, they were easily moved to Wakering.

20. They lay behind the high altar there for many years and worked many miracles, including the destruction of a sheep-stealer.

21. Æthelberht and Æthelred had a sister called *Eormenburh* or Domne Eafe, wife of Merewalh, king of the Mercians.

22. At Egbert's invitation, she came and chose as much land as her hind would run round.

23. The king and a large party crossed to Thanet in ships and the hind ran on with them following. Thunor objected but fell from his horse and was swallowed by the earth. The place was covered with a pile of stones and called *Thunerhleaw*. The hind finished its course and Egbert confirmed the grant.

24. Domne Eafe founded a church dedicated to the Virgin on Thanet.

25. Mildrith was sent abroad for education and, on her return, was consecrated by Archbishop Deusdedit with 70 virgins.

26. She succeeded her mother as abbess and performed miracles. Once, an angel of the Lord in the form of a dove guarded her from evil spirits.
27. She was buried in St Mary's Church.

## (b) The Bodley 285 Text

Rubric: *Prologus* or *Genealogia*

1. Pope Gregory sent Augustine and his companions to England. King Æthelberht, who had extended his power to the Humber, gave the missionaries a place in Canterbury. He was converted with his people and reigned for 21 years.
2. Eadbald succeeded him. He apostasized but later resumed his faith.
3. His sister Æthelburg was married to Edwin, king of the Northumbrians. She was accompanied by Paulinus, who converted the king and his people. After Edwin's death, Æthelburg and Paulinus returned to Kent and were received by Eadbald. Æthelburg brought back ornaments to the church of Canterbury; Paulinus became bishop of Rochester until his death.
4. The children of Eadbald and the Frankish princess Ymme were Eormenred, Eorcenberht and Eanswith, who is buried at the monastery of Folkestone which she founded.
5. Eadbald passed his throne to his younger son Eorcenberht, whose wife Seaxburg bore him Eorcengota, Eormenhild and Egbert, who succeeded his father.
6. The eldest son Eormenred had by his wife Oslafa two sons, Æthelberht and Æthelred, and four daughters, Domne Eafe, *Eormenberga*, *Eormenburh* and Eormengith.
7. Domne Eafe married Merewalh, son of Penda, and bore him Mildburg, Mildrith, Mildgith and Merefin who died in childhood. The parents then separated for love of Heaven. Their eldest daughter Mildburg rests at Much Wenlock; Mildrith was buried on Thanet but later translated to St Augustine's Abbey, before the High Altar; and Mildgith was buried in Northumbria.

Rubric: *Relatio* or *Passio*

8.  Æthelred and Æthelberht were orphaned and entrusted to King Egbert.

9.  Thunor, who was given authority over the realm and the princes, feared that they would be more popular with the king than he; so he told the king that they were a threat to his own and his children's power and asked for permission to kill them. Egbert weakened under repeated pressure and Thunor killed the princes in the royal hall at Eastry and buried them under the throne.

10. Awaking at cock-crow, Egbert saw a column of light over the spot and interrogated Thunor who was forced to disclose the princes' whereabouts. The council, which included Archbishop Theodore, advised Egbert to summon Domne Eafe to receive compensation for the killing.

11. She chose land of 40 *aratri* on Thanet by means of her hind running round it. Thunor tried to intervene in this process at a place called *Thunures hleaw* but he was swallowed by the earth and a mound heaped over him. The hind finished its course and the land was granted to Domne Eafe.

12. She built a church with the help of Egbert and gathered together virgins there.

13. Mildrith studied at Chelles under Abbess *Wulcume*, with a bishop's consent, and purchased relics, including a nail of the Crucifixion. When she refused to marry the abbess's relative, the abbess tried to burn her. When this did not harm her, the abbess tore out some of her hair which she sent to her mother in a psalter with a message requesting help.

14. Domne Eafe sent legates but they were refused permission to take Mildrith home and fled with her clandestinely, although she insisted on returning to collect the relics which she had forgotten. They were pursued but Mildrith's prayers produced a miraculous flow of the tide and they reached Ebbsfleet and then Minster safely.

15. Mildrith was consecrated with 70 virgins.

Rubric: *Translatio*

16. In the reign of King Æthelred, the bodies of Æthelred and Æthelberht were translated from Wakering to Ramsey.

17. At Wakering, a sheep-stealer had been struck dead at their shrine and some secular priests had tried to remove their relics but failed to do so.

## (c) The *Vitae Mildrethae*

1. Sent by Pope Gregory, Augustine baptized Æthelberht, the king of all the southern English up to the Humber. He reigned for 56 years, made laws and died 20 years after his conversion.
2. His son Eadbald succeeded him and apostasized, encouraged by the apostasy of Sæberht's sons. Mellitus and Justus fled from their bishoprics to Gaul but Laurence, archbishop of Canterbury, had a vision of St Peter which persuaded Eadbald to resume his faith. Laurence consecrated a chapel dedicated to St Mary, built by Eadbald to the east of the church of SS Peter and Paul. The children of Eadbald and the Frankish princess Ymme were Eormenred, Eorcenberht and Eanswith, who rests at the monastery of Folkestone which she founded.
3. The children of the eldest son, Eormenred, and his wife, Oslafa, were Æthelred, Æthelberht, Domne Eafe, *Ermenberga*, *Ermenburga* and Eormengith.
4. Domne Eafe's children were Mildburg, Mildrith and Mildgith, who rest respectively at Much Wenlock, St Augustine's Abbey (formerly on Thanet) and in Northumbria; and Merefin, who died in childhood. Domne Eafe separated from her husband, Merewalh, who had three brothers, Peada who converted the Middle Angles, Wulfhere who converted the Mercians, and Aethelred who succeeded Wulfhere and become a monk after a reign of 29 years; and two sisters Cyneburg and Cyneswith.
5. Cyneburg founded Castor. Cyneswith married Offa, king of the East Angles, but, encouraged by a vision of St Mary, remained virgin. Both rest at Peterborough with their alleged relative, Tibba.
6. Eadbald handed on his kingdom to his younger son, Eorcenberht, who ruled for 24 years and was the first English king to abolish the idols and institute a Lenten fast. His wife Seaxburg bore him Egbert, Eorcengota and Eormenhild. Eorcengota became famous overseas; Eormenhild married Wulfhere and bore him Werburg, who rests at Hanbury.

7.  Eormenred, who was pious rather than powerful, entrusted his
    sons Æthelberht and Æthelred to Eorcenberht to be cared for
    after his death. He respected this trust and bequeathed it to Egbert.
8.  Egbert ruled for nine years and gained control of all the southern
    and eastern kingdoms.
9.  Thunor feared the vigour and prudence of the princes and
    corrupted the king with talk of possible usurpation of the throne.
    Egbert eventually imitated Pilate and Thunor murdered the
    princes in the royal vill of Eastry and buried them under the
    throne. The king saw a column of light over the spot and was
    afraid; and the people murmured against him and Thunor.
10. Archbishop Theodore and Abbot Adrian called a council and
    accused the king of parricide, recommending that Domne Eafe
    should be summoned to receive compensation for the killing.
11. She chose as much land on Thanet as her hind would run round.
    The hind ran, followed by the king and his court and people, but
    Thunor tried to intervene and was swallowed by the earth. A
    mound was heaped over him and the place was called *Thunores
    hleaw*.
12. The hind finished its course and Domne Eafe received 48 hides
    of land, on which she built a monastery, dedicated it to St Mary,
    and gathered together virgins there.
13. She brought Mildrith to Thanet and then sent her to Chelles to
    study under an abbess called Wilcoma. When she refused to
    marry the abbess's relative, the abbess put her in a lighted oven
    but she was found unharmed three hours later. The abbess then
    tore out some of her hair which Mildrith put in a psalter and sent
    to her mother with a request for help.
14. Domne Eafe sent legates but, in conjunction with the bishop, the
    abbess refused to release Mildrith. The legates then fled with
    Mildrith who insisted on returning in order to collect some relics,
    notably a nail of the Crucifixion, which she had left behind. The
    party was pursued but, in answer to Mildrith's prayers, the
    pursuers turned their arms against themselves and the tide
    miraculously came into flood. Mildrith landed safely at Ebbsfleet
    and imprinted her footprints on a rock, which could not be moved
    afterwards and became the centre of a healing cult. A chapel was
    built round it.
15. Theodore consecrated Mildrith with 70 virgins and, at her
    mother's request, also made her abbess.

16. The devil blew out Mildrith's candle but an angel rekindled it.
17. An angel protected Mildrith from the devil as she slept.
18. Mildrith was distressed in church but the spirit of the Lord in the form of a dove settled on her forehead and comforted her.
19. After an illness, Mildrith died on 13 July and was buried in St Mary's Church.
20. Eadburg succeeded her. She built the church of SS Peter and Paul and had it dedicated by Archbishop Cuthbert. She translated to it the body of St Mildrith, which was found incorrupt.

### (d) The Gotha Text

1. Fearing that they would harm his kingdom or his children, King Egbert ordered Æthelred and Æthelberht to be killed, knowing that otherwise they would succeed to the government of the kingdom. The killing was done by Thunor who buried the bodies under the throne in the royal hall at Eastry. A celestial light shone over the place at night and terrified the king.
2. He summoned their sister *Ermenburga, alias* Domne Eafe, who had separated from the king her husband, and confessed to the killing. As compensation, Egbert gave her 80 *aratrorum iugera* on Thanet and she built there a monastery, dedicated to St Mary, where prayers were said for the martyrs.
3. Theodore consecrated *Miltrudis* with 70 virgins. She succeeded Domne Eafe as abbess.
4. While she was reading, her candle was blown out but miraculously rekindled. While she was lying down, an angel came in the form of a dove and sat on her head. While she was asleep, an angel protected her from the devil.
5. *Miltrudis* died on 13 July.
6. *Eadburgis*, daughter of Æthelberht and *proavia* of *Miltrudis*, succeeded her. She built a new church and translated *Miltrudis's* incorrupt body to it, burying it on the north side of the oratory where miracles still occur.
7. *Eadburgis* died on 13 December.
8. A few years later the Danish invasions forced the nuns to flee to Lyminge.
9. The church fell into disrepair but was taken over and restored by

the archbishops of Canterbury, who installed priests to serve the virgins.

10. Archbishop Lanfranc was persuaded to translate the relics to Canterbury.

### (e) The *Vita Mildburgae: Genealogia*

1. Augustine converted King Æthelberht.

2. The children of Æthelberht and the Frankish princess Bertha were Eadbald, a faithful Christian and builder of churches, and Æthelburg, queen of King Edwin of the Northumbrians. After his death she returned to her brother and built a monastery at Lyminge, where she is buried.

3. The children of Eadbald and the Frankish princess Ymme were Eormenred, Eorcenberht and Eanswith, who spent her life at the monastery of Folkestone, where she is buried.

4. Eocenberht married Seaxburg, daughter of King Anna and Hereswitha, and begot Egbert, Hlothhere, Eorcengota and Eormenhild. Egbert succeeded his father; Eorcengota went overseas and is buried there; and Eormenhild married Wulfhere, king of the Mercians, and bore him the virgin Werburg.

5. Eormenred was more concerned with piety than power. By his wife Oslafa, he begot Æthelred and Æthelberht. A ray of light from heaven informed everyone of their deaths and of the place of concealment of their bodies. Eormenred's daughters were Domne Eafe, *Hermenbirga*, *Hermenburga* and Eormengith.

6. Domne Eafe was married to Merewalh, king of the *Weste-hani*, in the western part of Mercian territory. Merewalh and Wulfhere, sons of Penda, reigned together. Peada ruled the Middle Angles and Æthelred succeeded Wulfhere, reigning for 29 years and then becoming a monk.

7. Their sisters Cyneburg and Cyneswith rest with their relative Tibba at Peterborough.

8. The children of Domne Eafe and Merewalh were Mildburg, Mildrith, Mildgith and Merefin, who died in childhood.

9. Merewalh's conversion and pious life.

10. Merewalh and Domne Eafe separated and Domne Eafe returned to Kent because she valued more the Kentish mausoleum of Augustine and his companions than the Mercian palaces; and she

preferred the company of Theodore and Adrian to that of the rude Mercians.

11. King Egbert welcomed her and gave her 48 *aratri* on Thanet, where she built a monastery dedicated to St Mary and became first abbess.

12. The archbishop of Canterbury consecrated Mildrith with 70 virgins and she succeeded her mother as abbess.

13. Mildgith spent her life in Northumbria and worked many miracles there.

14. Merewalh was buried at Repton.


### (f)  The *Vita Werburgae*: *Genealogia*

1. Werburg rests in Chester.
2. Her ancestor Æthelberht was converted by Augustine.
3. The children of Æthelberht and the Frankish princess Bertha were Eadbald, who succeeded his father, and Æthelburg who, after the death of her husband Edwin, returned to her brother and built a monastery at Lyminge where she rests with St Eadburg.
4. The children of Eadbald and the Frankish princess Ymme were Eormenred, Eorcenberht and Eanswith, whose remains are venerated at Folkestone.
5. The children of Eormenred and Oslafa were Æthelred and Æthelberht, who were killed but shown to be martyrs of Christ by a column of light, and Domne Eafe, *Ermenberga*, *Ermenburga* and Eormengith.
6. The children of Eorcenberht and Seaxburg, daughter of Anna, were Egbert, Eormenhild and Eorcengota. Eormenhild married Wulfhere, king of the Mercians, and bore him Werburg, whose aunt Eorcengota went overseas and was buried there.
7. Domne Eafe married Merewalh, brother of Wulfhere, and bore him Mildburg, Mildrith, Mildgith, who are illustrious in various monasteries, and Merefin, who died in childhood.
8. Werburg's relatives, Cyneburg and Cyneswith, daughters of Penda, rest at Peterborough with their relative Tibba.
9. Her uncles, Merewalh, Peada and Æthelred, were propagators of Christianity. Æthelred first spread Christianity among the Mercians.

## (g) The *Genealogia Regum Cantuariorum*

1. Led by Hengest and Horsa, the Anglo-Saxons first came to Britain in three ships. Horsa was killed in battle but Hengest won victory and began to reign as first king of Kent in 455.

2. Sent by Pope Gregory, Augustine converted King Æthelberht in 597, in the 35th year of his reign. Æthelberht built and endowed the church of SS Peter and Paul just to the east of Canterbury; and he built St Paul's Church, London, and St Andrew's Church, Rochester.

3. The daughter of Æthelberht and the Frankish princess Bertha was Æthelburg, who married King Edwin and built the monastery of Lyminge where she now rests.

4. Æthelberht's sister, Ricula, was queen of the East Saxons and bore Sæberht, saint and king of that people.

5. Æthelberht died in the 56th year of his reign and was succeeded by his son, Eadbald, who wished to favour the church and follow its teaching. By his queen, the Frankish princess Ymme, he begot Eanswith, who rests at Folkestone, and Eormenred, *regulus*.

6. The children of Eormenred and Oslafa were *Ermenberga*, who was the queen of Merewalh, king of the *West-Angli*, *Ermenburga*, Æthelthryth, Eormengith and the holy martyrs, Æthelred and Æthelberht, who were murdered by King Egbert's *praefectus*, Thunor, as he himself had ordered.

7. Eadbald died in the 25th year of his reign and was succeeded by his son Eorcenberht, who was the first English king to abolish the idols and to institute a Lenten fast. His queen was Seaxburg, daughter of King Anna, and she built a monastery on Sheppey.

8. Eorcengota, daughter of Eorcenberht and Seaxburg, was sent to Gaul and became a nun under her aunt, Abbess Æthelburg, in the monastery of Brie, where she rests. Their other daughter, Eormenhild, became the queen of Wulfhere, king of the Mercians.

9. Eorcenberht died in the 24th year of his reign and was succeeded by his son, Egbert, who died in the month of July in the 9th year of his reign and was succeeded by his brother, Hlothhere. He was wounded in a battle against the South Saxons, who had been stirred up by Egbert's son, Eadric, and died in February in the 12th year of his reign while being treated. He was succeeded by Eadric, who reigned for one and a half years and was succeeded

by his brother, Wihtred, who built St Martin's Church in Dover. Wihtred died in the 34th year of his reign and was succeeded by his son, Æthelberht, who died in the 36th year of his reign. He was succeeded by Eadberht Pren, who was captured by Coenwulf, king of the Mercians, and taken to Mercia. His successor, Cuthred, died in the 9th year of his reign and was succeeded by Baldred, who was driven out by the West Saxons in 823.

10. Up to that time, the kingdom of Kent had stood for 368 years; it now passed into the power of the West Saxons.


## (h) Þa halgan

1. Augustine baptized Æthelberht and his people.

2. The children of Æthelberht and Bertha were Eadbald and Æthelburg, who married Edwin, king of the Northumbrians. Paulinus went with her and baptized the king and his people. After Edwin's death, Æthelburg and Paulinus returned to King Eadbald, who gave Æthelburg land at Lyminge where she founded a monastery. She now rests there with St Eadburg.

3. The children of Eadbald and the Frankish princess Ymme were Eanswith, who rests at Folkestone, Eorcenberht, king of Kent, and Eormenred, *ætheling*.

4. The children of Eormenred and Oslafa were *Eormenburh*, Eormengith, Æthelred and Æthelberht.

5. The children of Eorcenberht and Seaxburg were King Egbert, King Hlothhere, Eormenhild and Eorcengota.

6. *Eormenburh, alias* Domne Eafe, married Merewalh, son of Penda, and bore him Mildburg, Mildrith, Mildgith and Merefin. Domne Eafe and Merewalh separated and the former returned to Kent to receive her brothers' *wergild* on Thanet from King Egbert, who ordered them to be killed.

7. Under the king's orders, Thunor his servant had killed them and buried them under the royal throne in his hall at Eastry. A celestial beam of light stood up through the roof of the hall at night and revealed where they were. The king saw it and was very afraid.

8. He ordered Domne Eafe to be fetched to receive their *wergild* and

she took 80 sulungs of land to found a monastery where prayers for their souls could be said.

9. Her daughter Mildrith was sent overseas to learn monastic practice and there she collected relics.

10. On her return, Domne Eafe gave her the monastery to rule and Archbishop Theodore consecrated her with 70 virgins.

11. She died there and miracles are often worked through her.

12. Her aunt Eormengith lived with her till her death and chose her own resting-place one mile to the east of St Mildrith's monastery, where miracles are worked through her.

13. St Eadburg became abbess after Mildrith and built the church in which Mildrith's body now rests.

14. Seaxburg founded St Mary's monastery on Sheppey. Her son Hlothhere gave her the land while they were still alive.

15. Seaxburg, Æthelthryth and Wihtburg were the daughters of Anna, king of the East Angles. Æthelthryth married King Ecgfrith but kept her virginity and was buried at Ely, where miracles are worked through her. Wihtburg rests with her. Eormenhild, daughter of Eorcenberht and Seaxburg, married King Wulfhere; and the Mercians were converted in their time. They begot Werburg, who was buried at Hanbury but later translated to Chester. Eormenhild rests at Ely with her mother and her aunt Æthelthryth; and miracles are worked through her.

16. Eorcengota was sent overseas to her aunt Æthelburg. She died there and her miracles are famous.

17. King Wihtred, son of King Egbert, built the monastery of St Martin at Dover in the place shown him by St Martin himself. He installed monks and gave lands which are still as they were. He rests in St Augustine's, in the *porticus* on the south side of St Mary's Church, built by his great-grandfather Eadbald.


## (i) Hugh Candidus's Text

1. Augustine baptized Æthelberht and his people.

2. He and Bertha, the Christian Frankish princess, begot Eadbald and Æthelburg who married Edwin, king of the Northumbrians. Paulinus accompanied her and converted the king. After the latter's death, Paulinus and Æthelburg returned to King Eadbald,

who gave his sister the vill of Lyminge. She founded there a monastery, where she rests with St Eadburg.

3. The children of Eadbald and the Frankish princess Ymme were Eanswith, who rests at Folkestone, King Eorcenberht, Eormenred, Domne Eafe, *Ermenburga* and Eormengith.

4. The children of Eorcenberht and Seaxburg were King Egbert, King Hlothhere, Eormenhild and Eorcengota.

5. The children of Eormenred and Oslafa were Æthelberht and Æthelred, whose sister, Domne Eafe, married Merewalh, son of Penda, and bore Mildburg, Mildrith, Mildgith and Merefin, who died in childhood.

6. Domne Eafe returned to Kent because Thunor had murdered her nephews [*sic*], Æthelred and Æthelberht, at Eastry and buried them under the royal throne. God indicated their bodies by a column of light and the terrified King Egbert sent for Domne Eafe. In order to placate the Lord, he gave her 80 *iugera aratrorum* of land to build a monastery and there Thunor was killed by being swallowed by the earth.

7. Domne Eafe sent her daughter Mildrith to Chelles to learn monastic discipline and she collected relics there.

8. On her return, she took the veil and was later made abbess of 70 virgins. Eormengith was with her and her body now rests there.

9. Mildrith was succeeded by Eadburg.

10. Seaxburg, wife of Eorcenberht, built the monastery of Sheppey and endowed it in cooperation with her son Hlothhere.

11. Seaxburg, Æthelthryth and Wihtburg were the daughters of Anna. Æthelthryth married King Ecgfrith but remained virgin. Eormenhild, daughter of Seaxburg, married Wulfhere and bore Werburg, who rests at Chester.

12. The children of Penda were Merewalh, Peada, Wulfhere, Æthelred, Cyneburg and Cyneswith. Tibba was their relative.

## (j) *S. Mildryð*

1. Augustine baptized King Æthelberht and all his people.

2. The children of Æthelberht and Bertha were Eadbald and Æthelburg, *alias* Tate, who married Edwin, king of the Northumbrians.

3. Paulinus accompanied her and baptized the king and his people.

After Edwin's death, she returned to King Eadbald, bringing treasures to the church of Canterbury. Paulinus became bishop of Rochester until his death.

4.  The children of Eadbald and the Frankish princess Ymme were King Eormenred, King Eorcenberht and St Eanswith, who rests in the monastery of Folkestone which she founded.

5.  The children of Eormenred and Oslafa were *Eormenburga, alias* Domne Eafe, Eormengith and Æthelred and Æthelberht.

6.  Domne Eafe married Merewalh, son of Penda, and bore him SS Mildburg, Mildrith, Mildgith and Merefin, a holy child. The parents separated and gave their goods and their children to God. Their eldest daughter Mildburg rests at Much Wenlock, Mildrith on Thanet and Mildgith in Northumbria. Merefin died in childhood.

7.  Æthelred and Æthelberht were orphaned and entrusted to King Egbert, son of their paternal uncle Eorcenberht and his wife Seaxburg.

8.  The princes' wisdom and virtue offended Thunor, one of the king's counts and his most valued attendant on his children, who feared that they would become dearer to the king than he. He suggested to the king that they might deprive him or his children of the kingdom and sought permission to kill them secretly. The king refused because they were relatives and dear to him; but Thunor asked many times and eventually murdered them secretly and buried them in [*sic*] the king's throne.

9.  Going out at cock-crow, Egbert saw a beam of light standing up through the roof of the hall. Terrified, he forced Thunor to tell him the whereabouts of the bodies. He then called his *witan* and, with the support of Archbishop Deusdedit, he summoned Domne Eafe to choose a *wergild* for them.

10.  She chose 80 hides on Thanet and, crossing over the river with the king, she demanded as much land as her hind would run around. The king consented and he and Domne Eafe followed the hind until they came to *Thunors hleaw*, where Thunor tried to dissuade the king from making the grant. The earth opened . . .

### (k)  The Lambeth Fragment

1.  [Mildrith's miracles] were known there and still are.

2. St Eadburg became abbess after Mildrith and built the church in which her body now rests.

3. SS Seaxburg, Æthelthryth and Wihtburg were daughters of Anna, king of the East Angles. Æthelthryth married Tondberht and then King Ecgfrith but remained virgin; she rests at Ely where her miracles are known.

4. Eormenhild, daughter of Eorcenberht and Seaxburg, married Wulfhere, king of the Mercians, which people received baptism in their day. They begot St Werburg who rests at the monastery of Hanbury. Eormenhild rests at Ely.

5. SS Seaxburg and Eormenhild took the veil at Milton. The Isle of Sheppey is a dependency of Milton and is three miles broad by seven miles long. Seaxburg built a monastery there, which took 30 years to construct. When it was built, an angel told her in a vision that a heathen people would soon conquer this people.

6. She had then held the kingdom for 30 years to deliver it to her son Hlothhere. She bought of him his share of the district to be free for the uses of the monastery as long as Christianity should be maintained in England. She obtained a blessing from Rome for those who undertook the charge for the service of God.

# Passio Beatorum Martyrum Ethelredi atque Ethelbricti

## (Bodley 285 Text; *BHL* 2641–2)

### Introduction

This text, which has never previously been published, is found only in Oxford, Bodleian Library, MS Bodley 285, fos. 116–21.[1] This manuscript is written in a thirteenth-century hand; and it was probably compiled as well as copied in the thirteenth century, for the latest dateable items in it include, on fos. 166–80, a letter of Pope Celestine III (1191–8) regarding the canonization of Peter of Tarentaise in 1191. Most of the manuscript consists of saints' lives, many of which are continental but some English, including lives of Edward the Confessor, Kenelm, Dunstan, Osith, Werburg and Ivo as well as the present text. There is no indication of provenance apart from the contents; but two items seem to provide strong evidence in favour of Ramsey. Firstly, the Æthelred and Æthelberht material in its present form clearly belongs to Ramsey: it is unlikely that the only manuscript in which it is preserved should be from any other house apart from Ramsey. Secondly, the material concerning Ivo, who was translated to Ramsey in the early eleventh century, is fuller in this manuscript than in any other, for it alone contains the *Miracula Sancti Yvonis*, which is principally of Ramsey interest.[2]

Punctuation has been modernized but the spelling of the manuscript has been retained, except in the case of a few purely orthographical errors which have been corrected. The words *luuione* on p. 99 and *anua* on p. 100 have not been identified and must be either neologisms or corrupt forms. Words supplied to correct apparent defects in the manuscript have been enclosed in square brackets.

INCIPIT PROLOGVS IN PASSIONE BEATORVM MARTYRVM ETHEL-
DREDI ATQUE ETHELBRICTI

Postquam mundo uenialis indulgencie dignatus est largiri munus (per
sue incarnacionis misterium) eternus Opifex, ac, eius feruore passionis,
condicionem a nexibus perpetue necis eruere propriam et de seuis
faucibus pestilentis inimici, opulenta radiantis uerbi doctrina disertorum
apostolorum toto innotuit orbi; atque catholica decora augmentacione
ecclesia continue fecundatur regeneratorum tironum, quos postmodum
flagranti animo triumphantes agonistas promeruit, et summi nominis
10    confessores habere. Qui radiis celestis perfusi gratie, scutoque fidei
uiriliter armati, contra liuidorum tela emulorum infatigabili animo ut
bellici uictores non segniter dimicauere, omnes illecebras lenocinantis
mundi, opes ac desideria aporiantes uoluptuose carnis pro supernorum
appeticione retributionum; magnificis effulsere actionibus uelut splen-
dentis radius solis in orbe, uirtute scilicet signorum et documento
multimode facundie. E quibus micuit prestantissimus Gregorius presul
apostolice sedis, pollens coruscacione actionum.[1] Cuius opinio late
admirabilis redolet, quantum diserte sciencie enituit lepore, quamque
competencium honestate morum lucide effulsit. Nempe isdem, digni-
20    tatem potitus excellentis facundie, inter residua decentissimorum in-
crementa operum, que infatigabili robore strenue gessit, hoc solummodo
ad indicium quam maxime glorie sue effecit, quod Anglorum nacionem
ab tetre gentilitatis errore ad iusticie cultum religionis honestissime
abduxit. Porro predictus reuerendus heros, cum decorosis effulgeret
meritis, ac pontificalis fastigium sortitus esset gradus, sollicite (ut
peruigil pastor) sategit diu optatum pie mentis desiderium ad congruum
fructuosi germinis perducere effectum, luculentissimumque Augustinum, quem in omni catholice pietatis institucione sufficientissime
compererat imbutum, aliosque probabiles delegit comministros, qui
30    euangelizare Anglorum genti uenirent dogmata euangelice predicacionis.
Suscepto itaque precepto, illustris diuini seminis sator Augustinus, cum
ceteris religiosis comitibus memorati presulis, perpropere iniunctum
officium exequitur; atque prompta deuocione inopiis repedauit uerbi,
appulitque tandem salubriter, post tanti effecti itineris spacium, in
citeriorem partem Angligeni ruris.

Eo tempore rex Ethelbrictus[2] in Cancia imperii gubernabat infulas
excellenti potencia, qui memorabili industria suarum uirium usque ad
confinium borealis plage dominatum nactus est regni. Denique disertis-

simus uir Domini in prefati regis applicauit oris, cum copioso agmine famulorum Christi quos isdem egregius rex gratantissima excepit ueneracione, atque in Doruernensi urbe,[3] que uniuersi regni sui fuit metropolis, eis gratifico affectu locum inpertiuit commorandi. Magnificus igitur diuine operacionis executor Augustinus, constancia religiose fidei roboratus, ac protectione superne benedictionis munitus, fluenta deriuare euangelici documenti uulgo sollicite mentis intencione non destitit, quo feritatem barbarice gentis a deuio cultu deuiare et ad noticiam Christiane credulitatis ualeret reuocare. Nec mora, inspirante Deo, nonnulli (abolitis cultibus ineptarum ceremoniarum) ad exhor-  10
tamenta eius clementis suggestionis summo pectoris conamine gregatim confluebant, quin pocius predictus rex, dulcedine spiritalis uerbi delectatus, opitulante Dei gratia, abdicatis erroribus parentalium idolorum, cedens Ihesu Christo, salutari unda tinctus est. Itaque, post suscepte fidei sacramentum cum per uiginti et unum annos iusta examinacionis lance (secundum equitatem diuini iuris) temporalis regni sceptra rite gubernaret, die uicesimo septimo[4] mundialibus rebus exemptus est, atque incunctanter subiit ouans superna gaudia indeficientis glorie.

Successit autem in administrationem regni eius filius et Berte coniugis  20
eius, uocabulo Edbaldus, qui primum cognicionem orthodoxe ueritatis dinoscere tempsit, sed postmodum, cum in nonnullis nefandis commissis sese immisceret diramque[a] ultionem terrentis Iudicis sensit super se inclementer decidere – ni ocius a prauitate tortuosi callis declinasset, propiciante Christo fallacis anathematizauit idolatrie fatuitatibus, ac, Christianam excipiens deuotissime religionem, gratiam sacre regenerationis indeptus est.[5] Erat uero huic (ex regali sobole uereque felici genita) soror nomine Ethelburga, que alia appellatione Tate uocitata est.[6] Hec namque in excercitio diuine actionis, sedula intencione flagrantis fidei, diligenter studuit proficere, ut incorruptibile brauium a remuneratore  30
premiorum bonorum adipisci mereretur. Que, cum incrementis adolesceret iusticie, ac probitate polleret et moribus, utpote nobilitati sue aptissime conuenerat, strenuissimo Eduino regi Northanimbrorum a germano eiusdem in matrimonium donata est legitimi conubii.[7] Cui etiam pudice uirgini acceptabilis Deo Paulinus episcopus in collegium tum solaminis asciscitur, quo comites eius (et Christiane) [ne] polluerentur ritu abominande gentilitatis, sacris exhortationibus ipsius et diuini

---

a MS: diraque

misterii sacramentis existerent corroborati. Sane religiosus antistes, munimine superne uegetacionis suffultus, non solum collegas (ne a proposito torpescerent celestis uite) continuit, uerum regem eundem, quem adierat, (Christi suffragante clemencia) ab infructuosi cultus exercitatione reuocauit suasione salutari, ac cum uniuersis nobilibus et uulgo innumero baptismatis tinxit ipsum spiritali ablutione. Post necem quippe impiam Eduuini regis, adiit regina Canciam cum prefato pontifice, efferens perplura ornamenta insignium rerum secum predicti regis, que in Christi templo (ob uenerationem sui magnifici nominis, pro
10  sibi adquisita specialissime interuencione peculiaris deprecationis, et pro anime redemptione memorati regis) gratifico affectu libauit, que hactenus ibi habentur conseruata in monumentum illustrissime regine. Recepti sunt igitur multum ab Edbaldo rege honorifice, atque antistes isdem pontificalem Rofensis ecclesie[8] suscepit (curam annuente rege) eamque uigilantissime regebat, usque quo gaudia, cum premio fructuosi laboris, penetrauit eterna.[9] At uero Eadbaldi regis et coniugis eius Emme (que erat filia regis Francorum) fuere filii, Eormenredus et Erconbrictus, ac soror eorum sancta Enstriht,[10] que condita iacet in monasterio quod Folk-anstan dicitur,[11] id quoque ad laudem edificauit ipsa altissimi nominis
20  Domini. Siquidem gloriosus pater horum, priuatus hac terrestri luce, incorruptibilis glorie palmam consecutus, Eorconbertus (filius minor natu) imperii suscepit fastigium, diutissimeque absque dedecore infortunii casuum nobiliter retinuit.[12] Sategit isdem, sollicitanti animo, obsecundare diuine institucionis legibus, ac cunctipotentis Domini inhianter efficere affectum, quo ei excellencior accumularetur augmen-tatio adepte bonitatis, in gloria quandoque future spei. Qui etiam, secundum generositatem regalis indolencie, felici ortu progenitam illustrem habuit coniugem, misericordiis refertam, cotidianis dapsilem elemosinis, que clarissime uirginis Etheldrithe erat germana soror,
30  nomine Sexburh.[13] Hec, placere pio iudici gestiens fideli famulatu, dispendia nociua deuitauit mundane iactancie, ne offenderet Dominum, quem toto affectauit nisu mentis cernere placatum. Quibus, fauente Christi gratia, beata erat proles – filie scilicet, uenuste castimoniam continentes illibate uirginitatis, Earcongata ac Eormenhild, speciosusque filius uocabulo Ecbrictus, qui (obeunte patre) regimen admisit regni.[14] Itaque Ermenredus rex, senior frater predicti regis, cum uiridante uigore pubertatis agiliter floresceret, non ludicra lenocinantis blandicie exercuit, sed pocius simplicis uite sectatus est mansuetudinem, iugiter adherens iusticie et fidei sincere religionis, cui benigna suffragabatur pietas
40  Domini, largiendo diffuse lucra terreni mercimonii et felicis sobolis

fecunditatem. Clarissimi uero fratres Ethelredus ac Ethelbrictus (Deo ab ipsa teneritudine rudis infancie acceptabiles) erant ipsius et Oslaue uxoris eius filii, ac insuper bis bine filie, his uocitate nominibus: Domneua, necnon Eormenberga, simulque Eormenburh, atque Eormengith, quas beauit largiflua bonitas Dei laude dignissime uite. Porro tradita est Domneua Meruueale, filio Pendan Merciorum regis, in consorcium legitime copulacionis, qui, Domini annuente clemencia, ibi amene prolis posteritatem adepti sunt, formosas uidelicet filias, sic pulcro uocitamine dictas: beata Mildburga, ac egregia Mildritha*a* et inclita Myldgith, ornatu uirgineo cuncte excellenter compte; sanctumque Merefin, qui 10 (dum adhuc infantiles gereret annos) ex hac molestia corporis corrupti-bilis ad mansura gaudia celestis regni subuectus est. Namque, post sacrati partus procreacionem, pii genitores, pro desiderio inmarcescibilis uite, se ab inuicem in hoc nutanti seculo constanter disiunxere, ac uniuersam supellectilem suam terrenarum possessionum Domino Christo in eterne hereditatis donacionem contulere, quo luce diuine contemplacionis mererentur frui in sempiterna sedis beatitudine. At filia maior eorum, Milburh, in terra Merciorum, in monasterio quod apellatur Winlocan,[15] condita iacet, ubi crebro eius miracula declarata sunt, immo prorsus (quamdiu scintilla in orbe uiget Christiane fidelitatis) perplura existunt. 20 Etenim Mildritha inclita in partibus Cantuariorum, in insula que nuncupatur Teneht,[16] honorifice sepulta est. Ubi etiam per multa temporum curricula iacuit, usquequo ad uotum ipsius diuine misericordie complacuit, ut eius sanctissimi corporis pignera ad decenciorem trans-ferrentur locum, ad monasterium uidelicet apostolorum principis Petri in Cancia honorifice constructum, in quo pastor apostolicus Anglorum, Augustinus, cum archipresulum gemmis, sacra tumulacione idem protegit et obseruat cenobium.[17] Hunc ergo locum Dei sponsa inhabitan-dum elegit; in quo ante principale altare, inter cancellos, digna ueneracione condita iacet, piis suos suorumque fouens patrociniis, et 30 fidelibus larga prestans beneficia populis. Ubi quoque usuali frequenta-cione eius patrantur signa, et crebra uirtutum exercitia, ad euidentis ostensionis declaracionem, quanta sit beate uirginis uirtus ante celsi Conditoris maiestatem. Sacra uirgo Mildgyth in terminis Northanim-brorum corpore deget,*b* per quam gesta sunt acta nonnulla mirabilium signorum, atque deinceps (Christo donante) geruntur ad eius integerrime castitatis ueneracionem. Enimuero genealogiam insignium martirum,

---

*a MS*: d *above* th
*b MS*: quiescit *over line*

Ethelredi ac Ethelbricti, sub compendiosi stili breuitate determinantes, ordinem exprimere geste rei libet nunc, ueraci narrationis relatu, quomodo agoniste idem fuere multati nefanda strage, per ministrum inique operacionis.

EXPLICIT GENEALOGIA BEATISSIMORVM MARTYRVM ETHEL-
DREDI ET ETHELBRICTI

INCIPIT RELATIO QUALITER PASSI SVNT IDEM GLORIOSI MAR-
TYRES ET DIVINITER REVELATI

Tempore illo, quo (per diuine gratie illustrationem) rudis ecclesie
10   pullulauit fides paulatim in terra Anglorum, documento ewangelici mysterii, floruere preciosi fratres, Ethelredus et Ethelbrictus, eximia pollentum coruscacione accionum, quos in Dominici amoris persistencia unice constancia innexuit spei. Qui preclare indoles, cum adhuc in iuuenilis imbecillitate etatis consisterent, regi Egberto, qui fuit filius (ut prelibauimus) Erconberti regis, commendati sunt ad sollertis institutionem prudentie, et ad humani subsidii sustentacionem, quia iam priuati uita affabilium extiterant parentum. In ipso namque inicio decoris adolescentie, nitor in eius uiguit sapiencie, ac experiencia erudite facundie; ultraque uires iusticie et pietatis sectabantur opera, ut (per
20   bone intentionis exercitia) indeficientis glorie adipiscerentur a Christo coronam. Sed execrandus hostis omnis equitatis inimicus, dum inuictos athletas ardui culminis attingere cerneret arcem, cum firmo humilitatis proposito, zeli fomite quendam non imparem sui malignitate inflammare satagebat satellitem, cuius dolorum opprobriis eosdem improperaret fraudulentis, aut nequiter probrosis necaret machinamentis. Huic sane (ex inquietudine austeritatis sue) erat rite seuum infixum uocabulum, quod latino tonitruus sermone sonat, uulgarique eloquio Thunur; cui prefatus rex (secundum uersuti anguis suggestionem) sui potentatum regni sub eo procurandi impertiuit, eundemque ut solos liberos specialius
30   adamauit pre ceteris familiari dilectione. Cumque isdem seuissimus satelles perpenderet beatos germanos proficere in dies ad excellenciora dona prudentis ingenii, liuore stimulabatur inuidie contra illorum beneficienciam, multum uerens ut, si diucius uita potirentur temporali, intimo amore efficerentur affabiliores pocius illo regi. Proinde acriter exarsit iniquus furore insane mentis, inclitos uiros deceptionis fraude gestiens elidere insidiando, odioque zelantis animi eis cepit inuidere; atque regem sedulo illos clanculo criminari accusando, simulque

uenenoso affirmans ore, quam, si forte hac presenti luce diu fruerentur, profecto ipsum natosque suos terreno priuarent regno. O quam subdole artifex mali machinabatur commenta mendacii aduersum insontes, quo laqueo eos contereret uersuto! Qui nefandus, post argumenta falsitatum, interpellare regem ceperat fraudulentis precibus, ut ipsos interimere eum occulte sineret. Sed, ut agnouit prudenter rex hoc fore dolum insidiantis maligni, refragabatur omnimodo consentire sue infauste peticioni, quia adamabat opido eos, eo quod affinitate sibi essent connexi sanguinee propinquitatis. At diuine iusticie rebellis, in uesani persistens cordis rigore, a cepto desistere proposito noluit, quo usque ad peruerse inchoacionis uotum proficeret, assidue regem crebris implorans flagitacionibus, blandimento false adulacionis, ut suo annueret affectui arbitrium agendi, quomodo de Dei famulis uellet. Porro rex Christianum cultum fide religionis excoluit, licet tum non perfecta mentis intencione, metuens nimium ipsum minime carere culpa, assentando reatum iniuste presumptionis, sicque inimico simulata uoce se nolle prorsus scire respondit (nosset uero ille quid ageret). Continuo iniquus innectere distulit moras, sed maturabat explere quantocius opere, quod iam longe pessima concupierat fieri ambicione. Igitur crudelis carnifex, plenus improbitate uiperei seminis, extimplo ut atra obtexit nebula noctem caligine, felices Dei tirones, sine respectu clemencie, in regis aula eiusdem cruenta interemit nece, in loco qui nuncupatur Easterige;[18] eosque clam sub regifico sepeliuit solio, autumans scelestus quod gloriosa martyrum funera in propatulo manifeste cognicionis numquam existerent prodita. Verum execranda mens inuisi tortoris, ignorans penitus euangelicam assertionem quoniam 'nil sit abditum quod non reueletur in publicum',[19] beatos quos feriit uiros iniuste occultare estimabat posse celando; sed pius Omnipresens desiderium nefandi cogitatus eius ad nichilum redegit, ac preciosos suos martyres ibi, quo humati iacebant uili contecti operimento, aperte dignatus est declarare mundo, euidenti indicio. Nam, instar flagrantis facis, emicuit super sanctos prolixe immense lucis radius, qui per summum regie aule culmen indeclinabiliter usque ad clarissimi arcem poli protendebat. Post uero primum gallicinium, rex (a sopore nocturne quietis euigilans) e stratu assurgit; reseratoque ostio, foras digreditur; uidet cominus iubar radiasse ipsius chorusci fulgoris; stupet magnanimiter; pauoreque concutitur ingenti formidinis. Imperat mox accersiri ad se celerrime impiissimum satellitem Thunur, quem minaci uultu sciscitabatur indignando, quidnam de suis adolescentibus propinquis actum foret, quoue obductu eos haberet occultatos. At ille, procaci responso, non quasi regi sed quasi simili sui

sciscitanti, reddidit responsum, inquiens, 'Tui ipse scias quo sint: ego
uero, nisi maiori coactione compellar, non diuulgabo hoc; quod, ut nulli
certum sit, prorsus exopto'. Cui cum rex minitando sepius diceret, 'Iam
nunc dicturus es; alioquin gratia mea priuaberis', ille, anxietate perfusus
animoque consternatus, in his uerbis confessus est, se eos habere
sepultos sub regali throno, in aula regis. Quod nefarium opus cum rex
perpetratum audisse, extimuit admodum, iramque diuine indignacionis
sibi ingruere pertimescens, pro consensu tante iniquitatis; concite cogi
imperat concilium et episcoporum suorum (inter quos primus erat
10  uenerabilis Theodorus archiepiscopus)[20] cunctorumque senatuum
consultu, percunctatur eos, quid sibi optimum esset faciendum. 'Timeo',
inquit, 'et ualde pertimesco pro consensu tante iniquitatis, ne iustam et
debitam iram Domini incurram, non enim (ut flens dico) me excusare
ualeo de consensu necis eorum, interpellante ac sepissime eos accusante
falsis criminibus (ut iam compertum habeo) ministro diaboli Thunur.
Vidi nuper non tacendum Dei miraculum, et (ut ordinabiliter possit
enarrari) subiungam clarius quid uiderim. Cum preterita nocte sompno
indulsissem, et corpori quietem contulissem, non casu (ut certum habeo
mihi) accidit quod, medio noctis silencio, experrectus sum; sed (ut
20  uereor) quin pocius ira Omnipotentis impulsus euigilaui et, a stratu
surgens, foras progrediens, ac sub diuo perstans, uidi omni luce clariorem
quasi solis radium de celo porrectum super aulam meam; et, ex insolita
contemplacione exterritus, animaduerti magni aliquid portendere'.
Cumque sui consiliarii (hec rege narrante) essent ignari et omnino
nescientes quid actum esset, rex eis ordinabiliter exposuit que gesta
erant. At illi (ut cognouerint rei ueritatem) dederunt ei pro futurum
consilium, quatinus deberet sororem illorum Domneuam (que tradita
fuerat Merweale in uxorem, in terra Merciorum) promittere, ut posset
fratrum suorum precium excipere, in quali negotio sibi gratissimum
30  esset; quod et fecit sine ulla dilatione. Veniente itaque illa ante presenciam
regis, benigne uoluntatis affectu concessit ei efficaciam mentis sue pro
meroris afliccione, quo afflicta erat pro interfeccione germanorum
suorum. Elegit itaque (secundum Domini disposicionem) pro eorum
precio terram quadraginta aratrorum, in loco qui appellatur Tenet.
Cumque rex (pro adipiscenda Domini misericordia) eius uoluntati in
omnibus pareret, et, amne illo transuadato, qui illic preterfluit, simul
cum innumero pergerent comitatu, ait rex ad Domneuam cum omni
hilaritate cordis, 'Quanti ruris partem uis habere pro precio fratrum
tuorum?' At illa dixit, 'Non amplius expeto quam cerua mea suo cursu
40  lustrare uult ineundo', asserens sic diuiniter sibi esse insinuatum ut

tantum ad usum sumere proprium deberet quantum prepete cursu cerua
giraret. Subiunxit rex, inquiens consentire se libenter uelle hoc, quod
sensit sibi celesti enucleatum indicio. Sane modestam femine mentem
spes nequaquam elusit; quippe agilis cerua celerem ante illos agebat
motum directo cursu, cuius uestigia rex cunctumque eius agmen
unimodo animo sequebantes, donec ad locum deuenirent qui uocitatur
Thunresleau. Quocirca eidem tale insertum est loco uocabulum, quia ibi
odibilis Deo Thunur funesta oppeciit morte, quem dextra horribiliter
tremendi percussit Iudicis (ob maliciam sue prauitatis) ulcione dire
inuectionis. Nam isdem malignus, cum prefatum attingeret locum,     10
appropiauit regi fraudulenta mente; ac, uultum pronus execrandi capitis
ad ipsum deflectens, uidelicet reuerenciam simulate humilitatis ei
adulanter exhibendo, taliter illum affatur: 'Gloriose rex, qui imperium
regis strenue proprii regni, quamdiu sequi uis gressum unanimiter huius
bruti animalis? Et si hec indocta fera omnem hanc circuire terram satagit
discurrendo, num tu cunctam huic immoderate femine perpetim largiri
moliris?' Ad hec dicta, malignus confestim a tergo frendentis equi
cecidit, atque tellus uasto patefacta est hiatu ad casum ruentis, ipseque
supremum mox flatum funditus amisit uite, ac ibidem humatus est;
super quem procere enormitatis exstructus est aceruus, qui hactenus    20
dicitur Thunresleau, scilicet ad insaniam superbe mentis omnibus
cernentibus propalandam, quantum Deo detestabilis foret ipsius uita,
qui tam ferociter repentina interiit dampnacione. Tali enim modo
scelesto excidente uita, rex anxius fuit nimium propter furoris Domini
ulcionem, seu diram sui satellitis internecionem; perpendit quoque
eundem magis exacerbasse Deum offensionibus infortunium malorum,
dum sic in eum celerrime uindicta superni arbitrii inclementer decideret.
Verum nequaquam dilacionem mansuetissima cerua distulit cepti differe
cursus, donec ad prefinitum locum (cui per gratiam Dei sibi intimatum
erat) deueniret, ibique paululum constitit, ac dein progreditur inde leui    30
incessu, nemine abigente. Porro rex simul et Domneua, ad eundem
aduentantes locum, grates persoluunt Christi bonitati inmensas, quod,
per irracionabile animal, ipsis optatum sue mentis uotum dignaretur
euidenter insinuare, qui etiam toto hoc affectauerit desiderio, ut beatis
martiribus (quorum illud precium erat) obtinerent eterne quietis
beatitudinem, dum iam ope priuati extiterant huius terrestris lucri. De
quibus animaduertendum est perspicue quam grata conuersacionis uite
religiositas extitit eorum Deo, cum post internecionem impiam mundo
eosdem tam micanti declarauit radio, ut undique notum foret quantus in
eis flagraret amor diuine equitatis, quos iniusta feriit ultio cruenti    40

tortoris. Sane hii iusticie cultores hanc temporalem cum dedecore amiserant uitam; sed clemencia pii Conditoris ipsos prouexit gloria in arce etheree sedis, immarcescibilibus decorans sertis radiantis floris, ubi uernant perhenniter cum omnipotente Christo, cui sit honor indeficientis laudis per omne euum.

Beata itaque Domneua sollerti cura fabricam inclite basilice in predicta insula Tenet, cum iuuamine regis Egberhti, inhianter fundauit; ac plurimam illic ancillarum religiosarum [congregationem] ad famulandum perpetuo Conditori coadunauit; eque suam scilicet filiam
10 Mildritham (ad imbuendam litteratorie studiis discipline) trans pontum uasti litoris destinauit, ad monasterium quod Cauul nominatur.[21] Erat in eodem cenobio abbatissa uocitamine Vuilcume, que gratantissime prefatam excepit uirginem cum honore dignitatis ad sacrorum apicum[a] erudiendam, cum consensione antistitis, qui super hoc procurator extitit potencia secularis dominii. Siquidem ipse eandem iuuenculam sedule ad bene agendum supernis informabat monitis, que intentissime ipsa capaci retinuit animo, actuque studuit diligenter patrare siquid utile (si expediret fore efficiendum) in cunctis nobiliter proficiens, secundum diuine iusticie prudenciam seu mundialis pericie disertitudinem. Hec
20 autem, cum propter exercitacionem studii diu in exteris exularet finibus, sategit strenue redimiri patriam dono insignium munerum, quippe sacras felicium sanctorum reliquias, necnon et residuas res ornamentorum ad decus templi pertingentes, ibidem adepta est – quin immo clavum (qui in Christi fuerat corpore infixus) sagaciter adquisitum, dans pro eodem precium inmensi census auri scilicet siue argenti, collatum sibi a genitrice, seu a nonnullis forte propinquis; atque eundem in aurea pyxide condidit, et in monasterio decenti honore suo collocauit seruandum, per quem[b] plurimi diuersis inualitudinibus obstricti impetrauere gratiam sanitatis et deinceps plenissime consequuntur, siqui integra exquisierint
30 fide.

Institutione ergo monasteriali prefata uirgo sufficienter celerrime imbuta proficiebat in dies, competentum honestate morum, in omni religiosorum exhibicione actuum – immo facundiam sollertis prudencie (utpote sue conuenerat nobilitati pocius quam cetere eiusdem cenobii famule) amplexata est sectando. Nempe abbatissa suadere illi admonicionibus

---

*a  MS*: sacris litteris *above line*
*b  MS*: quod

cepit blandis, ac intentis efflagitare precibus, ut sibi assentiret, atque in terra eadem, cum ipsis ad quos causa uénerat discendi, spacio sue uite stabili immutabilitate degeret, pollicens quoque illi lucrum affluentis gaze locupletanter collaturam, si libens ipsa suscipere eius amantissimum atque prestantissimum propinquum in matrimonium carnalis copule uellet, quia cum eadem adhuc seculari fruebatur habitu.

Verum clarissima uirgo abnuit constanter ullo modo abbatisse adquiescere uelle uotis, mallens pocius eterno obsecundare Conditori in castimonia incontaminate mentis, quam se immisceri lasciuiis fugitiui gaudii. Unde permota nimium abbatissa contra uirginis refragacionem,    10 mandat confestim uernacule caminum properanter succendere uehementi igne; ac eandem secrecius uirginem ad se euocat, imperans ut se celeri sequeretur calle. Cumque pariter ad locum quo fornax conflagracione ingenti torrebatur aduentarent, continuo sine clementi respectu pietatis, beatam Mildridam inter flammiuoma crepitantis incendia camini detrusit abbatissa, sueque iubet uernacule os ardentis clibani obserare ostio: quippe iniustissima sic cogitaret forte contingere, ut corpus uirginis contaminaretur ibi ustione eructantis flamme, propter inobedienciam qua sibi obtemperare recusabat.

Sed pius Conditor (qui quondam tres hebreos pueros a torrido redemit    20 caumate fornacis, ne flammis cremarentur atrocibus) sua potenti uirtute eandem non minus inuiolatam inter ignium uapores detinuit, quia minime attingere ferocitas ualuit flamme, quia munita erat integerrime uirginitatis pudicicia.[22] Post non modicum interuallum illuc abbatissa identidem iuit, imperauitque celerrime os reserare camini, autumans iam tum honesta uirginis membra exusta ab ignium conflagratione fuisse; sed reuera aliter quam rata est euenit. Nempe beata uirgo, suffragante Domini clemencia, inter horrisonos focorum ardores constiterat illesa, atque inde in publicum exiliuit innocua, sine ullo dispendio crepitantis incendii, utpote extranea ab omni fuerat luuione[c] illecebrosi luxus.    30

Tantum igitur abbatissa, cernens miraculum in uirgine esse patratum, mota est animo, iraque furenti inflammata; atque eandem crudeli apprehendit dextera, ac de sacri capitis cesarie crinem uiolenter abripuit, quem protinus de humo sancta tulit uirgo, eundemque clam diligenter occuluit, donec ipsum matri per legatum destinaret fidelem. Libellum

---

*c Sic*

uero psalmorum clarissima uirgo scripsit egregium, uti gratum genitrici
fore nouerat, ac in calce eiusdem crinem locauit, eidemque direxit,
simulque etiam cum eo pittaciolum permodicum in quo caraxatum erat
huiusmodi textus, ut, si incolumem eam cernere conaretur, ocissime
mandaret suis sine dilacione ipsam ad natiuum perducere solum. Quod ut
Domneua comperit in tanto angore animi dilectam esse filiam circum-
septam, mesta ualde effecta est, ac continuo cum plurimorum sociorum
iuuamine eosdem illuc misit identidem legatos, demandans eis, ut
episcopo intimarent et abbatisse, quare graui inualitudine corporis ipsa
10    opprimeretur, ac eos per omnipotentis clemenciam Domini obnixe
interpellarent, ut sue filie ad propria consentirent rura repedare, quo eius
contemplari aspectum quiuisset priusquam hac priuaretur uita.

Qui, iussa prompta mente exequentes domine sue, prope ceptum iter
peragunt, ac episcopo et abbatisse cuncta (ut eis fuerat iussionibus
iniunctum) per ordinem indicant, sed nullatenus illi annuere eidem
uirgini facultatem abeundi uoluerunt, quia confidebant adhuc posse eam
affatibus deuinci blandis, quo apud ipsos, incommutabili moraretur
stabilitate. Verum sacra uirgo uelociter innotuit actu, aliud se, quam illi
suspicati sunt, commodius scrutari consilium: quippe intempeste noctis
20    silencio, cum iam uniuersos fessus oppressisset sopor, abdite inde
aufugit; atque mox ad eam sui socii (uti inter se mutuo ante condixerant)
constanti animo aduenerint.

Illis igitur repedantibus celeri motu, cum iam essent digressi spacium
itineris, mencio beate uirginis repente menti irrepsit, minime sanctorum
reliquias, quas ibi difficulter conquisierat, secum tulisse; confestimque e
uestigio retrogradum arripuit iter, ac preciosum thesaurum ubi latenter
habuerat reconditum tulit, sicque iterum ceptam gradiebatur uiam. His
taliter gestis, abbatissa a sopore euigilans de stratu properanter consurgit,
cepitque sollicite eandem perquirere uirginem, suosque percunctari si
30    forte quo isset nossent. Qui omnes pari acclamacione protestati sunt, se
penitus ignorare quonam tenderet gressum. Unde ipsa uehementer
anua[a] effecta, basilicam cursim adiit, imperauitque cunctas pulsari
campanas; atque episcopo innotescit beatam Mildridam fraudulenter,
sine eorum consensu, uelocis fuge arripuisse cursum ad rura genitalis
soli. Qui hoc mutuo consilium decreuere consultum fore, ut post enorme
agmen destinarent uirorum, qui illam (si nollet ultro) saltem inuitam ad

---

*a Sic*

eos impellerent inuerso gradu uenire; quia affirmabant multo satius esse, ut tam indolem tamque egregiam apud se retinerent uirginem, quam aliorsum diuerti sinerent.

Ergo, cum uulgus (ut iussum fuerat exactum) insequeretur ueloci incessu beatam uirginem, contigit (secundum Dei disposicionem) ut ipsa iter quod ceperat prospero euentu ocius peragraret, ac litus acceleranter attingeret equoris; sed ex aduerso euenit continuo infestus casus, qui impedicionem intulit sibi ultra transfretandi, quoniam quidem ratis, recedente unda maris, eminus in sicco constiterat litore. Quocirca mesta nimium facta est sancta uirgo, afflictaque magnanimiter propter impedi-    10
mentum sui itineris, immo humanum formidans tremorem, que ocissime (ni solamen sublimis dextera impenderet Dei) super se ingruere uehementer extimuit. Que omni mentis nisu ad benignitatem conuersa est Domini, totam se potestati illius uidelicet corpus et animam commendans, ac intentissime implorans eius magnificentiam, ut, inter seuam procellam mundanorum turbinum, eam dignaretur uigore incrementorum corroborare uirtutum, et ab hostilium incursione ualida tueri protectione. Voto etiam se obligauit ipsius iugiter imperiis adherere; atque, reliquo dum uiueret tempore, absque residuo psalmorum concentu, mellifluum beati immaculati psalmum ad reuerenciam    20
eius nominis et intemerate uirginis Marie diatim concinere duodecies spopondit; quatinus ipsius adiuta presidio in se quantum aufugere posset manus, et patrie fines sine impedicionis laqueo efficaciter gratulabundo inuisere animo. Hec uero perorante, beata Mildritha assurgit protinus, intuensque se post tergum, et ecce conspexit, sibi appropiantem maximam uulgi cateruam, ad similem speciem quasi innumera esset acies nigrantum coruorum. Que mox ad suos conuersa, hortatur ut ocissime nauim altius in pelagus detruderent remis, asseuerans se contemplari mare ad litus per Dei gratiam redisse. Nec mora hi dicto cicius austri opem nacti carinam leui remorum tractu in alti gurgitis latitudinem    30
impellebant, ac sic cum prospero nauigio seculi flatus iter carpebant securum, sine ullo discrimine aduersi periculi. Cumque iam procul a terra esset ratis, sancta uirgo, ripam intuens quo rediit, ibi maximam consistere aciem se insequentum uidet uirorum. Unde leta effecta nimium propter quod ab eorum cruentis foret manibus; gratesque largitori omnis bonitatis Domino rependit immensas pro tanta sibi benificia collata, cuius pia annuente clemencia, ipsa eadem attigit nocte locum qui situs est in portu Tenet, qui ab incolis Ippesfleot uulgari uocitatur uocabulo.[23] Dum autem sol suo irradiaret mundum iubare,

dilecta Mildrida Deo, sompnolentum a se excuciens corporem continuo, monasterium (quod sibi mater insigni construxit opere) propere adiit, ac genitrici ocius intimare eius aduentum mandauit. At, ubi Domneua cognouit aduentum filie, gauisa est exultacione non modica; iussitque mox suis ut ipsam celeriter precarentur ad se uenire, ac eis cuncta obuiam signa propter aduentus eius reuerenciam pulsare imperat, nec minus subiecte familie contra moderanti ire incessu, atque ante se ut laudes omnipotenti Deo cum omni exhilaracione cordis concreparent, pro dilecte filie sue reuersione. Post intercapedinem exigui temporis, inhianter desiderauit uolui sanctimonialium habitu, spretis omnibus mundialibus superfluis pompis cum auctore suo: quod ad effectum (Christi annuente gratia) perduxit. Nam beate recordationis domnus archiepiscopus Theodorus, qui ea tempestate Christi gubernabat ecclesiam apostolica auctoritate, eam consecratam circumtexit sacris operimentis, una cum septuaginta uirginibus quas sua sancta mater inibi Domneua imbuit, et sacris exhortacionum sermocinacionibus suasit, ut spontanee et libenti animo se subici gauderent monachili proposito. Ad hoc quippe eas aggregauit et instruxit, quatinus commodius et facilius posset monachicum pensum (quod Domino nouerat persoluere) pro animabus uidelicet sanctorum preciosorum martirum Ethelredi et Ethelbricti (quorum precium erat) et pro remissione regis, qui illam hereditatem eis contulit honoris gracia, regnante rege eterno Christo, cuius regni imperium permanet in secula seculorum. Amen.

EXPLICIT PASSIO SANCTORVM GERMANORVM AC PRECIOSORVM MARTYRVM CHRISTI ETHELREDI ATQUE ETHELBRICTI

HIC INDICATUR QUALITER ET QUANDO ABLATI SVNT DE LOCO VBI SEPVLTI ERANT ET VBI MODO SVNT TVMVLATI

Igitur predicti sancti martyres Domini, Ethelredus atque Ethelbrictus, regnante rege Ethelredo[24] (filio famosissimi regis Edgari), concedente inclito duce Ethelwino[25] (in cuius uilla reperti sunt tumulati), exempti sunt a fratribus monasterii Ramesige et transuecti ad idem cenobium, quod isdem comes construxerat, cooperante sancte recordacionis domno Oswaldo archipresule,[26] itaque eundem locum Christo commendans eiusdem archiepiscopi consecratione, ac Ascwn (cuius diocesis erat) pretitulando commisit.[27] Utrosque spacium unius urne continuit: nam[a] fas erat eos corpore seiungi, quos diuina gratia per martyrii

---

*a* MS: n̄

triumphum pares fecerat eterna mercede. In priori monumento multis annorum curriculis eis positis, excelsus Dominus, qui humilia respicit, et alta a longe cognoscit, eos creberrimis ditare miraculis uoluit, de quibus unum posterorum noticie nunc propalamus presenti sermone.

Accidit ut quidam, alterius bonis cecatus, ouem cuiusdam pauperis tolleret secrecius, quam gestans in humeris, ligatis pedibus, deferre gliscebat secus archisterium sanctorum martyrum. Reus itaque huius sceleris continuo frustratur flatu uitali, humique prosternitur mortuus, ouem uiuentem habens in manibus. Eo insequente cui furtum fuerat illatum, recipit proprium, dimittit reum morte preuentum subitanea ultione sanctorum innocentium. Continuo currens ad edituos, sciscitatur si peremerint latronem illum: a nullo mortalium didicit iugulatum; acceptaque licencia reportandi quod suum fuerat, letus et hylaris reuertitur in sua, Deo ac sanctis martyribus eius multas gratias agens.[28]

Olimque (ut narratum est a plurimis) sagacissime temptauerunt duodecim presbiteri furtim eos abducere: quibus minime est concessus effectus desiderii eorum, quin insuper (propter temeritatis presumptionem, qua hoc conati sunt patrare) graviter multati sunt, non unimodo, nec unius uindicte plaga dire inuectionis plagati sunt (ut animaduertere cogerentur) quia uires uirtutis eorum excesserat, quod explere inexplorato meditatu studuerunt. Erant quippe sepulti in ecclesia eiusdem uille que uocatur Wakerynga,[29] cui inseruiebant segniter pauci incuriosi presbiteri, pro quorum ignauia et raritate competentis officii, quibus eos honorare debito seruicio debuerant, ut ita dixerim tediati sunt et amplius inibi noluerunt manere. Cum ergo eis placuit illinc aufferri, non elegerunt eorum seruiciis uenerari, qui eos absque eorum desiderio totis contatibus frustra molliti sunt auferre. Elegerunt siquidem quin pocius eorum ablacione auferri, quorum sine intercapedine uoces Dominum collaudantes sonant. Nichilominus eos libuit locari in loco quo iugis et continua laudacio Domini et sanctorum eius inest, scilicet inter monachice contionis cateruam (id est in conuentu cenobitarum) ubi rarissime uel nullomodo, opitulante Christi clemencia, expletur unius solummodo monachi seruicio monachile debitum pensum, licet insint pauci, quin magis duorum triumue, seu plurimorum, secundum mensuram monasterii substancie. Non enim per dies quosdam, sed per singulos instantes Domino seruiunt, nec semel ecclesie limina uisitant ut omnia ecclesiastica officia uno tempore expleant (sicuti mos est desidiosorum[b]

b *MS*: desidium

clericorum) sed omnia competenter suis propriis temporibus obseruant, iuxta decretum sanctionis regule, quod patris Benedicti institucio eos studiose admonicionis instituit admonitu. Iccirco talibus exercitiis se exercent, quia sperant se peruenturos ad eorum consorcium in celis, quorum patrocinia exposcunt in terris. Visum est senioribus iunioribusque eiusdem cenobii cenobitis fratribus eos singulos in singulis concludi mausoleis, et in capite ecclesie decenter collocari. Ibidem quippe semotim positi, sic meritis et signorum miraculis enitent, et locum habitationis eorum illustrant, quem admodum sol et luna
10  ambitum mundi suorum claritate radiorum illuminant. Dextrum uero chorum (quia ignorantibus dicam) sanctus Ethelredus sua presencia letificat ac patrocinatur, utpote senior frater: ast uero iunior frater, sanctus Ethelbrictus, sui germani meritis compar, sinistrum chorum nichilominus tuetur, et ibidem astantes sua iugi protectione protegit. Celebratur memoria translacionis eorundem sexto decimo kalendarum nouembris, quia eodem die aduecti sunt monasterio Ramesige, quod sibi elegerunt inhabitandum in diem resurrectionis omnium, quando cum sanctis omnibus percepturi sunt binas stolas celestis glorie, largiente Christo retributore omnium, qui uiuat et regnat per omnia secula
20  seculorum.[30] Amen.

APPENDIX C

# Vita Deo dilectae virginis Mildrethae

GOSCELIN OF CANTERBURY

(*BHL* 5960)

## Introduction

The *Vita Mildrethae* is preserved in the following manuscripts. All of them have been consulted and the letters here assigned to them correspond to those used in the textual footnotes.[1]

### A. London, British Library, Cotton MS Vespasian B.xx, fos. 143–63v

This manuscript is assigned to St Augustine's Abbey, Canterbury, on grounds of an *ex libris* inscription and dated to the early twelfth century on grounds of script. It is written in various hands and contains, in addition to the *Vita Mildrethae*, the lections of St Mildrith, the *Textus translationis . . . Mildrethae* and the *Contra Usurpatores*, works by Goscelin concerning St Augustine, lives of the archbishops of Canterbury (which are probably also by Goscelin), and a series of charters and papal bulls allegedly granted to St Augustine's Abbey.[2] This manuscript may be somewhat earlier than the other two early manuscripts, B and C, since its version of the *Textus translationis . . . Mildrethae* lacks a miracle concerned with the dispute with St Gregory's Priory which is found in B, fos. 184–5, and C, fos. 98–100.[3]

### B. London, British Library, MS Harley 105, fos. 134–53

Dated to the early twelfth century on palaeographic grounds and assigned to St Augustine's Abbey on the basis of its contents, this manuscript is closely related to A and contains the same texts concerning St Augustine and St Mildrith and the lives of the archbishops.[4] It formed part of the library of Sir Simonds d'Ewes in the seventeenth century.[5] I follow the ink foliation which fails to number fos. 1–5. The pencil foliation is also at fault because, although it does number these folios, it fails to number blank leaves. According to the pencil foliation, the *Vita Mildrethae* occupies fos. 137–56. In a later medieval hand on f. 133v (ink foliation) there appears the epitaph:

> Clauditur hoc saxo Mildretha sacerrima virgo
>> Cuius nos precibus adiuvet ipse Deus. Amen.

> Verbi incarnati m. xxx. Ego Aelfstanus abbas transtuli corpus
> beate virginis de Insula Taenet et hoc in loco honorifice condidi.
> + Ego abbas Rogerus II ipsum corpus sub testimonio bonorum virorum
> inspexi et iterato decentius in hoc loco collatum anno gratie
> m. cc. lix mense maii.

The first part of this is given by William Thorne who describes it as an epitaph on Mildrith's tomb.[6]

### C. London, British Library, MS Harley 3908, fos. 1–35

Script and contents show that this book was also produced at St Augustine's Abbey in the early twelfth century, but it is smaller than A or B and the twelfth-century section of it contains only the *Vita Mildrethae* and the *Textus translationis . . . Mildrethae*, together with two short texts of doubtful attribution, the *Missa de sancta Mildretha* and the musical *Historia de sancta Mildretha*.[7] Its production is perhaps some special indication of Mildrith's popularity at St Augustine's Abbey.

### D. Oxford, Bodleian Library, MS Rawlinson C.440, fos. 11–33v

This manuscript is a collection of saints' lives, written in a late twelfth- or thirteenth-century hand and of unknown provenance. Most of the saints whose lives are found in the collection are continental and apart from Mildrith the only English saints whose lives occur are Edward, king and martyr, and Edmund.[8] The *Vita Mildrethae* occurs alone and not in conjunction with Goscelin's other texts on Mildrith.

### E. Dublin, Trinity College, MS 172 (B.2.7), pp. 276–88

The first part of this manuscript is a collection of mainly English saints' lives written in a thirteenth-century script but of unknown provenance, its former assignation to St Peter's, Westminster, having been rejected.[9] The *Vita Mildrethae* breaks off abruptly in Chapter 13 and it is not accompanied by the other works concerning Mildrith. Other texts about

English saints in the collection include lives of Oswald, Werburg, Æthelthryth, Guthlac and Egwine. The second part of the manuscript is mainly occupied by various prophetic writings.[10]

F. Gotha, Forschungsbibliothek, Memb. I.81 (olim M.n.57), fos. 178v–85v

This large collection of English saints' lives is probably of English origin, as shown both by content and marginalia, but its precise provenance is unknown. On palaeographical grounds, it is dated to the late thirteenth or early fourteenth century.[11] The *Vita Mildrethae* occurs in an abbreviated form and is not accompanied by Goscelin's other texts about Mildrith. It is followed, however, by the *Vita sanctorum Æthelredi et Æthelberti martirum et sanctarum virginum Miltrudis et Edburgis* (the Gotha Text).

G. London, British Library, Cotton MS Otho A viii, fos. 1–5v.

This manuscript, which formerly contained various hagiographical texts, was almost destroyed by fire in 1731.[12] The only remaining folios contain fragments of the *Vita Mildrethae* (1–5v), of the *Textus Translationis . . . Mildrethae* (6) and of the Old English life of St Machutus (7–34).[13] The fragments of the *Vita Mildrethae*, which are not completely legible even under ultra-violet light, consist of passages from the list of chapter-headings, the prologue and chapters 2, 3, 4, 10, 23, 24, 25, 26 and 27. It is possible on palaeographic grounds that the manuscript from which these fragments come was written in the late eleventh century.[14] It would therefore have been written earlier than A, B and C, which are assigned to the early twelfth century.

The version of the Vita Mildrethae in E has been drastically truncated and that part of the text which describes Mildrith's career in France is found only in a much abbreviated form in F. Apart from these variations, the variations between the manuscripts are not great and the construction of a *stemma* has therefore not been attempted. The text given here is based on A as probably the earliest manuscript, although readings from the closely related manuscripts, B and C, have sometimes been preferred. The manuscripts D, E and F are later in date and, in the case of the last two, do not give full texts. Where they vary from A, this has been noted in footnotes.

Punctuation has been modernized. Following the practice of A, *c*s and *t*s have been distinguished. Forms such as *inp*- and *tan*-, which are frequent in A, have been emended, however, to *imp*- and *tam*-.

Orthographical variants and obvious scribal errors have not in general been noted.

Except in the title, the spelling of the subject's name has been standardized as *Mildritha*, which is the form most commonly occurring in A and B, although these manuscripts sometimes use *Mildrida*, *Mildretha* and *Mildreda* in an apparently random fashion. D follows this usage. C is fairly consistent in its use of *Mildretha* and in this it is followed usually, though not invariably, by E and F.

Square brackets have been used to indicate words supplied to correct apparent defects in the text. Suggested translations of passages of exceptional difficulty have been offered.

INCIPIT PROLOGUS IN VITA DEO DILECTAE VIRGINIS MILD-
RETHAE[a]

Diuinus interpres Ieronimus, Iob secundo transferens, de stercore eum eleuasse se gloriatur.[1] Nulla species, nullus decor, nisi in luce uidetur; quantum quid monstratur, tantum cognoscitur; sol in nube, aurum in terra, gemma in luto, nucleus in testa, triticum in palea, uirtus est inexposita. Res digne preconio iacent scriptore sub tepido, sordent sub garrulo, lucent claritate sua sub diserto. Quocirca, O karissimi mei, in uita beatissime uirginis Mildrithe mortalem sensum superante, cum non
10 sufficiam beniuolentie uestre satisfacere, sit tamen aliquid me dulci amicitie obedisse. Parui non ut uolui sed ut modo inter innumeras mentis et temporis ablationes raptim et cursim ualui – si gratiam non meretur repulsa facultas, uel ueniam habeat prompta uoluntas. Sententiam autem ueritatis obnixe exequimur, non ex nouis testibus, sed ex ipsa uita eius et meritis antiquitus descriptis uel ab antiquis historiis collectis. Valeant qui hec fastidiunt tamquam ad se non pertinentia, dummodo uobis domesticis a Deo date domine dilectoribus sint parata.[b] Satis uero docent presentia uel assidua eius signa quam sint prisca credenda.

EXPLICIT PROLOGUS

20 INCIPIUNT CAPITULA

I. Virgo Domini Mildritha tam sancta quam regia progenie pollet ab utroque parente.

---

a  B *reads in an early modern hand*: Prologemena et Capitularum elenchie. Libr. 4.;
   C, D, E, F *and* G *show minor variants on* A.
b  F: pergrata

VIVS interpres ieronimus. Iob sedo transferens: de stercore eum eleuasse gloriatur:
Nulla species. nullus decor. nisi in luce
uideatur. Quantu quid monstratur: tan-
tu cognoscitur. Sol in nube. auru in terra.
gema in luto. nucleus in testa. triticu in palea. uirtus est in-
terposita. Res digne preconio. iacent scriptore sub tepido.
sordent sub garrulo. lucent claritate sua sub diserto. Quo
circa o knu mei in uita beatissime uirginis aldride mortalem sensu supante. cu non sufficia beniuolentie uire satisfacere: sic tam aliquid me dulci amicitie obedisse. Parui. ni ut uolui. sed ut modo inter innumeras mentis et
temporis ablationes raptim et cursim ualui. Si gram ni me-
reatur repulsa facultas: uel ueniam habeat prompta uoluntas. Sententiam aute ueritatis obnixe exequimur. ni ex nouis
testabuis sed ex ipsa uita eius et meritis antiquitatis descriptis uel ab antiquis historiis collectis. Valeant qui hec fastidiunt tanquam ad se non pertinentia. du modo nobis domesticis a deodate dne dilectorib sint parata. Satis uero
docent presentia uel assidua eius signa: qua sint prisca
credenda. INCIPIVNT CAPITVLA.        I. De arda dignitas.
VIRGO dni aldreda. tam sca qua regia pgenie. polleret abutroq parente.
Iacet et uirgin magna regalitas qua athelberti pm anglor regu. xpiani irra. II.
Rex eadbaldus et aranus. diuinitus concec. poplin sui ad xpianitate trahit. et ex. III.
Iiangog regis filia parentale stancia aldrede prerogat.        IIII.
Ab eaibaldo rege ermenredus filius matre et primos uirginis pducet. a regio
quoq mercior meruita huic pac erecut. et scim pgenie addidit.        V.
Maroru auunclor uirginis qua gra cantui coniungutur. abi mare ecclam funda-
tur. et uirginis septuaginta ordinauit.        VI.
Ear nor sce matris et scissime filie. quo illa suasir et ista siruit. celeste philosophia
erudiendo querere.        VII. De auunica tempana
Orantur transmarie diuinis litteris et disciplinis erudienda nec minia cessant

3. London, British Library MS Harley 105, f.134: the beginning of the *Vita Mildrethae*.

II. Lucet uirgini materna regalitas, quam Athelberti primi Anglorum regum Christiani irradiat dignitas.

III. Rex Eadbaldus eius atauus, diuinitus correctus, populum suum ad Christianitatem trahit et ex Francorum regis filia parentalem Franciam Mildrithe prerogat.

IIII. Ab Eadbaldo rege, Ermenredus filius matrem et proximos uirginis producit. A regno quoque Merciorum Meruuala huic pater exitit, ad sanctam progeniem addidit.

V. Martyrium auunculorum uirginis qua gratia Cantiam commigrauit ubi mater ecclesiam fundauit et uirgines septuaginta coadunauit.

VI. Feruor sancte matris et sanctissime filie, quo illa suasit et ista sitiuit, celestem philosophiam exulando querere.

VII. Mittitur trans mare diuinis litteris et disciplinis erudienda, nec in uia cessant dauitica timpana.

VIII. Docentes precurrit diuina intelligentia amabilis omnibus et gratiosa.

IX. Exempla uirtutum que ab omnibus humiliter expetit omnibus impendit; quas Christus gemmas in Anglia habeat, in hac lucescit; contra diabolum insurgit.

X. Abbatissam blandientem et terrentem ut nubat tota constantia et contradictione reuerberat.

XI. In ardenti fornace obtrusa, manet flammis illesa ut uirgo immaculata.

XII. Diu in igne persistentis auditur canor uirginalis et martyrialis, *Igne me examinasti Domine*, et contra exit a flamma.

XIII. Iterum patitur pro castitate. Cesa et lacerata ad repatriandum a Domino est exaudita.

XIIII. Auulsos crines mittit matri ceu martyrialia xenia. Legatis maternis natam reddere dissimulat abbatissa.

XV. Noctu cum legatis egressa repetit tamen relicta sacra, et euadit ad mare, uotis potita.

XVI. Videt persequtorum cuneos minitantes pudicitie sue, pro qua mallet (et pro sociis quibus timebat) animam dare.

XVII. Clamantibus nautis uoce et illa corde, hostes in se ipsos arma uertere; iamque pacati, quo magis properabant, eo diuinitus remotiores erant, donec estus maris succurreret.

XVIII. Precibus et uotis dominice sponse pelagus obtemperat: nec mora absortos fluctus uno impetu reumatizat, naues sulleuat et uirginem nauigat. Hostis, amissa preda, se exasperat; uirgo canoris laudibus in Domino triumphat.

XIX. Lapis egredientis a naui uirginis perpetuo signo seruat uestigia; et diuersis morbidis dat medicamina; et impatiens mutare loca circumdatur ecclesia.

xx. Colligit reducem filiam Domneua solenni letitia cum uirginum chorea et tota plebe obuia.

xxi. Consecratur a sancto presule Theodoro cum uirginibus septuaginta; simulque, petente, matre, ordinatur abbatissa.

xxii. Beata Domneua, migrans ad celestia, reliquit Mildrethe sue monasterii sceptra.

xxiii. Consurgens pro genitrice, Domini uexillifera totius uirtutis erat forma, ut magistra.

xxiiii. Pro grege uigilantis et legentis, lumen malignus spiritus extinxit, quod ilico angelus lucis clarius restituit. 10

xxv. Sopita in Domino, uidit demonem sibi insidiantem, sed econtra amicum angelum illum procul absterrentem, seseque luciferis alis amabiliter obuelantem.

xxvi. Oranti in ecclesia toto corde, spiritus Domini apparuit in specie columbe candidissime, sedens in eius uertice et fauens illi amicissimo alarum uerbere.

xxvii. Ut diu desiderauerat multisque lacrimis optinuerat, uenit ad extrema et, pacem commendans omnibus, transit in thalamum Domini sui speciosa,$^a$ quam flentibus reddunt salutifera signa et presentia patrocinia. 20

xxviii. Succedit Eadburga$^b$ abbatissa, que in edificatum sibi templum transferens illam inuenit post tot annos toto corpore et uestibus integram et incontaminatam.$^c$

INCIPIT VITA DEO DILECTE VIRGINIS MILDRETHE$^d$

Regum proles,[2] dignissima uirgo Domini Mildritha, tam pollet stemmate quam sanctimonia. Gentem Merciorum clarissima natiuitate, populum Cantuariorum perpetua illustrat mansione. Inde genitorem, hinc sortita est genitricem. Ab utroque uero regno et ab utroque parente, non solum regificum sed et sanctificum genus trahit, terreque nobilitatem celo attollit. Quod ut lucidius comprobetur, progenitores eius et cognatos, ab 30 his modo qui Christo initiati sunt, retexere dignum uidetur, ut horum natiuo auro et gemmis uel rosis ac liliis corona uirgini formetur: per quos nouella Anglorum ecclesia sumpsit augmentum, sicut per apostolicos

---

a  F: sponsa
b  F: Edburga
c  C omits capitula
d  F adds Idus Iulii

patres exordium. Nec fastidiat lector florulentum hoc diuerticulum uel supplementum adiacentium alueorum; quo refectus, irriguis pratis currat iter ceptum.

II

Huius itaque decentissime sobolis*ᵃ* tritauus, antecessorum et parentalium regum potentissimus ac felicissimus rex choruscat Athelbertus.³ Primus*ᵇ* Anglorum regum fide Christi ac baptismate canduit, primus celeste regnum de terreno obtinuit. Hunc illud precluentissimum Romani orbis decus et magnum mundi luminare Augustinus,⁴
10 excellentissimi Gregorii⁵ (immo Christi) legatione functus, eterni solis agnitione in angelum conuertit, quem ut magnum maris cetum apostolica beati Petri sagena cum sua gente celo triumphauit. Imperauit usque ad Humbram fluuium⁶ cunctis australibus prouinciis late Brittannie, fouebat et subiectos reges grata dicione. Nec contentus sua salute, omnes certabat Domino lucrifacere et Christianitatem ubique propagare. Gaudebat Dei famulis obedire magis quam regnare, reuerebatur uerba sacerdotum potius quam bella augustorum. Quinquaginta et sex annis regnauit, longe felicior, qui Christum uidere in sua gente nasci et Christo renasci meruit, quam Cesar Augustus, qui totidem annis imperauit*ᶜ* sed
20 Christum, suo tempore humanatum, fide non attigit. Post uiginti autem annos sue in saluatore regenerationis (anno uidelicet Incarnati Verbi sexcentesimo sextodecimo) assumptus ad supernum solium, conditus est in porticu sancti Martini, intra ecclesiam beatorum Petri et Pauli apostolorum, ubi et Berta regina possidet monumentum. Multa adeo diuine et humane honorificentie bona indidit idem pater patrie sue, decernens attente quicquid sanctius didicisset a patribus et transmarina comitate. Maxime autem amore beati Petri euangelicique progenitoris sui Augustini, Romanis legibus ac decretis informauit patria iura, ut Anglia, sicut alter orbis, ita altera uideretur Roma, tamquam filia tante
30 matris emula. Quarum omnium institutionum exemplaria adhuc habentur, Anglico eloquio descripta, sicut tunc in concione*ᵈ* sapientum sancita fuerant et accepta.⁷

------

*a* D *and* F: prolis
*b* F: Hic primus
*c* D: regnavit
*d* F: constitutione

III

Huic succedens, filius Eadbaldus*e* interim a paterna pietate declinauit et in idola ac stupra defluxit.[8] Unde traditus ei, cui se mancipauerat, Satane, crebra agitabatur*f* uecordia et inuasione demonica ac uexatione, ut a tam seuo tyranno disceret, iugum Christi quam suaue esset; et a casu firmius staret. Roborabat hanc apostasiam transitus ad ethera Christianissimi regis Orientalium Saxonum Saberti,*g* nepotis digni regis Athelberti,*h* cuius tres filii cum indisciplinata plebe in paganismum sunt conuersi.[9] Pulsi antistites sacrati, Mellitus a Lundonia, Iustus a Rofensi ecclesia, consulto beato Laurentio archipresule Cantie,[10] transmigrant in Gallias, amissa spe, sanius esse reputantes cum Loth animam suam saluare, quam cum ardente Sodoma perire, cui non possent prodesse. Hos etiam ipse Laurentius eadem desperatione sequuturus, noctem ipsam matutine fuge in supradicta apostolorum Petri et Pauli ecclesia*i* iugibus precibus et lacrimis cum anxiis suspiriis continuat, lugens miserabiliter dilecte gentis errorem priore peiorem, orans mundi saluatorem, ne redemptionis sue plebem suique fidelissimi signiferi Augustini laborem daret in perditionem et antiqui predonis insultationem. Tandem sopor fessum et mestum occupat; adest in uisu*j* memor ouium sibi a Christo in pignus dilectionis sue commissarum supernus ianitor Petrus, increpat perfugam Domini uerbis et uerberibus acerrimis per longa spacia noctis. 'Quomodo,' inquit, 'oues Dominicas tibi creditas in medio luporum dimittis? Nondum ad sanguinem restitistis et fugitis.[11] *Bonus pastor animam suam dat pro ouibus.*[12] Hoc Christus fecit et docuit, in hoc me seipsum sequi precepit. Ego uincula, uerbera, carceres et ipsam mortem crucis post Dominum pertuli, sueque redemptionis gregem uite impendio defendi. Decebat et te eius seruare exemplum, cuius tenes officium, sciens repositam coronam certaminum.' Talibus celestis clauigeri castigationibus [admonitus] beatissimus archipontifex arma uirtutis induit. Nactusque diluculum, quo fugam intenderat, ad ipsum quem fugiebat regem irrumpit, datoque loco, indumenta deicit, lacerum corpus et liuentes uerberum plagas ostendit. Ille regaliter*k* indignatus pro tanti uiri iniuria, et 'Quis,' exclamat, 'hoc scelus in te presumpsit?'

10

20

30

---

*e* B: Ædbaldus
*f* E: uegetabat
*g* A, B, C, D and G: Sigeberti
*h* D: Ethelberti
*i* F: basilica
*j* D: per uisum
*k* D: legaliter

Cui episcopus, 'Tui,' inquit 'causa sic affectus sum.' Ingressusque narrationem apostolice in se animaduersionis exponit ordinem. Tum úero rex tremefactus tam euidenti miraculo, recolensque, si innocens pro alieno errore[a] neglecto hec passus sit, quid patietur qui corripientem contempserit, execratis simulacris cum omnibus diabolicis figmentis, plena fide Christi baptismum suscepit, omnemque populum suum ad Christianitatem traxit et ecclesiam Dei opibus, obsequiis, auxiliis extruxit, confirmauit, dilatauit. Mellitus et Iustus, reuocati a Galliis supplici eius legatione, sedes suas perpetua recipiunt libertate. Ipse

10 etiam, in oriente monasterii sanctorum apostolorum, basilicam sancte Dei genitricis edificauit,[b] quam Mellitus, archiepiscopus post sanctum Laurentium (ipso rege adhuc superstite) consecrauit. Dignum scilicet atauum successure nepti Mildrithe se exibuit, cui etiam regios parentes non solum ex Anglia sed etiam ex augustali Francia addidit. Nam ex regina Emma, Francorum regis filia, Ermenredum et Erconbertum[c] filios, ipsiusque auos, et beatissimam uirginem Christi Eansuiðam[d] genuit, que requiescit in monasterio Folcanstan[e] quod ipsa condidit.[13]

### IIII

Primogenitus regis, Ermenredus, ex regali coniuge Oslaua gemellas et
20 martyriales Christi laureas Athelredum[f] atque Athelbertum[g] germinauit, sanctas quoque paradisiaci et euangelici fontis filias quattuor,[h] Domneuam, Ermenbergam,[i] Ermenburgam,[j] et Ermengitham,[k] sanctissimos scilicet nostre uirginis auunculos et materteras et matrem beatissimam. Gloriosa autem Domneua tres pretiosissimas Sancte Trinitatis gemmas, tres sanctissimas Christo sponsas, Mildburgam,[l] Mildritham et Mildgitham florificauit, et hoc quasi trifolium lilium pro sceptro tulit. Nomina simillima, par formarum gloria, equalis gratia, mens et amor et sanctitas trium erat unica. Hinc Mildburga ut fides, inde

---

a  *F*: delicto
b  *F*: construxit
c  *F*: Erkonbertum
d  *C*: Eanswiðam; *D*: Candidam; *E and F*: Eanswitham
e  *E*: Folcastan
f  *F*: Ethelredum
g  *F*: Ethelbertum
h  *A*: tres
i  *B, C, D, E and F*: Ermenbirgam
j  *C adds* alias *in a later hand over word*
k  *C and D*: Eormengitham
l  *D*: Milo- and *throughout*

Mildgitha ut spes, media choruscat Mildritha ut caritas. Nam et in Cantico Canticorum, *Media caritate constrata sunt*,[14] et ut aliquid hic de poetarum fabulis adiungamus, *Tres erant pariles gratie sorores.*[15] His tribus sidereis lampadibus, tria Brittannici orbis regna Siderum Conditor irradiauit. Sancta Mildgitha in partibus Northanimbrorum,[m] sancta Mildburga in natiua terra Merciorum, monasterio Winlocan[n] dicto,[16] sancta uero Mildritha in parentali regno et principali Anglie regione, apud principem et protoparentem Anglice regenerationis, post multos annos de Taneto translata, requiescit Augustinum.[17] Que singule Deo sacrate uirgines singula loca celestibus assiduant miraculis. Quartam quoque sobolem uirginum, fratrem Merefin dictum, quasi croceum florem in medio liliorum produxit, quem Christus paruulum suscipiens paradisi floribus addidit. Post tanta pignora, pii parentes, renuntiantes coniugio et regno terrenis cum possessionibus, se transtulere in hereditatem incorruptam conseruatam in celo. A patre quoque prelustrissima Mildritha regibus patruis cum pia et sacra progenie claruit, per quos nichilominus Christiana propago floruit. Nam Meruuale[18] genitoris tres germani reges, Peada[o] Mediterraneos Anglos,[19] Wlferus[p] Mercios ad Christum conuertit, subiectosque reges, dato prouinciarum et amplioris potestatis premio, Christi cultores effecit.[20] Successorque Wlferi fratris, Æthelredus,[q] post uiginti nouem annos imperii sui monastice professioni se mancipauit.[21] Quorum beatissime sorores,[22] Cineburga et Cineswitha,[r] uelut gemelli oculi Domini, Burgensem beati Petri ecclesiam[23] clarissimis meritis illustrant, et condigne amite[s] Mildrithe gloriam et honorem inter ceteros natales accumulant. Cineburga regina sui nominis castrum[24] immo preclariora uirtutum insignia dereliquit. Cinesuuitha, regi Occidentalium Anglorum Offe desponsata, a mundi domina Maria, sibi splendide apparente et 'Tuis lacrimis irrigata uenio' dicente, perpetue uirginitatis palmam extorsit, regnumque celorum uiolenta rapuit.[25] His etiam, in eadem apostolica ecclesia, beata uirgo Tibba,[t] in Sancte Trinitatis gratia adiuncta tercia, consanguinitate (ut fertur) Mildrithina proxima, meritis uero certissimis, est cognatissima.

10

20

30

---

m F: Northanhumbrorum
n D: Wenlocan; F: Winelocan
o C: Weade
p E: Wulfer-, *and throughout*
q D: Ethelred-; E: Athelred- *throughout*
r C, E *and* F: Kineburga et Kineswitha
s F: alme
t D: Tidda

V

Adhuc autem inmorantes in parentela tam splendide uirginis Mildrithe, poscimus legentis uel audientis patientiam, dum exponamus causam, qua illam adducamus Cantiam. Iam Eadbaldus, rex fidelissimus, Dei cultor et ecclesie deuotissimus adiutor, migrans ad eternum regnum, iuniori filio Eorconberto sceptra imperii delegauit, que ille uiginti quattuor[a] annis excellentissime tenuit. Hic igitur, accinctus fortitudine, primus regum Anglorum ab uniuerso regno idola exterminauit, primus etiam ieiunium quadragesimale, proposita pena transgressoribus, per omnes summa auctoritate obseruandum sanciuit.[26] Coniunx illi sanctissima Sexburga,[27] Anne regis Orientalium Anglorum Christianissimi ac piissimi[28] filia, beatissimeque uirginis Etheldrithe[b] germana,[29] que peperit ei Egbrihtum filium successorem[30] duasque filias sanctissimas, Ercongodam[c] et Ermenhildam.[31] Quaram Ercongoda, uirgineo flore Deo sacrata, missa est trans mare sacris litteris et religione imbuenda; sancta uero Ermenhilda,[d] data supradicto Wlfero regi Merciorum, sanctam Domini uirginem Werburgam protulit,[32] que in monasterio Henuburch,[e] signis preclara, requiescit.[33] Ermenredus autem, regia dignitate decentissimus, qui paternum regnum pietate attentius quam imperio decorabat, ubi uite finem uidit, filios suos Æthelredum atque Æthelbrihtum,[f] geminum sua lumina sidus,[34] fratri Eorconberto regi[35] adhuc infantulos commendauit, ut pro patruo eis pater et seruator esset et hereditatem suam, usque ad maturum euum procurando, reconsignaret. Quod ille benignissime impleuit[g] dum uixit, qui et ipse, in anniuersario sancti archiepiscopi Deusdedit[36] obiens, fraternum depositum cum regno Egbrihto[h] filio reliquit. Isque successor nouem annis regnauit[37] et omnia orientalia atque australia regna optinuit, qui et commissos sibi consobrinos suos uice patris habuit. Erat tunc regis prefectus et popularis impius, Thunor[i] uocabulo, quod Latine resoluitur in tonitruum. Hic nigro felle metuens uigore et prudentia crescentem regalium puerorum industriam et indolem diuina atque humana prerogatiua omnibus

---

a  *B*: tribus
b  *B, C, and E*: Ætheldrithe
c  *E*: Eorcongodam
d  *C*: Eormenhilda
e  *B*: Henuburh; *D*: Heneburch; and *F*: Kenuburc
f  *F*: Æthelburtum
g  *D*: compleuit
h  *F*: Egbrichto
i  *E*: Thunre

amabilem et gratiosam, naturalem regis affectum, crebro sibilo sub-
plantandi regni, exterritat, corrumpit et inclinat, ut sibi hanc culpam
permittat, quo regis caput contra insurgentes tyrannos defendat. Qui
tandem, audiens regem quasi inuita uoluntate et quasi uoce Pilati et
Iudeorum dicentem, 'Quid ad me? Tu uideris', data nocte[38] tenebrarum
satelles in uilla regia Hestrie[39] utrosque innocentes obtruncat et sub ipso
regis solio tamquam commune nefas occultat, donec altis gurgitibus ab
humana notitia dimergat. Sed qui reuelat abscondita tenebrarum, mox
effuso instar solis radio a corporibus sanctorum et ipsis regalibus tectis
usque ad celi fastigia, multis intuentibus publicauit et carnificis uesaniam    10
et martyrum gloriam. Rex quoque uidit et, quasi in caput suum libratum
hoc fulmen conspexisset, expauit, dum tamen cogitaret potius quam
certum haberet cui malo frenum[j] relaxauerit. Hoc celesti indicio reperte
regales glebe regaliter funerantur, patratum scelus ubique uulgatur,
plebis querimonia in regem et detestabilem ministrum grassatur et
gemellum patrie iubar impie extinctum defletur. His tumultibus sanctis-
simus archipresul[k] Theodorus,[40] a primicerio Anglice fidei Augustino
septimus, cum beatissimo patre Adriano[41] se medium interserit, quos per
sanctum papam Vitalianum perpetuos patronos Roma Anglie miserat.
Denique Adrianus impositum sibi primitus hunc apostolatum in    20
Theodorum transtulit et ultimum locum in nuptiis Domini celo
promouendus occupauit, laborem uero fructumque peregrinationis et
euangelii pro honore inglorius inuasit, nec minus prelato prodesse
ecclesie concertauit.[42] Hi itaque, habito concilio pontificali et[l] populari,
regem arguunt parricidii. Qui enim consensit, fecit. Cui, ultro ad
penitentiam manus danti, suadent ut primitus neptem suam, sororem
martyrum, reginam Merciorum Domneuam, accersiat et ab eius orbitate
ueniam dignis beneficiis expetat. Accersita uenit. Rex, ingemiscens non
solum suum reatum sed et tam amabilium ablatam sibi iocunditatem
consobrinorum, benignissimis uerbis et rerum satisfactionibus illam    30
sanare consurgit. Thesauros auri, argenti, gemmarum, uestium aura-
tarum, ceterarumque opum regalium proponit. At regia liberalitas
Domneue omnia respuit, crudele esse iudicans ut quasi fraternum
sanguinem alieno precio uenditaret, que pro eternis diuitiis propria
reliquisset. Sed que euangelica erat discipula gratis mauult ignoscere.
Tum[m] rex beneficus insistit cum patribus ut ibi, in natiuo regno et in

---

j  B, C and D: frena
k  F: presul
l  D: pariter et
m  D: tunc

splendore ortus sui, regia matrona perpetuo remaneat, ubi, inter sanctorum luminaria et populos diuina religione florentes, beatius quam inter rudes adhuc Christicolas Domino seruiat. At illa, quamquam speciosa Tempe[43] et rerum opulentia et cantici maris faustitas et transmarini orbis commeatus et diuitie ac populositas ibidem arrideat, certius tamen principali sanctorum apostolorum Petri et Pauli monasterio,[44] sancta conuersatione et innumeris sanctorum pignoribus clarissimo, maxime autem primi institutoris sui Augustini amore et presentia uel uicinia, capitur ac tenetur. Unde regem obsecrat quatenus sibi in

10 Taneto, insula proxima, locum concedat ubi monasterium pro sancta germanorum memoria et regis indulgentia constituat. Rex uero in eius preces deditissimus rogat edicere quantum uelit. Tum illa, 'Quantum,' inquit, 'cerua mea uno curriculo ambire poterit'. Nec cunctatus rex promptissime annuit simulque cum turba procerum et patrum ac populi ad incompensabilem distributionem in insulam transit. Cerua, diuino arbitrio emissa, instar sagitte euolat. Rex cum omni comitatu prosequitur. Mira omnium expectatio, quo fera pertingat. Tum uero infandus Thunor, non se ferens a stimulis inuidie, exclamat in principem, 'Flos et thalamus, O rex, hec insula est regni tui et tu eam, heu, bruti animalis

20 iudicio auferendam tradidisti. Quem modum, quem terminum tibi insensata bestia ponet? Quanto probabilius portionem modestam et consultam ipse distribuisses, quam in cantatricis femine et effrenate fere conditionem seculis ridendam subisses?' Vix ea fatus erat et ira Dei ascendit super eum, excussusque equo more impiorum retrorsum cecidit, quem subito tellus infinito hiatu dehiscens uiuum inuerso capite absorbuit et in uentrem inferni ad Dathan et Abiron consortes traiecit.[45] Nec aliud in toto mundo[a] sepulchrum meruit, qui innocentibus quos extinxit partem etiam aliene terre detraxit. Agger uastus illi loco impositus, qui Thunoreshleap[b] dicitur, infamis nominis infandum

30 memoriale pretendit. Diffugiunt[c] omnes procul a pereunte cum clamore et horripilatione. Nec humus satis tuta sub pedibus uidebatur, que unius raptu ceteris minitabatur. Regia uero industria eo erat trepidantior, quo crimini uicinior. At cerua, iam excurso termino, in longum et latum quadraginta octo aratrorum substitit atque inde passim ad notam dominam domestica fide se recepit. Nec mora gloriosa regis deuotio, magnificas gratias rependens Deo, auctori tam euidentis electionis sue,

---

*a* D: uicinio

*b* F: Thunoreshlep; *B and C*: Thonores hleaw; *D*: Thonereires heleap; *and E*: Thunres leap

*c* F: Tunc diffugiunt

totum hoc spacium tradidit illustrissime proxime sue Domneue omnique posteritati sue ecclesiastice, beato Theodoro cum omnibus patribus benedicente et confirmante. Que ibi, ipso rege indefessa munificentia administrante opes et impensas edificiorum diuitiasque et$^d$ necessaria rerum, constituit uirginale cenobium in honore sancte$^e$ Dei genitricis et uirginis uirginum, et a deuotissimo$^f$ patre Theodoro dedicari optinuit, turbeque uirginum religiosissime, quas ibidem prima fundatrix ecclesie prima$^g$ coadunauit et instituit, prima mater prefulsit.[46] Sicque beatissimam filiam suam Mildritham secum uel ad se transductam huic genitiue regioni sue perpetuauit. Qua adducta et reddita maternis natalibus ut supra proposuimus, iam uia uite sue, qua supernos thalamos attigit, procedamus.

VI

Ea igitur tempestate, quamquam per apostolicos pedagogos Theodorum atque Adrianum tam Greca quam Latina eruditione passim Britannia polleret, Gregorianis quoque concentibus in Romanam timpanistriam transisset,[47] tamen feruor fidei illustrium Anglorum certatim soboles suas transmarinis scolis et disciplinis informandas mittebat, prudentissime scilicet considerantium quia ad plenam morum posituram genialis patria non sufficiat.[48] Hinc beata Domneua, uidens in filia Mildritha prerogatiuam electionis diuine et spem perhennis glorie, sacris studiis imbuendam et diuinis nuptiis parandam destinat ultra mare, proponens Domino, quasi uiscera sua offerentem$^h$ uirili mente Abrahe. Nec illa uero minus prompta extitit usque ad inmolationem Isaac matri obedire. Hec enim non ut terrigena sed ut celigena id est non quasi in terris sed in celo nata, ita a tenera etatula spernebat infima et anhelabat ad superna. De luce uigilauit ad Dei sapientiam, in$^i$ foribus suis assidentem inuenit illam. Ultro eam spiritus sanctus eterna caritate allactauit, ultro sibi Christus perpetue uirginitatis sponsam adamauit, et in illo aromatico totius sancte dilectionis pectore thalamum collocauit. Hanc preclara genitrix non aurotextis uel gemmatis purpuris, sed uirtutum monilibus et diuinis dotibus adornare atque ad ardentem lampadem ipsius oleum indeficiens amministrare satagebat. Ipsi uero angelici duces Theodorus

---

d *Omitted in A, D and E*
e *Omitted in A, C, D, E and F*
f *D*: beatissimo
g *E omits* ecclesie prima
h *MSS*: offerendam
i *C, D and F*: et

et Adrianus estuantem ad sidera dextra leuaque celesti fomento raptabant. Hanc itaque sacra Domneua exosculans benignitate materna, sic ad appetendam Dei philosophiam prophetica excitat suadela: *Audi filia et uide et inclina aurem tuam et obliuiscere populum tuum et domum patris tui et concupiscet rex decorem tuum quoniam ipse est Dominus Deus tuus.*[49] At uirgo Domini, iam ciuis non tam Anglica quam angelica, iam amore diuino in toto mundo peregrina, iam mente concipiens ethera, exilium pretulit alumne patrie, et ipsi (qua nil in uita dulcius habebat) parenti melliflue, ardens ad Christum pennis columbe euolare, in quo
10   possit requiescere. Quicquid sibi inter parentes dulcescebat, quasi mundi catenam a Domino prepedientem, exuere flagrabat. Non illam externe conuersationis aduersitas terrebat, iras maris et pericula ridebat.

VII

Mittitur ergo (adhuc quidem in seculari habitu quo liberius disceret) in Gallias ad celeberrimum monasterium uirginum cui Kalum erat uocabulum.[50] Nam in hoc uel*ᵃ* in Andilegum[51] conciues Angli maxime transibant. Parentum opes et Anglica gaza uirgini ibant comites, nequaquam scilicet ad auaritie uel ambitionis instrumentum, sed ad peregrinationis et necessitatis solacium. Torquebat altus discessionis
20   dolor alterna uulnerate caritatis precordia, inde matris, hinc filie: sed fortissima pectora ingenitum affectum uicerunt, Christi amore et spe cohabitationis in celo sempiterne. Sulcabat turgidos undarum*ᵇ* montes carina ueliuola et iter accelerabant impulsa Zephiris carbasa: sed pennas uentorum anteuolabant alta suspiria et sancta puelle desideria. Nec inter fluctuum miracula cessabat diuina tympanistria Dauitica modulare tympana, *In mari uia tua et semite tue in aquis multis.*[52] *Beati immaculati in uia Domini et qui scrutantur testimonia eius*ᶜ *et in toto corde exquirunt eum. Vtinam dirigantur uie mee ad custodiendas iustificationes tuas.*[53] Beata itaque et immaculata hoc erat quod canebat, hoc agebat quod beati-
30   ficabat, in toto corde exquirens eum quem optabat, et ad consideranda reuelatis oculis mirabilia de lege diuina directa est quo tendebat.

VIII*ᵈ*

Preerat Kalensi arcisterio genere et rebus potens abbatissa litterisque eruditissima, nomine Wilcoma,[54] quod in salutationem uirginis *Bene*

---

*a  A adds above line* in Brigum vel
*b  F*: aquarum
*c  F*: Domini
*d  F gives only a minimul summary of Chapters VIII–XVIII*

*uenias* resonat Anglica lingua.[55] Hec regalem et dominicam gemmam Mildritham solenni letitia, secundam matrem professa, colligit et nouam natam ut unicam inter omnes habere incipit. Promuntur certissime genitricis supplicia mandata et regifica xenia, unde tota illa tam uirginis gratie quam munificentie congaudet ecclesia. Lucet omnibus regalis forme specula ceu stella matutina. Grandeue filiam, adolescentule sororem amplectuntur amantissimam. Quibus omnibus illa uelut aromatum apoteca respondebat et intimam benignitatem mellificabat. Tradita ergo litterali discipline, docentes se precurrebat diuina capacitate. Vix audierat et docta erat. Thesaurizata memorie nec uolucres    10 celi nec fures poterant auferre. Condiscipulas superabat, magistras equiperabat uel preueniebat.

## IX

Quid*e* morum puritatem et uite industriam memorem? Que ab omnibus probitatis exemplum discere uenerat, omnibus erat. Documenta uirtutum que a singulis petebat cunctis prebebat. Cum huius humilitatem, illius patientiam, alterius abstinentiam, alterius uigilantiam, quorundam caritatem et beniuolentiam, mansuetudinem et modestiam emulari decertasset, omnes omnia singulorum bona in ea uidebant et ab ipsa accipiebant, dignisque meritis sine liuore affectabant, quam primam    20 dignitate, extremam subiectione, imitari nequibant. Cunctosque ipsa monasteriales adhuc in seculari habitu uincebat. Ita erat affabilitate mellitula, deuotione lacteola, caritate nardiflua, obsecutione nectarea, modestia aprica, uisceribus pietatis in cunctos diffusa, congratulatio felicium, consolatio destitutorum, copia inopum, compatientia miserorum. Tam multimoda gratia gratiosa ipsi quoque dioceseos pontifici uenerabilis habebatur et gratifica. Quos uero ignes irarum ille antiquus draco tunc effulminabat, qui tyrannica quondam arrogantia et rapina dixerat, '*Super astra Dei exaltabo solium meum; ero similis altissimo*',[56] cum modo uideret se puellari calcaneo conteri et illam, se alliso, ad    30 celestia niti. Specula Sion in monte sita et undique munita nullum aditum prebebat hosti: procul absterrebatur insidiator a presidente intus maiestate Christi; defecerunt framee inimici. Impatiens tamen cedere et quicquam intemtatum relinquere,[57] externis auxiliis, in curribus et equis Pharaonicis et machinis Babylonicis, id est subiugalibus sibi animabus uentosis et lubricis, hanc a foris expugnare aggreditur, quo maioribus triumphis deiectius obruatur.

---

*e   E omits* Quid . . . miserorum

X

Erat eiusdem monasterii abbatisse propinquus, iuuenis spectabilis
opulentiam et stemma iactitans nobilitatis. Hunc temptator in amorem
uirginis accendit et his flammis, hoc ariete, arcem Dei impetit. Amator, et
per se et per amicos eius, conubia non mediocriter petit: possessiones,
oppida, castella, familias, thesauros rerum, diuitias et honores Francie in
dotem proponit.ᵃ Sed abbatissa acrior insurgit: ea uero tota uesania
huic amatam⁵⁸ adiungere contendit, ea precibus, blanditiis,ᵇ donis et
promissionibus infinitis puellam occupat, gloriam mundi insibilat, uiros
10   illustres, matronas nobiles, sorores simplices, quasi auctoritate ecclesie
uerendas, in nuptiarum suadelam concitat, immotamque minis ac
terroribus arietat. Ipsum etiam episcopum uel fautorem uel consen-
taneum apparat. Quas autem illecebras, que incitamenta que ferrea corda
domarent non dixit.

'Filia miᶜ eximia, rosa regum clarissima, stella Anglorum fulgida,
proles Francorum augusta, te digna audi monita. Generositas precelsa et
formositas amanda et districtionis impatiens etas delicata et cultus
secularis ac licentia nulli professioni celibatus addicta, uetant te in
monasterio delitescere, et habitum profiteri rigide continentie, et a regali
20   libertate inferiorum ancillatu et abusione degenerare. *Melius est* iuxta
apostolum *nubere quam uri.*⁵⁹ Et idem testatur alibi, *Volo adolescentulas
nubere, filios procreare, matres familias esse.*⁶⁰ Est hic consanguineus
noster, etate et uigore iuuenili floridus, morum et aspectus elegantia
amabilis, inter Gallicos heroes, inter potentes et amicos regis inclitus, et
pars imperii gratissima, tui solius diligens et te omnibus rerum deliciis ac
diuitiis preponens. Auge in eo, obsecro, splendorem Francie, cum sis
regaliter Francigena. Rex propinquam approbans et omnes optimates
regii omniumque decus et potentatus, ego quoque cognatius atqueᵈ hec
abbatia amplissima et opulentissima, cum hoc sponso pariter tui erimus.
30   Quos si repudiaueris, ut damnosa peristi.'

Talibus dictis ecclesiastice primicerie instrepit fauor amicorum et
matronarum, et Mildrithe decentissime omnes orant assensum. At uirgo
Domini, in simplicitate columbina, armata prudentia serpentina, et supra
firmam petram contra omnes impetus fluctuum et tempestatum fundata,
uelut letiferos cantus Sirenarum aut fedos crepitus ranarum auertit et

*a  D*: promittit
*b  D*: blandimentis
*c  E*: mea
*d  E*: et

respuit uana molimina; ipsamque erroris magistram hac repercutit sententia:

'Quid pulueri et*e* cineri generositatem, quid sacre religionis discipule diuitias intentas? Quomodo, doctrix castimonie et dux uirginum, ad corruptionem illicis? Mater me huc ad scolas direxit, non ad nuptias. Pudicitie hic documentum quesiui, non maritum. Ad uirtutum instrumentum ueni, non ad matrimonium. Doceri posco disciplinam Domini et timorem, non seculi ambitionem. Et quid te longa morer ambage? Plus me terrent blanditie tue quam mine. Torque, lania, incende, eneca: non potero separari a Christi caritate et sibi decretam pudicitiam prodere.' 10

Hec et huiusmodi dicta protestantem inflammata tyranna totam*f* transuersa tuetur.[61] Clamat Christi rebellem et aduersariam uel anti-Christam magis quam Christianam, que in uice Christi iubentibus non paruerit, de quibus precipit: *Omnia quecunque dixerint uobis seruate et facite;*[62] et iuxta apostolica et regularia precepta: *Obediendum esse prepositis non solum bonis et modestis sed etiam discolis;*[63] omne autem matris sue imperium penes se esse, ex quo eam miserit et addixerit sue discipline talem uero presumtricem, adulteram Christi censendam, non sponsam. Deinde insequitur suppliciis, cedibus, uerberibus, iterumque lenimentis, precibus uel horrendis diuine uirtutis, ut adquiescat, adiura- 20 tionibus. Que tandem constantia, que fides martyrum a tanti nominis maiestate impulsa non nutaret, cum carnifices et mortes non timeret. O*g* certamen durius cum Christiana auctoritate, quam cum Neroniana impietate! Nam ab idolatra[64] occidi propter Christum certissimum*h* est premium: Christiano uero contraria urgente per Christum, quo erit euadendum. Sed bellatrix Domini et in hoc argumento conculcauit Eue serpentem tortuosum et milleformem scorpionem in angelum lucis se transfigurantem, audiens contra improbos preceptores Petrum apostolum proclamantem, *Obedire oportet Deo magis quam hominibus.*[65] Didicit etiam in fide, que per dilectionem operatur, et implet omnia mandata 30 Domini quia, secundum apostolum Paulum, *Littera occidit, spiritus autem uiuificat*[66] et *ubi Spiritus Domini ibi libertas.*[67] Docuit eam pura ueritatis columba et unctio eius intima Scripture discernere sacramenta. Que in psalmis cum martyribus cantare nouerat, *Nisi quia Dominus erat in nobis, cum exurgerent homines in nos, forte uiuos deglutissent nos.*[68] Itaque adamantina duritia insuperabilior existit, et ut rupes uasta resistit. Utque

---

*e* D: aut
*f* A: totum
*g* E *omits* O certamen . . . evadendum
*h* A, C and E omit certissimum . . . Christum

quondam pretiosa martyr Lucia a mille hominibus et mille boum paribus
ad lupanar trahentibus moueri non poterat corpore, sic Spiritus Sancti
domicilium Mildritha inmobilis perstat*ᵃ* mente.[69]

## XI

Iam uero abbatissa, non ferens furorem sue deuictionis et repudii, tota in
necem grassatur agnicule Dei. Caminus uasto incendio acriori ira
uentilante inflammatur, et terribiles flammarum globi ore eructantur.
Astat hostia Domini inuictissima, que, uirginitatem uite et exitium
matrimonio preponens, optionemque in triumphum uertens, mox in
10   mediam candentis clibani uoraginem contruditur. Tum,*ᵇ* ore fornacis
attentius obstructo, omnis uapor intrinsecus constringitur, ut trucius in
extinguendam animam animetur. Verum in protectione Dei celi et in
umbra alarum Domini sperantibus omnis malorum conatus inanescit.
Nullus omnino ardor, nullus estus eam tetigit, sicut nulla libido
maculauit. Quid enim materialia incendia in illam possent, aduersus
quam incentiua uitiorum et porte inferi non preualebant, mira uero Dei
gratia pene eam formidabant contingere, quas ipsa non formidabat*ᶜ* pro
Domino perferre, quas et interrita ipsa magis uisa est absterrere.
Fremebant undique flagrantes rogi in obstrusa cauerna, illa uelut
20   forenses turbines ridebat in aula tranquilla. Ambiebant lucentes facule
Dominam serena*ᵈ* reuerentia, et lumina sua non tormenta, splendorem
suum non terrorem ministrabat flamma, atque in obstructo ergastulo
diem reddiderunt incendia. Thalamus uirgini fit fornax torrida, ten-
torium apricum domus ignita, prunarum area quasi rosarum atria, et
fulgurantes torres lampadarum uincebant obsequia. Tutior hic erat
innocentia inter flammicomos*ᵉ* uigores quam inter humanos furores, et
quam homines suppliciis impegerant, supplicia defensabant. Sic sanctus
Daniel securus inter leones Deum suum adorabat, quod inter homines
impune non poterat. Seruabat sodalitas beluina quem beluis tradiderat
30   inmitior rabies humana, escamque ab hominibus sibi appositam fere
esurientes contuentur intactam. Quanta letitia tunc triumphabas Dei
amica, cum, celesti rore perfusa, stares in ignibus uelut in amenitate
paradisiaca et, quasi clauso cubiculo solitaria, orares patrem tuum mente

---

*a*  *D*: persistit; *B*; prestat
*b*  *D*: Tunc
*c*  *D*: dubitabat
*d*  *D*: seuera
*e*  *D*: flammiuomos

tam secura quam pura! Quanta gratiarum actione eructabant labia tua ymnum trium puerorum Domino,[70] quos et animo imitabaris et martyrio, quanta etiam deuotione expansis manibus cum beatissima Agnete consimili uernabas passione ac flore.[71]

## XII

Dehinc post trium horarum interuallum, cum iam sacratissima Domini uictima non solum carnibus sed ipsis etiam ossibus consumta funditus crederetur, magistra indisciplinata ad fornacem redit, aperiri eam et purgari precepit. Inter reserandum uero,[72] cigneum uirginis ab intus audiunt canorem et claram martyris uocem, '*Igne me examinasti Domine et*   10 *non est inuenta iniquitas in me.*'[73] Sic, patefacta egrediendi ianua, apparuit uirgo splendidissima tamquam aurum decocta, uelut a croceo cubili consurgens aurora, uti de thalamo procedens sponsa, quasi columba ad fenestram suam speculata. Perculerat omnes alto stupore audita, terruit altius uisa, et a tantis ignibus ornata, non lesa, et quasi a sepulchro resuscitata. Euocant et excipiunt egredientem prona deuotione, de qua, ut pessumdata, nil aliud quam cineres uenerant eicere.*f* Ad tantum miraculum urbs confluxit, populi accurrunt. Non domus, non atria, non platee uel campi sufficiunt irruentibus. Beatus sibi censebatur qui triumphantem uirginem spectare mereretur. Nam quis mirari sufficeret,   20 ne*g* unum quidem in corpore crinem, ne unum in uestibus filum a tanto lesum caumate, nec odorem estus, nec maculam inesse. Addita est potius uictrici gloria pro pena, casteque pudoris illuxere faces. Rutilabat flamma genarum, lacteolosque rosis infecit purpura uultus. Fideles uenerantur et inmanitatem persequentum detestantur: aduersarii confunduntur et uel inuiti obsequuntur.

## XIII

At bona castigatrix, unde resipiscere debuerat uel proficere, inde acriori (prauorum more) armatur furore, et uirginalis palme impudentius quam proprie tyrannidis cepit erubescere.[74] Que, post aliquot dies, sola solam   30 humilem Dei ancillam nacta obuiam, subito irruit, inaudit, impetit: ut leena uitulam, ut ursa agnam, ut aquila columbam. Itaque, insertis utrisque manibus ceu ferratis carpentis in sanctam cesariem, teneram puellam allidit in terram, calcat pedibus, terit calcibus, tundit pugnis acsi

---

*f*  C: reicere
*g*  *B omits* ne unum . . . crinem

plumbatis et cestibus, lacerat et laniat uenenatis unguibus, discerpit et
exstirpat crines furiosis tractibus. Nec*a* cessant uirulenta oculorum
iacula et serpentine lingue conuitia, tranquilla lacescere et transuerberare
pectora. Horrebat ira acsi Thesiphoneis anguibus crinita.[75] Iam denique
hanc suffocasset, extinxisset, enecasset, nisi aliquo forte interueniente
diuina manus succurrisset. At prouida*b* uirgo Domini auulsam laceri
uerticis comam arripit et in tempus oportunum recondit. Videns ergo
uirtutis detrimentum, ubi quesierat instrumentum, et castitatis peri-
culum, ubi sperauerat subsidium, contrito et intimo spiritu rogitat
10   unicum refugium, suum Dominum, quatenus eam a tantis diaboli laqueis
eripiat, uel natali gremio reddat uel in paradisum suum fessam animam
recipiat. O ineffabilem diuine benignitatis dispensationem! Qui pleros-
que sanctos, translatos feliciter ab Anglis, perpetuos transmarinis
patronos prerogauit, ipse dilectissimam suam Mildritham externis
tantum in exemplum et miraculum ostendit et desideranti patrie tandem
multo prestantiorem restituit. Hanc autem extraneorum non solum
doctrinis et institutionibus, uerum etiam diuersis temtationum generibus
(id est blandis et asperis aduersitatibus) exerceri uoluit, quatenus et sibi
proficeret ad celestem coronam, et genti sue, cui preferenda erat, ad
20   illuminationem glorie perpetuam, quibus eo doctius consuleret, quo
multiplicius terrarum moribus composita fuisset. Maxime autem ipsum
transmarinum orbem elegantia Christi arguit uel docuit in ipsa, insinuans
quod aurum quas gemmas ipse possideret in Anglia.[76] Quomodo itaque
pupillam et aduenam suam susceperit, quas aures clementie ad eius
preces inclinauerit, quibus miserationum oculis anxiam respexerit, finis
reditus sui tandem comprobauit.

## XIIII

Interim instinctu diuino psalteriolum uirginea manu scriptitat, forma et
habilitate qua certissime matri Domneue placiturum nouerat, prolixos
30   crines suos cruento liuore erutos, quasi reliquias, quasi pignora uel
stigmata martyrii, in summa libelli margine collocat, ipsique genitrici per
diuinitus oblatum gerulum destinat. Simul et uerbis et scriptis lacri-
mosis expostulat, quatenus non tam uite sue, qua absumpta a tribula-
tionibus in Domino requiescat, quam uirginali corone uita cariori inter
omnia Satane uenabula periclitanti succurrat. Talia nuntia uel xenia ubi
materna Domneue uiscera attigerant, plaga doloris icta concidit, sanguis

---

*a   E omits* nec cessant . . . crinita
*b   E ends abruptly*

et mens fugit et tamquam intestinam prolem aut torreri flammis aut absorberi fluctibus oculis conspexisset, commori querebat, cui subuenire nequibat. Clamat se ream filie et parricidam, que ignotis tradidit puniendam. Volebat ad liberandum eam per se proficisci, sed non sat rationis erat huic pietati, cum et iugis languor, quo ad celestia parabatur, uetaret et ipsa aduena contempni posset.[77] Verum in spem reducta de ipsius palma intemerata et seruata Dei prouidentia, missis nauibus cum honestis legatis (ut decebat) et numerosis sociis, tam episcopum quam abbatissam orat, obtestatur, quatenus desiderata genitrici nata per hos citius remittatur, que se in supremo morbo et merore languentem consoletur. Abbatissa uero confusa de rabie et inmanitate, qua insontem extinguere certauerat,[c] et uerita ne tante crudelitatis apud Anglicas nationes infamis fiat, aut, eruta a suis rictibus, preda sibi insultare gaudeat, cum pontifice idem sentiente actitat qualiter decus regni Mildritham tamquam ciuem Francigenam perpetuo retineat. Et legatos quidem magnifica[d] hospitalitate utrique suscipiunt, puellam uero omnimodis suasionibus, satisfactionibus, rerumque pollicitationibus allicere et incorporari sibi contendunt. Hoc populus, hoc uniuersa uirginum contio ut dominam suam orat et implorat, ne se sua pietate saucias deserat. Transeunt dies et materni legati nil proficiunt.

## XV

At uirgo Domini, equa uirtute contemnens et dolos [et] iras Antiqui Corruptoris, consulta et accepta legatorum fide, in umbra alarum Dei sperans, statuta nocte egreditur, paratoque fido comitatu uel equitatu excipitur atque deducitur. Iam preterierant custodias urbis et municipia, iam arridebat profugis expedita uia, et amica dux repatriaturis ratibus respondebat aura, iam Israelita Domini, acsi Egyptia seruitute liberata, cum Maria tympanizabat Redemptori gratiarum modulamina. Percussere ilico uirgineum pectus preciosissima pignora, memorie relapsa, que fuge precipitatione hostili hospicio reliquerat oblita. Iamdudum enim, ut erat totius boni amantissima et apis florigere emula feruentissima, quicquid decere patriam suam et nouellam genitricis ecclesiam uidisset uel digno pretio, uel gratifico exterorum beneficio, adeptum thesaurizauerat; unde et in ecclesiasticis ornamentis et preciosissimis sanctorum pignoribus plurimum ditescebat. Clauum uero Dominice confixionis, multo auri et argenti pondere ut opes incomparabiles

c  D: conauerat
d  D: magna

obtinuerat, que omnia uel matri mitteret, uel ipsa quandoque afferret. Tanta itaque damna diuinorum carismatum, ubi modo recordatione nubila sensit anima, subito sibi omnis serenitas in turbinem procellosam est redacta. Ipsa diriguit et intremuit, retentoque equo, impatiens progredi ut lapis hesit, planctus et gemitus et alta suspiria uerberabant aurea sidera. Turbati comites graui afficiuntur angore, dum durum sit tam inestimabilem thesaurum perdere, et durius in mortis discrimina redire, ubi si fugisse deprehendantur, et ipsi puniantur, et uirgo perpetua captiuitate dampnetur. Adesto Ihesu Domine, adiutor inoportunitatibus
10　in tribulatione! Certa et affixa est ancilla tua omnia perpeti, antequam careat sancte passionis tue et redemptionis sue priuilegio salutari. Redire igitur in hostiles fauces quas euaserat perdurat, uel si sola et incomitata debeat. Redit; nec possunt socii pro qua uenerant deserere dominam: simulque participant sortem suam. Redit et, angelo pacis preeunte nulloque occurrente uel sciente, ad desideratum thesaurum felicitate uictricis Iudith peruenit, omnia sua fide Saluatoris integre salua inuenit, rapit et recurrit:[a] tanto scilicet iam securius, quanto felicius, sanctorum et Christi sui comitata pignoribus. Sic Gallica rura iam post aliquantos annos transmissionis sue pertransiuit suusque iam sol mundo, et uerus
20　sol glorie sponse sue reluxit; atque ad mare nauesque paratas peruenit. Talibus ergo non tam temptationibus quam uictoriis, armigeram suam ineffabili[b] dispensatione Christus exercuit et triumphauit, quam et in angustiis innoxie seruauit, et coronas perpetuas sibi secundum pericula multiplicauit. Decebat etiam, ut Dominice plage tropheum, quod auro emerat, suimet tribulatione redimeret, et in hoc ipsum Christum eo familiarius possiderat, quo laboriosius recepisset.

## XVI

Ipso interea diluculo, ubi uirginis fuga apud Kalense monasterium deprehenditur, tunc motus et turbo[c] exoritur, discursus et excursus[d]
30　querentium passim peruagatur. Omnis chorus uirginum in planctum conuertitur, pontificis inertiam calumniantur, principis uero sue tyrannidem in tam innocente extrusa execrantur. Tunc plane intellexere quid in presente habuerint, quid in absente perdiderint: quod lumen, quod decus, quod mel et lac, quam dignitatem, iocunditatem, festi-

---

*a* *D*: occurrit
*b* *D*: inestimabili
*c* *Apart from A, all manuscripts read* turba
*d* *B omits* et excursus

uitatem in amissa amiserint. Persequutrix, quia furor suus derisus sit, amplius furit ubique limphata omnia turbat; pulsatis signis omnes aduocat; episcopi auxilium efflagitat et cum eo cetum persequutorum diriuat,[78] quicquid arma ferre potest in Dei puellam exundat. Et forte ad hoc tam ualidam manum misit, ne illi, qui tam prouide exierint, prouidentius sibi auxilia[e] a sua Anglia concitauerint[f] et defensionem si expediat parauerint. Verum diuina columba, ambulans quam simpliciter tam confidenter, non cruentam sed innocentem euasionem meditabatur; nec in humana sed in Dei uirtute innitebatur. Iam uero beate Mildrethe omnis comitatus et equitatus et supellex una cum ipsa nauibus erat    10 imposita et cuncta suis sedibus ordinata; et uenti obsequentes inflabant carbasa; solummodo contracti maris expectabatur reuma. Ecce autem iterum nubes tribulationis eminus oculis offertur, que fluctuosam tempestatem in ipso litore minitabatur. Apparuere cohortes Francigene, et uolucres equitum turme, et exerta bellatorum arma sole repercusso radiantia, et hastilia splendenti ferro cacuminata. Aspiciunt naute in se turbido fremitu properantes; *gelidusque per ima cucurrit ossa tremor,*[79] formido mortis incumbens spem, consilium et auxilium obruit. Nulla resistendi ut paucis et pacificis fiducia, nulla fuge uia. Hostis occupat, refugium maris abscesserat, totas naues siccum litus alligabat. Carnifex    20 impellit, aqua repellit. Incerti erant an domine an uite proprie magis timerent. Clamor in celum tollitur ut impunitatem uel ueniam mereantur. Risisset hec discrimina promptissime martyrio Mildrithe constantia; si suum tantum gladiator sanguinem appeteret, nec sociis suis nec sue integritatis brauio metueret.

XVII

At illa de profundo cordis longe eminentius spiritu Moysi ad Dominum clamabat, utque ille, tacita uoce sed mentis tonitruo, super omnes Israelitas fugientes et Egyptios prementes ab altissimo exaudiri atque audire meruit, *'Quid clamas ad me?*[80] *Nunc uidebis quid faciam Pharaonice*    30 *parti,'*[81] sic alma uirgo re ipsa et ipso uisu diuinum responsum accepit. Repente enim, ut fabulis utamur, exemplo fraternorum cuneorum qui uipereis dentibus sati et e terra progeniti mutua cede interiere, persequutores agnicule Dei in sese arma uertere et, signa infesta signis, pila pilis, in sua uiscera contorsere.[82] Scuta inaurata,[83] lorice, galee ensesque

---

*e B*: auxilium
*f B, C and D*: conciuerint

prefulgentes in se collidebantur suisque reddidere quod alienis*ᵃ* mina-
bantur. At tamen complacati inuicem, ut Pilatus et Herodes in insontis,
predam uel penam festinabant. Sed rursus, alio Dei miraculo atque alia
repulsa, quo anhelantius properabant, eo remotiores erant. Currebant
equi crebris calcaribus icti et, cum iam quasi captis insultare se putarent,
ita recutiebantur quasi quos petebant fugissent. Hec uidens Domini
famula, ut magis audiatur, maiori armatur orandi fiducia cum hac uoce
Dauitica: *Ego clamaui quoniam exaudisti me Deus. Et ut magis ac magis
clamem, inclina aurem tuam michi et exaudi uerba mea.*[84]

10    XVIII

Extenso itaque in celum ore, manibus et corde:
'Uniuersorum,' inquit, 'Conditor et Domine, omnia quecunque
uoluisti, in celo et in terra, in mari et in omnibus abyssis fecisti. Tu
pendulis fluctibus terminum intransgressibilem posuisti et super-
eminentia terris montuosa equora ultra limitem defluere uetuisti. Ad
tuum imperium quondam stetit unda fluens, donec pertransiret populus
tuus. Per medium undosi profundi sicca patebat uia, et a dextris et a
sinistris pro muris et presidiis stabat unda. Moxque inimicos per-
sequentes mare operuit, et idem elementum illos deduxit et protexit, istos
20   interclusit et absorbuit. Alia item omnipotentatus tui euidentia:
tempestuosissimos montes fluctuum sicco uestigio superambulasti, disci-
pulumque fide ambulantem et diffidentia submersum erexisti comitemque deduxisti;*ᵇ* et eodem igne Babilonie pueros tuos intus fouisti et
noxios foris combussisti; Danielisque intacti accusatoribus belue quid
essent ostendisti. Tu columna lucis, tu a serpente percussis spectaculum
in cruce salutis, tu ergo es refugium meum, Domine, a tribulatione que
circumdedit me, libera me a persequentibus me quia confortati sunt
super me. Et nunc me tibi dedo perpetuam famulam, ut nullum unquam
preter te amatorem admittam et semper legem tuam custodiam.
30   Psalmum quoque Beati inmaculati[85] ad gloriam sancti nominis tui et
memoriam beate genitricis tue uoueo me per singulos dies uite mee
duodecies decantaturam, preter reliquam psalmorum orationumque
uictimam, tantummodo redimas in pace animam meam ab his qui
appropinquant michi, et in beneplacito tuo illesam reddas patrie et ancille
tue mee genitrici.'

--------

*a*  D: aliis
*b*  B *omits* comitemque deduxisti

Vix talia perorauerat, et natura elementi obedire Dominice sponse laborat; citiusque quam lex eterna uocabat, ad eius obsequium mare prouolat – nec iam solitis momentis uel morositate maline*c* augmentatur, uerum uno impetu acsi de alta rupe ruens impellitur. Tunc, patente uia et euadendi et persequendi, hostilis acies permittitur paululum approximare, uidelicet uacuos rictus in preda erepta Dei prudentia eludente, ut tantum uiderent euadentes et tabescerent, dum se putarent perfugas comprehendisse nec tangerent, in manibus tenere nec caperent, uiuos deglutisse nec lederent, et cum omnia in ipsos posse uiderentur, nil possent. Omne litus subito pontus erat, pontus naues eleuat, militares cuneos longius proturbat, pro nautis militat. Illi armis naualibus incumbunt, uela attollunt, rapiuntque, ruuntque. Insidunt transtris et uerrunt equora remis.[86] Alis suis et pennis carina preteruolat. Hostes elusi elata signa et tela in auras crispant, ensibus rotatis aera uerberant, arcubus sagittis et iaculis uentis et mari comminantur, surde procelle et inania*d* litora clamosis increpationibus obtunduntur, belliger sonipes huc illuc uacuas frustra preuertitur auras. Quid uos tam copiosa manus in unam puellam ualuistis? Persequendo uos exinanistis, et illam amplius clarificastis, dum omnibus notificaretis, tanti eam esse quam bellico apparatu reposceretis, uosque tam inbelles ut totis conatibus nil possetis. Usque ad mare compulistis; cur non et in ipsum profundum cum antiquis persecutoribus percurristis, ut quam inuictissimam tam in fluctibus quam in ignibus probastis etiam uestris armis uictoriosiorem undis obruti probaretis? Itaque ne ex toto inaniter uenissetis, in uos ipsos bellastis, et uel uictores uictis profugis palmam reliquistis, uosque crudelitatis et ignauie obprobria domum retulistis. Interea alma Mildritha cum suis triumphans flagrantissimas gratiarum hostias inmolat et, ut filii Israel excusso iugo Egyptiorum, decantauerunt, Domine, nomen sanctum tuum, et uictricem manum tuam laudauerunt pariter. Vere mirabilis Deus in sanctis suis, quos uariis temptationum palmis deducit in uia mirabili, ut per anfractus et transuersa aduersitatum itinera mirabiliter deducantur in uia recta. Via enim Domini et per auia recta facta est, et iter sanctorum preparatum in latitudinem caritatis, perducens ad certum locum et tendens semper (licet diuerso calle) ad mercedem laborum. 'Benedictus Deus,'[87] inquit apostolus, 'qui semper triumphat nos in Christo Ihesu.'[88]

---

*c* D: marine
*d* D: marina

## XIX

Iam uirgo Domini*ᵃ* angelico ductu et felici cursu patriam attigit et puppis
currens in portum uirginalis insule qui Ipples fleot*ᵇ* dicitur successit.⁸⁹
Adiacebat quadratum saxum ut marmor niueum, granditate uires
uincens quattuor uirorum, duritie basium et columnarum que lacesseret
ferrum, egressure uirgini ita accomodum, ut diuinitus credatur ibi
preparatum. In hoc itaque infinita Domini*ᶜ* benignitas indelebile dare
dignata est indicium, quam gratiosum in electa sibi uirgine habuerit
affectum, ut omni posteritati perpetuo sit in salutem et exemplum ipsius
10   meritorum. Nam ubi a naui descendentis domine uestigia subiectus
[lapis] excepit, ita ea sibi quasi recenti niui aut luto infixa subito ostendit,
ipsiusque comites et affluentes ad tam insigne miraculum populos
obstupefecit.⁹⁰ Nec solum eternaliter durat hoc signum uirginea planta
informatum, uerum etiam uariis languoribus iuge operatur remedium
pro fide credentium. Norunt enim*ᵈ* adhuc febricitantes et ceteri morbidi
ex antiqua consuetudine lapidem radere et, hoc puluere potato, certam
medelam haurire. Patet et alia superne uirtutis gratia.*ᵉ* Lapis non solum
impressum sibi pignus domine semper seruat, uerum etiam in eodem
loco super ripam fluminis, quo ei a naui suppeditauerat, inuictus et reses
20   perhenniter durat. Sepe temptatum est, sepe ab eodem loco remotus est,
sed post modicum iterum in sua sede repertus est. Plerumque in altum
ipsius amnis gurgitem est dimersus, sed citius quam humano officio
posset sue mansioni est redditus. Nocte quoque sullatum uideres ante
luciferum uel post pusillum*ᶠ* in sua relatum. Quod et nostro tempore
satis compertum habemus. Miroque modo quasi ramus arboris trahentibus cedit ac dimissus uelut naturaliter in suum locum resilit. His
populi accensi uirtutibus de hoc sacrario uirginis oratorium in memoriam
eius fecere et sacra porticu ipsum ipsius saxum cinxere; quatenus hic cum
diuinorum beneficiorum augmento cresceret fidelium deuotio, et instar
30   uirginalis templi uocaretur domus Dei lapis positus in signum et titulum
eius qui *factus est in caput anguli.*⁹¹ Hic ergo assiduantur carismata
uirginis et, inter ceteras frequentias, in diebus rogationum sacras hic

---

*a  F*: Christi
*b  C*: Ippeles fleot; *D*: Ipples fleoth; *F*: Ippesflet
*c  F*: Dei
*d  F*: etiam
*e  F*: medela
*f  F omits* uel post pusillum

populus agit letanias. Hic infirmi, ut prenotatum est, uirginei lapidis
rasuras in aque potu*g* gustantes, non solum ipsi curantur, uerum etiam,
asportato lapidei pulueris antidoto, ceteris languidis medentur. Hic
etiam, post typum Ierusalem Christique et ecclesie sacramentum,
impletum Isaie uidetur uaticinium: *Venient ad te qui non nouerunt te et
adorabunt uestigia pedum tuorum et puluerem pedum*h *tuorum lingent.*[92]
Linxerunt hunc salutiferum puluerem qui biberunt et in uestigio
uirginis*i* adorabant Dominum, cuius ipsa erat templum. His itaque
uberius loco suo expositis, ne alibi repetere cogeremur, ad uirginem
deducendam superius reuertamur.                                          10

## XX

Amabilis itaque Deo et humano generi Mildritha uix puppim reliquerat
et lucifera eius fama plebes ob uias attraxerat. Felicem se qui uidere
meruisset credebat, nec credentem fallebat quam uidere salus erat. Dolet
amissam Gallia, gaudet receptam Anglia, quam uere matri reddidit ueri
Salomonis machera. At uero beatissima Domneua, que de eius reditus
desperatione pene erat moritura, tanta nunc exultauit letitia, ut totius
egritudinis omniumque dolorum oblita et tota sibi uideretur sana acsi
ipsa uel filia, ut euangelica puella, a morte sibi esset reddita. Continuo
ruit obuia cum uniuersa sororum ac*j* plebis caterua. Virginea carmina,   20
organica cymbala in terris et angelica modulamina in supernis emulantia,
laudibus diuinis mulcebant ethera. Cuncta simul tintinnabula, summa
festiuitate hec concrepabant gaudia. Amplectuntur uirgines uirginem et
circumdant *uirgulam fumi ex aromatibus*[93] ut flores rosarum, ut lilia
conuallium, ut castra apum melligerantium, ut lumina lampadarum, ut
incensa thimiamatum. Amplius autem consecrabant et auctorizabant hec
solemnia celestia beate Mildrithe munera, que triumphaliter afferebat in
Domini clauo et sanctorum pignoribus ueneranda. Tunc inter sancta
oscula et lacrimas letitie uoce Iacob clamitat caritas sanctissime
Domneue, '*Iam leta moriar*, filia mi, *quia uidi faciem tuam.*'[94] O     30
sanctorum mater dilectio que et in hac peregrinatione quodammodo
paradysi amenitatem representat! Nam pia Domneua,*k* dum maternis
uisceribus ab afflictione externa refouet et mulcet dulcissimam sobolem,

---

*g*  *F*: in aqua
*h*  *B omits* pedum . . . uirginis
*i*  *A and F add*: uel uestigium interuentricis
*j*  *F omits* ac plebis
*k*  *F*: mater Domneua

exemplum estimabile terris dedit illius superne matris Ierusalem, que
pias animas ab hac Egypto uel Babilone ad se reuertentes eo blandius
colligit, quo amarius afflictas in mundo nouit, omniumque dolorum
infinitis ulterius deliciis obliuisci facit.

## XXI

Sed nimirum sicut filias ethnurusque[95] alienigenas quondam impro-
babat[a] Rebecca, sic uestes seculares quamuis mediocres, quibus adhuc
sanctitatem tegebat celica Mildritha, mutare in diuinum cultum certabat
Domneua. Que iam spiritualis mater ex carnali facta hortatur hanc, ut
10   armatura Dei induta tota transeat in Christi federa. Illa postulat; ista, ut
hec uota sua ac desideria longa acceleret, implorat. Quid, O benigna,
benignissimam hortaris, ad fontem sitientem trahis, estuantem accendis,
currentem impellis? Quamuis sit una rogantis et optantis beniuolentia,
noli desiderantem rogare sed adiuua. Re magis quam prece egent
suspiria. An hoc parum est quod iam bis Domino hostiam uiuam se
sacrificauerit: primo in fornace pro uirginitate tradendo, deinde in mare
perpetuam uirginitatem uouendo? Pro qua defendenda, inde subiit
flammas, hinc confugiebat ad undas. Sed, ut nichil ei desit in ulla gratia,[b]
consecretur iam tercio, ut quod erat mente, corpore, uita, sit habitu,
20   professione, religione, scilicet sancta in fide, spe, caritate summe
Trinitatis perfecta.[96] Consecretur et quarto ab ecclesia,[c] mater
ecclesiastica, ut quaterni euangelii ministra, ut quadrifide crucis
uexillifera, ut uirtutum quadriga, prudentia, iustitia, fortitudine,
temperantia, subnixa. Venit ergo paranymphus Christi Theodorus,
benignissime genitricis et nate caritate attractus; agit dominica[d] sacramenta festiuus. Accedit regia sponsa ad perhennia regis sui pignera et
cum ea turba decies septena[e] septiformis spiritus gratia in Decalogum
testamenti Dei federanda. Ardebant in singulis dextris, ut nuptiales
facule, ut uirginales lampades, sua luminaria. Stellata suo celo uidebatur
30   ecclesia. Virgo Domini inter electas electissima, inter omnes unica,
pulchra ut luna, sua secum adducebat sidera. Cui clamat uox sponsi
epithalamica, *Una est columba mea, una est matri sue electa genitricis sue.*[97]
Te noui ex nomine, quod os Domini nominauit.[98] *Ostende michi faciem*

---

*a*  F: improperabat
*b*  F: nulla gloria
*c*  F *omits* ab ecclesia
*d*  D: diuina
*e*  D: septuagena

*tuam, sonet uox tua in auribus meis.*[99] *Pulchre sunt gene tue ut fragmen mali punici,* [100] *collum tuum sicut monilia.*[101] At sponse caritas inpatiens silentii non tam uerba reddit quam ingerit: *Dilectus meus michi et ego illi.*[102] *Inueni quem diligit anima mea, tenebo eum nec dimittam, donec introducam illum in domum matris mee et in cubiculum genitricis mee.*[103] Congaudet assistens cognatissima uirginitati angelorum caterua et inuitat ad thalamum Domini laude prophetica, *Specie*[f] *tua et pulchritudine tua intende, prospere, procede et regna.*[104] Specie tua accipe *speciosum pre filiis hominum forma.*[105] Tali prerogatiua accedentem reginam in oblationem Dei sanctam, diuinus ierarcha adducit regi gratissimam,[g] prece inmolat, benedictione oppignerat, fideli[h] anulo subarrat, et inseparabili caritate summo principi confederat. Conclamant angeli, collaudant[i] archangeli, fauent dominationes, cherubin et seraphin subscribunt dotem regni indelebilem. Hinc, uelut quondam a spiritu Moisi in administros septuaginta fluxerunt, in ceteras eiusdem[j] numeri sorores diuina carismata, quibus omnibus almifluus Theodorus imposuit apostolicam manum, ut et ipse acciperent spiritum sanctum et fierent Domini sacrarium et hortus et germen suarum gratiarum. Has omnes cum precellentissima Mildritha, uel post eam, sacris uelis impositis, Domino desponsauit et dedicauit, forte Domneua ad hoc eas hactenus differente, ut profiterentur pariter cum expectata sobole et congrueret eis diuino dictamine uox psalmiste, *Adducentur regi uirgines post eam.*[106] Felix quecumque cantare poterat cum ipsa unica, 'Ipsi sum desponsata cui angeli seruiunt, cuius pulchritudinem sol et luna mirantur.' Quantum gaudium, quantum spectaculum prebuit dies illa supernis et infimis conuentibus! Nam si gaudium est in celo super uno peccatore conuerso, quanto magis super tam candido tot animarum contubernio. Venerabili autem Domneua supplicante et pre diuturna egritudine se excusante, adhuc sacratissimus archipontifex superaddidit benedictionem dignissime Mildrithe, et pro ipsa matre tamquam spiritualem Saram prole innouandam ordinat in principem domus ac familie diuine, et abbatissam consecrat sanctimonialis choree. Hinc Dominum suum, cuius familia est uniuersitas rerum, pulchra gratia imitari uisa est, et numero fere discipularum facta modo dux siderea et mater lactiflua consecratarum sibi septuaginta uirginum. Ita de uirginalibus uirginei sponsi nuptiis,

---

f  F *omits* Specie . . . regna
g  B: sacratissiman
h  D: fidei
i  D: congaudent
j  D: eiusmodi

uirginalem germinauit pascuam et progeniem semper floridam. O sancte indolis repentina senecta et filia in matrem mutata! Senectus enim uenerabilis est non tam annosa quam sensu et uita probata. Quam cito desponsata tam cito fetata, et uirgo Syon filias suas simul peperit et omnes uno partu caritatis effudit.

### XXII

Iam per plures annos regia et materna primiceria Domneua ad cumulum perhennis glorie longo languore decocta festinante Domino in meritorum premia uenit ad extrema. Circumstant matrem, cum unico pignore sue
10   primitie, sue plantationes nouelle, lactentes sicut nouelle oliuarum filie, sed iam radicate et fundate et solidate in diuina caritate. Omnia uirtutis documenta proloquitur, omnia in omnibus protestatur, seruare fidem Deo, perseuerare in sancto proposito, accensis iugiter lampadibus obuiam procedere sponso, iugum Christi suaue amabiliter ferre sub uberibus mellifluis a Deo date matris Mildrithe. Sic, commendatis omnibus Domino, migrauit ad angelicam sanctorum ciuitatem Ierusalem, relinquens prestantissimam natam totius loci et possessionis ac familie Dominice eternam heredem. Tetigit hic gladius Domini piissimam Mildritham, perueniens usque ad animam, sed non distulit
20   sanctus paraclitus consolationem et salutem suam, ut posset et ceterarum acutam sanare tristitiam. In hac omnes reclinabant fessa capita, in hac respirabant orbata pectora, in hac reperere omnia, hec reddebat uberiora[a] solacia.

### XXIII

Consurgens ergo pro genitrice signifera Domini, quasi tunc demum cepisset preteritorum oblita, cum Apostolo in anteriora se extendit. Tropheum uirtutum in astra attollit, calcato mundo in celum exardescit. In columna ignis et lucis antecedens, igne sequaces accendit, luce attrahit. Ire uirtutis uia non tam imperat quam monstrat, non tam
30   documentis quam exemplis comites prouocat. Ut omnibus precellentior,[b] ita apparebat humilior. Ministra esse malebat quam magistra, prodesse quam preesse, famulatu quam precepto caritatis obsequium docere. Mansuetudine magis quam rigore, patientia quam terrore uincere curabat, diligi potius quam timeri satagebat. Iugi abstinentia et

---

*a*  D: uberima
*b*  F: excellentior

uigiliis, psalmis et orationibus assiduis, redolebat suauitatem boni
Christi odoris. In egentes elemosinis, in cunctos homines uisceribus
clementissimis, mel et lac erat humani generis. Portabat Dominicum
gregem iuxta uocem Domini ad Moisen, *sicut portare solet nutrix
infantulum suum*, [107] ac diffusa in omnibus precordiis maternis trahebat
omnes ad Dominum spiritu eterne dulcedinis. Sequebantur dignam[c]
matrem bone filie unanimi feruore, nec ab ea se patiebantur degenerare.
Una cunctis beniuolentia, una in Christo concordia. Nocte et die psalteria
in manibus, psalmodia et preces in oribus, obsequium sororitatis et
reuerentia in moribus. Preueniebat princeps sua coniuncta psallentibus,      10
in ecclesia sua benedicens Deo in medio suarum tympanistriarum.[108] Una
erat in eis contentio, que humilior, que obedientior, que uigilantior, que
in omni probitatis emulatione sanctissime matri esset proximior. Illa
omnes astringebat in Christo, uno dilectionis uinculo. Sic itaque, ad
uocem sponse ordinata in uicem caritate, inuincibilis et impenetrabilis
apparebat hosti hec conserta sibi chorea et terribilis ut castrorum acies
ordinata. Cessent inmitia Amazonum bella, nil egit mauortia Pentis-
lea,[109] nil Thamaris heroibus metuenda,[110] horrent Lemniadum
parricidia;[111] hic potius sulphureas et infernales acies expugnant uere
pudicicie castra et uictricia signa cum coronis feruntur in astra.          20

## XXIIII

Sic Deo dilectam puritate uirginali animam angelorum tuebatur
custodia, et se illi adesse frequentes uel uisu uel claris ostendebant
obsequiis, sicut subsequentibus lucet sententiis. Sorores post ymnos
matutinos solito sopor reficiebat, una philomela Dei noctem sacro cantu
mulcebat, adeo cum Bethleemitis pastoribus uigilabat et uigilias noctis
supra gregem suum custodiebat. Supplicationes, gratiarum actiones,
suspiria, lacrime incendebant thimiamata sanctorum desideriorum et, de
fiala aurea plena odoramentorum et de manu angeli tenentis thuribulum
aureum, ascendit in conspectu Domini fumus dulcis aromatum. Ab        30
oratione repetebat lectionem et alterna uicissitudine reparabat uirtutem.
Ibi Domino uel cum Domino, hic Dominus sibi uel cum ipsa loquebatur.
Ibi ipsa interpellabat, hic ipse docebat. Cum ergo ut apes melligera
canonicis scriptuarum floretis incumberet, et ad celestem mensam
ardente lumine esurientem animam pasceret, totius boni aduersarius
candelam eius exsufflauit ac penitus extinxit, ut quam in nullo uincere
poterat saltem cursum ipsius uel absterreret uel retardaret. Cuius insidiis

c  D: bonam

amicissimus uirginis angelus lucis[a] repentinus obstitit, hostem longius in suas tenebras excussit eodemque momento diuino lumine lumen legenti restituit, candela suo splendore clarius recanduit. Sensit filia lucis angelicam presentiam et uisitationem diuinam, ampliusque exultans se temtatam ad maiorem gloriam, securior reddidit protectori Domino gratiarum uictimam. Nec mundi nox illi oberat, quam declaratio sermonum Domini illuminabat, cuius et lampas ab eterno sole indeficienter radiabat.

## XXV

10   Sic prostrata sed nunquam quieta, inimici malignitas alias in suam perniciem molitur insidias. Nam, ut quondam suus satelles Datianus dixerat in martyrem cuncta uincentem Vincentium, *Si non potui superare uiuum, puniam vel defunctum*,[112] sic teterrimus[b] bellipeta[113] occupare uirginem aggreditur dormientem, quam usque in[c] baratrum aufugerat uigilantem. Nil agis improbe tuis semper machinis obruende, cum sponsa in sopita fide custodi suo dicat, qui nunquam dormitat, *Ego dormio et cor meum* ad Deum[d] meum *uigilat*,[114] et Deus Deus[e] meus, ad te de luce tua etiam dormiens uigilo. *Sub umbra alarum tuarum protege me[f] et in umbra alarum tuarum sperabo donec transeat iniquitas*.[115] Cui et beate

20   Agnetis fiducia aduigilabat dicentis, *Mecum enim habeo custodem corporis mei angelum Domini*.[116] Talibus itaque armis fidei et caritatis munita, signato super se lumine uultus Domini, signaculo diue crucis, uirgo quiescebat et seruator huius sancti templi Domini angelus aduenit ac propter dulce soporantem familiarissime assedit, et (O mira dulcedo caritatis angelice in uirginem!) splendentibus complexam alis amicissime obtexit. Sic arca propitiatorii[g] alis cherubin uelabatur. Venit econtra draco tortuosus suis fantasiis sopitam illudere meditatus. Videt angelum sicut fulgur choruscantem; utque quondam sui ministri sepultum Dominum custodientes hoc aspectu sunt exterriti et facti uelut mortui,

30   sic ipse ex animi pauore retrorsum ruit et cum horrendo eiulatu procul aufugit. Omnia hec letis oculis per suauem soporem dilecta Deo anima contemplabatur et suum propugnatorem secum triumphantem et

---

*a*  *Omitted in D*
*b*  *A, B and C*: deterrimus
*c*  *D*: ad
*d*  *B*: Dominum
*e*  *F*: Dominus
*f*  *F adds* et in umbra alarum tuarum protege me
*g*  *D*: propitiationis

hostem ruina sua tabescentem. O beata uirginitas, que tam grata Deo et amabilis supernis uirtutibus et terribilis infernalibus potestatibus ostenderis, que sicut omnibus es incomparabilis ita preminentior es cunctis preconiis! Angelis sociaris et ipsi Domino copularis.

## XXVI

Currens ergo celica Mildritha de die in diem, de uirtute in uirtutem ad ardua, iam transcensa scala Iacob tenebat ethera, iam in celis erat conuersatio sua et, solo corpore in terris posito, tota mente et anima degebat inter siderea agmina. Iam olim cupiebat dissolui et cum Christo esse et propter dilectas quidem filiarum animas hactenus moras tolerabat 10 in carne; sed diuturnius non poterat ferre. Cotidie uero moriebatur pro illarum gloria in Christo, quam mortificabat fortis ut mors dilectio. Quadam ergo die, plus solito rapta in supernam contemplationem percussaque eternis amoribus, nec iam ferens diuinos impetus et mirabiles uulnerate caritatis cruciatus, tandem irrupit[h] peculiarem sibi ecclesiam sancte Dei Genitricis. Tum ibi coram eius cognatis patrociniis frena relaxauit oculorum riuulis altisque celestium desideriorum suspiriis. Clamor, gemitus, luctus, ululatus implebat oratorium. Non tam uerba quam planctus, non tam preces quam eiulatus agebat. Rugiebat a gemitu cordis sui. Oculi eius sicut columbe super riuos aquarum, *sicut* 20 *piscine in Esebon.*[117] Tota adeo affectione erat sicut hortus irriguus cuius non deficiunt aque. Quos tunc questus dabat in celum, quos mugitus et susurros in aures Domini, in qua hec sancta uota clamabant: Quis det *ut Omnipresens desiderium meum audiat?*[118] Heu michi *quia incolatus meus prolongatus est, habitaui cum habitantibus cedar, multum incola fuit anima mea.*[119] *Ut quid Domine recessisti longe?*[120] *Usque quo obliuisceris me in finem, usque quo auertis faciem tuam a me?*[121] *Quando respicies?*[122] *Quando ueniam et apparebo ante faciem Dei mei?*[123] *Surrexi aperire dilecto meo at ille declinauerat atque transierat. Anima mea liquefacta est ut* dilectus *locutus est.*[124] *Per noctem quesiui quem diligit anima mea, quesiui et non* 30 *inueni illum;*[125] *uocaui et non respondit michi. Filie Ierusalem nuntiate dilecto quia amore langueo.*[126] Tota denique nocte persistens in templo uirgo uigilantissima non oculis, non labiis,[i] non manibus, non pectore cessabat. Amicum inquietabat, celo uim faciebat. Non somnum dabat oculis, non requiem timporibus suis donec inueniret locum Domino, donec ipsum Dominum luctando cum Iacob uinceret et teneret ac

---

h *A, B, and C*: irripuit; *D*: erupit
i *D omits* non labiis

gratulabunda diceret, '*Inueni quem diligit anima mea, tenebo illum nec dimittam.*'[127] Venit enim subito Deus dilectionis, dulcis et suauis Dominus spiritus Domini Iesu et, ut flumen pacis et torrens inundans et fluminis impetus letificans ciuitatem suam,[a] fonte caritatis sue repleuit et inebriauit eam, quamque misericordia eius preuenerat ut fleret, subsecuta est ut amplius ad ipsum fleret. Cui uelut in Iordane lacrimarum baptizate apparuit, ipse spiritus Domini in specie columbe, super niuem candide, super solem splendide, seditque familiarissime in eius capitis uertice. Sedit in arce sua ales mitissima et ipsa potestas altissima. Virgo
10 gemebat[b] et columba columbam suam permulcebat. Ipsa ore placido pacem ferebat, alis blandifluis[c] per timpora uirginea applaudebat, faciem et ceruicem gratissimis pennis reuerberabat, totum caput amicabiliter uelut corona florida astringebat. Loquebatur intus ad cor Ierusalem dulcesque susurros et intima uerba eius pectori inserebat, foris quoque piis nutibus quasi sermonibus dicebat:

'Amica, quid ploras? Quam queris? Mecum uenit tibi, et tecum est quem diligit anima tua. Ego sum amor dilecti tui. Ab illo processi et ueni et in me ille uenit tibi. Ego te illi federaui, illum tibi dedi. Iungeris ipsi, me mediatore. Per me ipse uocat te; me acutore et nuncio accede. *Surge,*
20 *propera, amica mea, columba mea, formosa mea, et ueni. Iam hiems transiit, pluuia[d] abiit, tempus putationis aduenit.*[128] Audiui omne desiderium tuum, auribus percepi lacrimas tuas. *Veni de Libano ueni;*[129] decoraberis corona quasi sponsa.'

His affectionibus et dictis inenarrabilibus, Dominus paraclitus consolatione et unctione sua letificabat dilectam sibi animam, diuque persistens et amplexans caput eius ostendebat super eam inestimabilem[e] misericordiam suam, ut pre splendore non posset uideri per unam fere horam. Tandem gratissimum sibi uirginei cordis templum subintrauit et in ea mansionem faciens requieuit uel celos[f] cum claritate sua repetens
30 hanc non deseruit.

### XXVII

Prosequitur itaque dolor corporis beatissimam Mildritham, insinuans a cunctis doloribus iam liberandam et, diruta mortalitatis fabrica, ad

---

a  *F*: Dei
b  *D*: gaudebat
c  *F*: blandissimis
d  *D*: imber
e  *D*: ineffabilem
f  *D*: celum

immortalia se exituram gaudia. Intellexit se exauditam et hoc sibi suam prenuntiasse columbam, ne timeret mortem transitoriam per quam transiret ad uitam sempiternam. Non eget iam longa narratione nota ipsius flagrantia, que gratiarum libamina, que orationum incensa, que totius sancte deuotionis cinnama et balsama Domino adoleuerit, quod eam ab hac mundi uoragine ad suam misericordiam uocare dignatus sit. Gaudebat, exultabat, triumphabat tamquam ad supernas epulas inuitata et in thalamum Domini sui producenda. Reuerebatur tamen, quamquam purissima conscientia esset, ne quid decoris, ne quid ornamentorum sibi deesset, quo minus sponso nimium eleganti placeret. Que nil presumens 10 de$^g$ sua iusticia innisa est tutius in Saluatoris misericordia. Torrebat languor in sacrificium Domini exhausta membra, sed plus estuabat sitiens in Deo anima et mens celo intenta. Orabat, psallebat; semper Domini benedictio, semper laus eius in ore suo. Ipsa inmolabat et ipsa inmolabatur Deo sacrificium laudis. Iam beata attigit diem supremum diu desideratum. Contremuit chorus sororum acsi terre motus totum concussisset uel deiecisset monasterium. Desertus uisus est mundus, dies nebulosus, sol obscurus. Dominabantur desolatio et orbitas, meror et gemitus. Aduocat totum contubernium suum, hortatur et obtestatur seruare omnes in Christo caritatis uinculum et uotum suum inuiolatum$^h$ 20 et memores esse parturitionis$^i$ et uiscerum suorum. Ad hoc uulnerabant materna pectora filiarum lacrime tamquam sagitte acute, et anhelantem ad Dominum retorquebant ad se. Quas pia mater obsecrabat ut mallent se sequi ad gloriam quam hic retinere ad erumnam. Cumque ab ea flagitarent extreme allocutionis et ualedictionis aliquod hereditarium memoriale sic memoratur dixisse:

'Pacem et sanctimoniam inter uos habete, carissime, caritatem Dei et proximi stabili integritate seruate. In communi necessitate communiter, ut decet domum Dei, sperantes in Domino consulite, maiores audite, prudenter discernite, inuicem onera uestra portate, inuicem obedite, 30 unanimi obsecutione unum corpus et unus spiritus in Domino atque una domus Dei estote et Deus pacis ac dilectionis maneat semper cum omnibus uobis.'

His et huiusmodi hortatibus$^j$ cum$^k$ consolationibus maternis domesticas Christi docebat et omnibus oscula sancta dabat. Iamque,

---

g  D: in
h  F: immolatum
i  F: participationis
j  D: orationibus
k  D: et

refecta uiuifico Dominici sacramenti uiatico, splendidam animam effudit
in manu Domini, facta corona glorie et diadema regni in manu Dei sui.
Transiit tertio Idus Iulii[130] ad eternum diem et infinita secula,
sepultaque est in ipsa sancte Dei Genitricis uirgo uirginali ecclesia, que
(ut premonstratum est) a matre fundata et ipsa post matrem eidem est
principata. Deflent mortales tantam lucem terris sullatam; gaudent
superne uirtutes tantam ciuem sibi collatam. Damnaque terrena tranant
in celica lucra. Quin et terrigenis iterum redditur maiori tripudio,
multoque presentior nobis est celesti patrocinio, quam ante fuisset
10   mortali contubernio. Versa est tristitia in gaudium, luctus in iubilum,
obitus in eternum solemnium. Iam cum Domino et in Domino nobiscum
est usque in seculum. Hoc diuinis uirtutibus, hoc miraculis, hoc
reuelationibus crebro attestatur et claris signis nobis loquitur. Benedictus
Dominus qui in omnia secula dominatur et in sanctis suis mirabilia
semper operatur. Amen.

## XXVIII

Suscepit itaque pupillam domum regendam alma uirgo eiusdem
monasterii Eadburga[a] et prelata est tam coacta quam inuita, tam addicta
quam refuga.[131] Hec, ueluti naturalis filia plerunque refert faciem
20   genitricis pulcherrime, sic uitam, mores et studia sanctimonie emula-
batur sanctissime matris[b] Mildrithe. Orationi, lectioni, ceterisque sancte
obseruationis exercitiis intenta, peruigili exemplorum lampade sorores
irradiabat, sacrisque hortamentis et documentis quasi manu ducebat,
utque secum omnibus castum Deo templum exhiberet decertabat. Tanta
autem contritione et humilitate cordis se deiecerat, ut se cunctis
inferiorem estimaret, iuxta quod Gregoriana sententia docet, *Iustus aut
omni potestate seculari exuitur, aut si aliqua cingitur non sub illa curuatur, ne
superbus tumeat, sed eam sibi subicit, ut humilior innotescat.* Et alibi, *Qui
intra sanctam ecclesiam bene temporaliter imperat, sine fine in perpetuum
30   regnat et de gloria seculi huius ad eternam gloriam transmeat.*[132] Verum,
cum hoc templum sancte Dei genitricis in benedictione Dei nate
multitudini non sufficeret et artiora claustra Dominicum gregem
constringerent, dux solertissima aliud iuxta maius et honorificentius
cenobium condidit, totumque cenobialibus officinis et habitaculis
perfectissime[c] instituit atque in honore principum apostolorum Petri et

---

*a   F*: Edburga
*b   D*: genitricis
*c   D*: plenissime

Pauli ab archipresule Cuthberto[133] dedicari fecit. In hoc enim beate
Mildrithe decentissimam glebam transferre decreuerat, ut ei$^d$ maxime
hoc habitaculum preparauerat. Statuto ergo die sacre translationis,
celeberrimo confluente affatim clero et populo, dant manus uirginali
sarcofago. Hic non citius amoueri operculum, nec aperiri poterant clausa,
quam inclusa erumpebat suauitatis gratia. Hinc myrra electa, hinc
balsama non mixta, hinc incensa et cuncta late effluebant aromata. Tum
miracula miraculis occurrunt. Inueniunt uirginem uestibus mundissimis
et toto corpore post tot scilicet annos integram et incorruptam, ita ut
uideretur magis dormire in thalamo quam putrescere in sepulchro. Hac 10
quippe incorruptione et odoris suauitate diuina benignitas dignata est
propalare, quanta sibi seruierit mentis et corporis puritate. Cuius oratio
directa est sicut incensum in conspectu Domini, que ut terebintus non
incisus uaporauit habitationem suam, et ut nardus Marie ac sponse odor
unguenti repleuit domum Domini totam. Hic uero et pia uiuentis
memoria et tam clara dormientis miracula letificabant et uulnerabant
liquefacta sororum pectora. Passim uoluebantur lacrime et gaudia,
eratque quodam modo leta mestitia et mesta letitia. Tum beata
Eadburga, inmensas Deo gratias agens et laudum cantica cum tota
ecclesia attollens, inclitam glebam a priori domicilio et sepulcro sustulit 20
et in nouum apostolorum templum transposuit, atque in aquilonali parte
presbiterii in nouo sarcofago glorifice recondidit. Huc etiam sacrum
collegium filiarum ad ipsam matrem perpetuam transduxit, relicta parte
quo primitiue ecclesie sancteque sue memorie iugiter deseruiret. Erat
autem utraque domus quasi unum monasterium et una chorea sub una
auriga, spacio ad claustri modum tantum bipertita. Prior et hereditaria
uirginis ecclesia suam possiderat et uiuam et defunctam, secunda
suscepit a priore concessam. Hunc ergo locum sue translationis preciosissima margarita perhennibus illustrat beneficiis. Cunque iam ad summum
patrem Augustinum diuina operatione atque amore (ut proprio textu 30
exponetur) transierit ibique se adesse multimodis uirtutibus compro-
barit,[134] hic quoque se non deesse uberrime ostendit, Deo auctore qui in
sanctis suis omnia cooperatur in bonum in secula seculorum.

EXPLICIT VITA DEO DILECTAE VIRGINIS MILDRETHAE$^e$

---

d  A and B add *above line* vel sicut
e  B *omits* EXPLICIT . . . MILDRETHAE.

# Notes

## Introduction

1. B. de Gaiffier, 'L'hagiographie et son public au XIe siècle', *Miscellanea Historica in Honorem Leonis van der Essen*, I (Brussels, 1947), 137–66, reprinted in *idem*, *Études critiques d'hagiographie et d'iconologie* (Subsidia hagiographica, XLIII, Brussels, 1967), 475–507; and 'La lecture des actes des martyrs dans la prière liturgique en occident', *AB*, LXXII (1954), 134–66. On the vernacular homily, see A. K. Fortescue, *The Mass: A Study of the Roman Liturgy* (2nd edn, 1937), 284–5; and J. A. Jungmann, *The Mass of the Roman Rite* (1959 edn), 289–90.
2. *ASS, Novembris*, III, 436, cited and discussed by De Gaiffier, *Études critiques*, 475–6.
3. Cited by De Gaiffier, 'La lecture des actes des martyrs', *AB*, LXXII (1954), 148, from Gregory of Tours, *Liber in gloria martyrum*; Monumenta Germaniae Historica, *Scriptores Rerum Merovingicarum*, Iii, ed. B. Krusch (Hanover, 1885), 531.
4. N. Herrmann-Mascard, *Les reliques des saints: formation coutumière d'un droit* (Société d'Histoire du Droit: Collection d'histoire institutionelle et sociale, VI, Paris, 1975) is a recent account of saints' relics with further references. See also M. Foerster, *Zur Geschichte des Reliquienkultus in Altengland* (Sitzungsberichte der Bayerischen Akademie der Wissenschaft, Philosophisch-historische Abteilung, Munich, 1943), 3ff.
5. See P-A. Sigal, 'Maladie, pèlerinage et guérison au XIIe siècle: Les miracles de saint Gibrien à Reims', *Annales: Économies, Sociétés, Civilisations*, XXIV (1969), 1522–39; and R. C. Finucane, 'The use and abuse of medieval miracles', *History*, LX (1975), 1–10, and *Miracles and Pilgrims: Popular Beliefs in Medieval England* (1977).
6. Helgaud of Fleury, *Vie de Robert le Pieux: Epitoma Vitae Regis Roberti Pii*, ed. and trans R-H. Bautier and G. Labory (Sources d'Histoire Médiévale, I, Paris, 1965), 127. In general, see J. Sumption, *Pilgrimage: An Image of Medieval Religion* (1975).
7. In general, see B. Toepfer, 'Reliquienkult und Pilgerbewegung zur Zeit der Klosterreform im Burgundisch-Aquitanischen Gebiet', *Vom Mittelalter zur Neuzeit: Zum 65. Geburtstag Heinrich Sproemberg*, ed. H. Kretzschmar (Berlin, 1956), 420–39. On Conques, see *Liber Miraculorum Sancte Fidis*, ed. A. Bouillet (Paris, 1897), 120–2. On Fleury, see *Les miracles de saint Benoît écrits par Adrevald, Aimoin, André, Raoul Tortaire et Hugues de Sainte Marie, moines de Fleury*, ed. E. de Certain (Société de l'Histoire de France, Paris, 1858), 63–5.
8. É. Faral, *Les jongleurs en France au moyen âge* (Bibliothèque de l'École des Hautes Études, Sciences historiques et philologiques, CLXXXVII, Paris, 1910), 44–55.

9. For Anglo-Saxon England, see Foerster, *op. cit.*, 15–22; in general, see Herrmann-Mascard, *op. cit.*, 235–70.

10. *Ibid.*, 193–234.

11. A. S. Napier, *Wulfstan: Sammlung der ihm zugeschriebenen Homilien nebst Untersuchungen über ihre Echtheit* (Berlin, 1883), 170 and 173.

12. B. de Gaiffier, 'Miracles bibliques et vies de saints', *Nouvelle Revue Théologique*, LXXXVIII (1966), 376–85 (reprinted in his *Études critiques*, 50–61) and 'Mentalité de l'hagiographie médiévale d'après quelques travaux récents', *AB*, LXXXVI (1968), 391–9. See also W. F. Bolton, 'The supra-historical sense in the *Dialogues* of Gregory I', *Aevum*, XXXIII (1959).

13. C. Grant Loomis, 'The miracle traditions of the Venerable Bede', *Speculum*, XXI (1946), 404–18. See also C. W. Jones, *Saints' Lives and Chronicles in Early England* (Ithaca, 1947), esp. 57–64 and 75–6.

14. *Two Lives of St Cuthbert*, ed. and trans. B. Colgrave (1940), 198 and 200–2; *Gregorii Magni Dialogi Libri IV*, ed. U. Moricca (Rome, 1924), 97 (II.10) and 42 (I.6).

15. F. Graus, *Volk, Herrscher und Heiliger im Reich der Merowinger: Studien zur Hagiographie der Merowingerzeit* (Prague, 1965), 62–88, and L. Zoepf, *Das Heiligen-Leben im 10. Jahrhundert* (Beiträge zur Kulturgeschichte des Mittelalters und der Renaissance, I, Leipzig and Berlin, 1908), 31–62 and *passim*.

16. For examples related to relic-thefts, see P. J. Geary, *Furta Sacra, Thefts of Relics in the Central Middle Ages* (Princeton, 1978), 143–52.

17. Graus, *op. cit.*, 113–16. See also De Gaiffier, 'Hagiographie et historiographie', *La storiografia alto-medievale* (Settimane di studio del Centro Italiano di Studi sull' Alto Medioevo, XVII, 1970), 141–5.

18. J-C. Poulin, *L'idéal de sainteté dans l'Aquitaine carolingienne d'après les sources hagiographiques (750–950)* (Laval, 1975).

19. De Gaiffier, *Études critiques*, 452–74.

20. S. Roisin, *L'hagiographie cistercienne dans le diocèse de Liège au XIIIe siècle* (Université de Louvain, Recueil de Travaux d'Histoire de la Philologie, 3rd ser., fasc. 37, Louvain and Brussels, 1947).

21. Zoepf, *Heiligen-Leben*, 12–24, discusses this and other material aims. See also B. de Gaiffier, 'Les revendications des biens dans quelques documents hagiographiques du XIe siècle', *AB*, L (1932), 123–38.

22. A. Gransden, *Historical Writing in England c. 550 to c. 1307* (1974), 68 and 77.

23. Zoepf, *op. cit.*, 24–30.

24. Gransden, *op. cit.*, 68.

25. Ed. De Certain, especially 90–172. See K. F. Werner, 'Die literarischen Vorbilder des Aimoin von Fleury und die Entstehung seiner *Gesta Francorum*', *Medium Aevum Vivum: Festschrift für Walther Bulst*, ed. H. R. Jauss and D. Schaller (Heidelberg, 1960), 69–103.

## [1] *The Content of the Mildrith Legend*

1. For a list of versions and their contents, see below, Appendix A.

2. See below, pp. 39–40.

3. See below, p. 27.

4. See below, pp. 25–7.

## [2] *The Diffusion of the Mildrith Legend*

1. *SO*, II, 3–13.
2. *SO*, II, 3–283. On the date of the *Historia Regum*'s compilation, see *ibid.*, xii–xv; P. H. Blair, 'Some observations on the *Historia Regum* attributed to Symeon of Durham', in *Celt and Saxon: Studies in the Early British Border*, ed. N. K. Chadwick (1963), 63–76; and D. N. Dumville, 'The Corpus Christi "Nennius"', *Bull. Board of Celtic Studies*, xxv (1974), 369–80.
3. This statement occurs in *SO*, II, 4, in a passage which has apparently been inserted between the rubric mentioned above and the beginning of the *passio* proper.
4. See below, pp. 17–18.
5. *SO*, II, 13.
6. This is the earliest possible date of *CS* 149, the latest charter in which Mildrith is referred to alive. For this and all pre-Conquest charters subsequently referred to, see P. H. Sawyer, *Anglo-Saxon Charters* (1968), which lists manuscripts, editions and modern commentaries. *CS* and *KCD* numbers are correlated with Sawyer's own numbers on pp. 26–38. An interim discussion of the early charters of Minster-in-Thanet is given in my 'The Mildrith Legend: A Study in Early Medieval Hagiography in England' (Ph.D. thesis, University of Birmingham, 1978), 418–46. A definitive discussion will not be possible until the cartularies of St Augustine's Abbey, Canterbury, which contain the Minster-in-Thanet charters, have been fully studied. For the comments of D. Whitelock, see *Anglo-Saxon Writs*, ed. F. E. Harmer (1952), 456–7. See also *The Register of St Augustine's Abbey, Canterbury, Commonly Called The Black Book*, ed. G. J. Turner and H. E. Salter (British Academy Records of the Social and Economic History of England and Wales, II, pt 1, 1915), xxxiii–xxxix.
7. The dating-clause is inconsistent and could refer to 748 or 746.
8. See below, pp. 142–3, and, on the authorship, pp. 20–1.
9. *DHE*, 5 (sec. 17), and *Leechdoms*, III, 430. In addition, the *Vita Mildburgae* confirms that Domne Eafe's church was dedicated to St Mary (London, BL, Additional MS 34, 633, f. 208v); and *CS* 189 records a grant to Eadburg's successor Sigeburg and her *familia* in the church of St Peter. The Latin version of the Old English text, *þa halgan*, refers to Eadburg's construction of the church of SS Peter and Paul and the translation of Mildrith's relics to it, but it may not be independent of Goscelin's work: *DHE*, 6 (sec. 17) and below, p. 21.
10. J. K. Wallenberg, *Kentish Place-Names: A Topographical and Etymological Study of the Place-Name Material in Kentish Charters Dated Before the Conquest* (Uppsala, 1931), 73.
11. *SO*, II, 10; and E. Ekwall, *The Concise Oxford Dictionary of English Place-Names* (4th edn, 1960), 491.
12. *SO*, II, 9–10.
13. *Ibid.*, 10.
14. *Ibid.*, 9–10.
15. See below, p. 89, and *Chronicon Abbatiae Ramseiensis*, ed. W. D. Macray (RS, 1886), 55.
16. On Eastry, see S. E. Chadwick, 'The Anglo-Saxon cemetery at Finglesham: A reconsideration, *Medieval Archaeology*, II (1958), 5–7 and fig. 3.
17. See below, p. 57, *Chronicon Abbatiae Rameseiensis*, 55; and *DHE*, 13 (sec. 25).
18. D. W. Rollason, 'Lists of saints' resting-places in Anglo-Saxon England', *ASE*, VII (1978), 68.

19. M. Lapidge, 'Byrhtferth of Ramsey and the early sections of the *Historia Regum* attributed to Symeon of Durham', *ASE*, x (1981), 97–122.

20. M. Lapidge, 'The hermeneutic style in tenth-century Anglo-Latin literature', *ASE*, IV (1975), 67–111.

21. Blair, 'Some observations', 113–18, whose interpretation seems to supersede T. Arnold's, given in *SO*, II, xii–xiii. See also P. H. Blair, 'Symeon's History of the Kings', *Archaeologia Aeliana*, 4th ser., XVI (1939), 87–100, and H. S. Offler, 'Hexham and the *Historia Regum*', *Trans. Architectural and Archaeological Soc. of Northumberland and Durham*, II (1970), 51–62.

22. C. Hart, 'The Ramsey *Computus*', *EHR*, LXXXV (1970), 37, and, for an edition of the annals, 38–44.

23. See below, pp. 90, 24 and 102.

24. See above, pp. 17–18.

25. See below, p. 96, and *SO*, II, 8.

26. See below, p. 93, l. 29.

27. F. Barlow, 'Two notes: Cnut's second pilgrimage and Queen Emma's disgrace in 1043', *EHR*, LXXIII (1958), 650–1, discusses this dating. Although his conclusion that 1035 is the correct date seems sound, his statement that Goscelin gave this date in his *Textus translationis . . . Mildrethae* (*BHL* 5961 and 5964) and *Contra usurpatores* (*BHL* 5962) (on which see below, p. 22) is incorrect. In both cases, Goscelin gave the date as 1030; see *TT*, c. 12, and *HP*, 84.

28. W. St J. Hope, 'Recent discoveries in the abbey-church of St Austin at Canterbury', *Archaeologia*, LXVI (1915), 390.

29. See below, p. 89.

30. See below, pp. 105–7.

31. This translation is said to have taken place in the fourth year of Abbot Wido (*ASS, Maii*, VI, 413). He took office in 1087. For his dates and those of Abbot Scotland, see C. N. L. Brooke, D. Knowles and V. C. M. London, *The Heads of Religious Houses, England and Wales 940–1216* (1972).

32. *TT*, c.1. There is also a reference to this text in the *Vita Mildrethae*; see below, p. 43, ll. 29–32.

33. *ASS, Maii*, VI, 395 and *Acta Sanctorum Ordinis Sancti Benedicti, Saeculum Primum*, ed. J. Mabillon (Venice, 1633), 525. This argument is based on T. J. Hamilton, 'Goscelin of Canterbury: A critical study of his life, works and accomplishments' (Ph.D. thesis, University of Virginia, 1973). I am grateful to the author for permission to use his work, to which my debt is very great. For accounts of Goscelin's career, see *ibid.*, 130–93; *The Life of King Edward Who Rests at Westminster Attributed to a Monk of St Bertin*, ed. and trans. F. Barlow (1962), 91–111; *DNB*, XXII (1890), 253–4; and C. H. Talbot, 'The *Liber Confortatorius* of Goscelin of St Bertin', Analecta Monastica, 3rd ser., *Studia Anselmiana*, XXXVII (1955), 1–22.

34. This and the Latin text are printed in *DHE*, 1–10.

35. Wihtred's translation occurred at the same time as Mildrith was translated to the crypt; see reference given in n.28.

36. *DHE*, 6 (sec. 17).

37. W. Levison, *England and the Continent in the Eighth Century* (1946), 182–4, 187, 199 and 201.

38. The *Contra usurpatores* is printed in *HP*, 68–96. It states (p. 73) that the canons made their claim to possess Mildrith's relics about three years after the

translation of the relics of St Eadburg and an unnamed saint, later claimed to be
Mildrith, to St Gregory's Priory. This took place in 1085 (see below). The
priory's earliest charter, which is dated to 1086 or 1087, also makes the claim;
see *Cartulary of the Priory of St Gregory, Canterbury*, ed. A. M. Woodcock
(Camden 3rd ser., LXXXVIII, 1956), 1–2. The priory's foundation date is given
as 1084 or 1085 in *ibid.*, ix. The date 1086, given by D. Knowles and R. N.
Hadcock, *Medieval Religious Houses, England and Wales* (2nd edn, 1971), 349, is
probably incorrect.

39. *HP*, 108.
40. *Ibid*, 72–3.
41. *Ibid.*, 77.
42. Printed in *HP*, 97–108. There is an abbreviated version in *NLA*, I, 308–9, the
    compiler of which states specifically that he is drawing on a text preserved at St
    Gregory's Priory (p. 310).
43. *HP*, 72, 78–9 and 80, compared with 103 and 107.
44. P. Grosjean, 'De codice hagiographico Gothano', *AB*, LVIII (1940), 90–103.
45. *NLA*, I, 310.
46. *HP*, 97–9 and 102; and below, pp. 137–40.
47. *DHE*, 2–10.
48. See above, and Appendix A.
49. See above, n.38.
50. *DHE*, 1 (sec. 5).
51. *NLA*, I, 309–10.
52. *DHE*, 1 (sec. 5). This information is also found in its Latin translation; see *ibid.*,
    2 (sec. 5).
53. *HP*, 107–8, and below, pp. 62–3.
54. *TT*, c. 4. She was the successor of Sigeburg who was last mentioned in charters
    of the early 760s; see *TT*, c. 2 and 3 and *CS* 188 and 189. The identification
    proposed here was suggested by R. C. Jenkins, 'St Mary's minster in Thanet
    and St Mildred', *Arch. Cant.*, XII (1878), 190–1. His view that there were two St
    Mildriths, one of Lyminge and one of Minster-in-Thanet (*ibid.*, 191–2) seems
    speculative.
55. N. P. Brooks, *The Early History of the Church in Canterbury* (forthcoming).
56. W. G. Searle, *Onomasticon Anglo-Saxonicum* (1897), s.v.
57. N. P. Brooks, 'The development of military obligations in eighth- and ninth-
    century England', in *England before the Conquest, Studies in Primary Sources
    presented to Dorothy Whitelock*, ed. P. Clemoes and K. Hughes (1971), 79–80.
58. G. Ward, 'The age of St Mildred's Church, Canterbury', *Arch. Cant.*, LIV (1941
    for 1942), 62–8, identified this refuge with the church dedicated to St Mildrith.
    He was, however, shown to be wrong by R. U. Potts, 'St Mildred's Church,
    Canterbury: Further notes on the site', *ibid.*, LVI (1944 for 1943), 19–22.
59. London, BL, Additional MS 34, 633, fos. 206–9.
60. Additional 34,633 f.210r. H. P. R. Finberg, *The Early Charters of the West
    Midlands* (2nd edn, 1972), 200, argued that the text was by Goscelin. This was
    also the view of Talbot, '*Liber Confortatorius*', *op. cit.* in n. 33, 13, and Barlow,
    *Life of King Edward*, *op. cit.* in n. 33, 111. There is, however, no documentary or
    internal evidence to justify such an attribution and the text differs markedly in
    wording, style and emphasis from the *Vita Mildrethae*, which is certainly by
    Goscelin. The single exception to this is the occurrence in both texts of the

phrase *regni flos et thalamus* to describe Thanet (f. 208v and below, p. 18, ll. 18–19; but this alone does not prove identity of authorship.

61. Additional 34, 633, f. 207r; *The Chronicle of Hugh Candidus*, ed. W. T. Mellows (1949), 50–1, and *ASC* (E), s.a. 963.

62. Finberg, *op. cit.*, 199.

63. *Ibid.*, 197–8.

64. *PL*, CLV, cols. 97–110.

65. *DHE*, 7 (sec. 24).

66. *The Chartulary or Register of the Abbey of St Werburgh, Chester*, pt I, ed. J. Tait (Chetham Society, Remains Historical and Literary Connected with the Palatine Counties of Lancaster and Chester, n.s. LXXIX, 1920), xv–xviii, citing *CS* 1041 and *ASC*, s.a. 894 and 907. Higden dated the translation to 875 but his account is probably based on *ASC*, s.a. 874, which records the presence of the Danes at Repton in the general area of Hanbury; see *Polychronicon Ranulphi Higden Monachi Cestrensis*, ed. J. R. Lumby (RS, VI, 1876), 364 and 366.

67. See above, n. 61.

68. *PL*, CLV, cols. 106–7. The place in question may be Threckingham in Lincolnshire (*Chartulary of St Werburgh*, ed. Tait, x–xi). Hanbury emerged from the Danish invasions as a property of St Werburg's, Chester (*ibid.*, x), so this cannot represent a later attempt at Hanbury to reclaim the relics.

69. *PL*, CLV, col. 107–8.

70. *Fl.Wig.*, II, 258–60.

71. *Ibid.*, 258–60. The history of Mercia also has a little material associated with the Mildrith Legend, dealing briefly with Eormenred and Merewalh (*ibid.*, 264–7). On the manuscripts, see *Monumenta Historica Britannica or the Materials for the History of Britain from the Earliest Period, I, Extending to the Norman Conquest*, ed. H. Petrie and J. Sharpe (1848), 86–7, and *The Chronicle of John of Worcester, 1118–1140*, ed. J. R. H. Weaver (Anecdota Oxoniensia, XIII, 1908), 4–9. A new edition of the chronicle is to be published by Dr P. McGurk of Birkbeck College, London.

72. *Fl.Wig.*, II, 276; *John of Worcester*, ed. Weaver, 7–8.

73. For discussion of the chronicle, see *ibid.*; *Fl.Wig.*, II, viii–x; W. H. Stevenson, 'A contemporary description of the Domesday Survey', *EHR*, XXII (1907), 76–7; *The Vita Wulfstani of William of Malmesbury*, ed. R. R. Darlington (Camden 3rd ser., XL, 1928), x–xvi; and R. R. Darlington, *Anglo-Norman Historians* (1947), 14–15.

74. *DHE*, 1–9.

75. It is printed from this manuscript alone in *Liber Vitae: Register and Martyrology of New Minster and Hyde Abbey, Winchester*, ed. W. de G. Birch (1892), 83–7. On the date of this part of the manuscript, see N. R. Ker, *Catalogue of Manuscripts Containing Anglo-Saxon* (1957), 338–40. Birch preferred to date it a few years earlier; see *Liber Vitae*, xvi, xviii, xix and lvii–lviii. The other manuscript, Cambridge, Corpus Christi College, MS 201, is of mid-eleventh-century date; see *ibid.*, 82–90, and *DHE*, xiv.

76. *DHE*, 7; see Appendix A.

77. *Liber Eliensis*, ed. E. O. Blake (Camden 3rd ser., XCII, 1962), 120–3.

78. *DHE*, 7, n. 0, and xvii.

79. See above, p. 26.

80. F. M. Stenton, *Anglo-Saxon England* (3rd edn, 1971), 326.

81. *Hugh Candidus*, ed. Mellows, 56–9. The version appears to have been translated into Latin from Old English; see *ibid.*, xxxv.
82. *Ibid.*, 58, and above, p. 26, n. 56.
83. See above, p. 26, n. 61, and *Hugh Candidus*, ed. Mellows, 58. The three saints appear also in the *Vita Mildrethae* (see below, p. 115, ll. 22–32).
84. *Hugh Candidus*, ed. Mellows, 64.
85. *Leechdoms*, III, 422–32, is cited as it is the most accessible edition. A better edition of the Lambeth Fragment has been published by M. Foerster, 'Die altenglischen Beigaben des Lambeth-Psalters', *Archiv für das Studium der neueren Sprachen und Literaturen*, CXXXII (1914), 333–4, and of both texts by M. J. Swanton, 'A fragmentary life of St Mildred and other Kentish royal saints', *Arch. Cant.*, XCI (1975), 15–27.
86. Ker, *op. cit.*, 172–3 (cf. 343); for kalendars, see *English Kalendars before A.D. 1100*, ed. F. Wormald (Henry Bradshaw Society, LXXII, 1934), nos. 2, 3, 6, 7 and 14. Wormald never published in detail his reasons for attributing the kalendars in this volume to particular areas or churches.
87. Ker, *op. cit.*, 343, and M. R. James, *Descriptive Catalogue of the Manuscripts in the Library of Lambeth Palace* (1930), no. 427.
88. N. R. Ker, *Medieval Libraries of Great Britain* (1964), 78.
89. Caligula A. viii, fos. 108v and 119v, and *ASC*, s.a. 832.
90. Caligula A. viii. fos. iiiv, and 113v, and *Leechdoms*, III, 432. See also G. Herzfeld, 'Zu *Leechdoms* III, 428ff.', *Englische Studien*, XIII (1889), 140–2.
91. See above, p. 30.
92. See above, p. 19, n. 27.
93. See above, pp. 18–20.
94. For an example, see A. Vidier, *L'historiographie à S. Benoît-sur-Loire et les miracles de S. Benoît* (Paris, 1965), 137.

## [3] *The Genesis of the Mildrith Legend*

1. See above, pp. 15–17.
2. *DHE*, 7 and 8 (section 27) and *Fl.Wig*, I, 260.
3. *The Historical Works of Gervase of Canterbury*, ed. W. Stubbs (RS, II, 1880), 287.
4. *EH*, IV.19, and Caligula A.viii, f.117r.
5. See above, p. 28.
6. *CS* 35 could be dated 675 or 690: the latter is much the more likely in view of what is known of the history of its grantor, King Oswine. For this and the date of *CS* 42, see K. Harrison, *The Framework of Anglo-Saxon History to A.D. 900* (1978), 142–6, citing an unpublished lecture by D. Whitelock.
7. For this and other Minster charters, see above p. 16, n. 6. The name referred to here appears as *Eaba* in *CS* 96. For a comparable mutation of the same name, compare Bede, *EH*, IV.13, where the name *Eaba* appears, with *The Old English Version of Bede's Ecclesiastical History*, ed. and trans. T. Miller (Early English Text Society, O.S. XCV–XCVI, 1890), 302, where the same name appears as *Æbbe*.
8. Elmham, *Historia Monasterii Sancti Augustini Cantuariensis*, ed. C. Hardwick

(RS, 1858), 249–50, regarded *CS* 44 as a confirmation of *CS* 42 whereas in fact the reverse must have been the case; see Harrison, *op. cit.*, 69–70 and 142–5.

9.  This is disputed by P. Chaplais, 'The origin and authenticity of the royal Anglo-Saxon diploma', *J. Soc. of Archivists*, III (1965–9), 48–61, who would prefer to attribute the introduction of charters to Augustine. Even if he is correct, the fact remains that there are no authentic charters extant which antedate Theodore's pontificate. The use of charters for grants to churches before his time is unlikely to have been general.

10. W. Page (ed.) *The Victoria History of the County of Kent* II, (1926), 127.

11. W. Levison, *England and the Continent in the Eighth Century* (1946), 139 and 150. P. Sims-Williams is sceptical of the identification; see his 'An unpublished seventh- or eighth-century Anglo-Latin letter in Boulogne-sur-Mer MS 74 (82)' *Medium Aevum*, XLVIII (1979) 22, n. 119.

12. N. Herrmann-Mascard, *Les reliques des saints: formation coutumière d'un droit* (Société d'Histoire du Droit: Collection d'histoire institutionelle et sociale, VI, Paris, 1975), 82–4.

13. See below, p. 143. For further references to this translation, see above, p. 16.

14. *TT*, c. XV.

15. See below, pp. 127–8: cf. *DHE*, 5 (sec. 13); and p. 132. There was a gospel-book of St Mildrith, which may have been connected with her cult at St Augustine's Abbey by Elmham's time in the early fifteenth-century: *Historia Monasterii S. Augustini*, ed. Hardwick, 97–8.

16. G. Ward, 'Saxon records of Tenterden', *Arch. Cant.*, XLIX (1938 for 1937), 241–3; E. Ekwall, *The Concise Oxford Dictionary of English Place-Names* (4th edn, 1960), 463.

17. *The Register of St Augustine's Abbey, Canterbury, Commonly Called The Black Book*, ed. G. J. Turner and H. E. Salter (British Academy Records of the Social and Economic History of England and Wales, II pt 1, 1915), 29.

18. A. M. Everitt, 'The making of the agrarian landscape of Kent', *Arch. Cant.*, XCII (1977), 17–20.

19. *Leechdoms*, III, 430–2 (on which, see above, pp. 30–1) and *DHE*, 5 (sec. 18).

20. *Fl.Wig.*, II, 258.

21. *SO*, II, 10.

22. *DHE*, 9 (sec. 28) and *EH*, II.6.

23. *DHE*, 6 (sec. 17).

24. *Ibid.*, 1 and 2 (sec. 6).

25. See above, p. 24.

26. F. M. Stenton, 'Pre-Conquest Herefordshire', in *Herefordshire, III – North-West* (Royal Commission on Historical Monuments in England, 1934), lvff., reprinted in *Preparatory to Anglo-Saxon England, Being the Collected Papers of Frank Merry Stenton*, ed. D. M. Stenton (1970), 195, n. 2.

27. The name also occurs in the witness-list of *CS* 45, a charter dated to 679 and thus after the period which the legend assigns to the death of Eormenred, son of Eadbald. The witness of *CS* 45, however, may well have been a different person bearing the same name.

28. *Fl.Wig.*, I, 259, and *Leechdoms*, III, 422.

29. J. M. Kemble, *The Saxons in England*, rev. W. de G. Birch, I (1876), 148–9; H. M. Chadwick, *Studies on Anglo-Saxon Institutions* (1905), 271–4; and P. H. Blair, 'The letters of Pope Boniface V and the mission of Paulinus to

Northumbria', in *England before the Conquest, Studies in Primary Sources presented to Dorothy Whitlock*, ed. P. Clemoes and K. Hughes (1971), 7–8.

30. *EH*, II.3.

31. One difficulty is that *CS* 88, recording a grant made to Mildrith, is probably earlier than *CS* 96, recording a grant made to Domne Eafe. The explanation may lie in Goscelin's statement that Mildrith was consecrated abbess in her mother's lifetime (below, p. 135, ll. 27–32).

32. See above, p. 21; and *Leechdoms*, III, 402.

33. *De Gestis Regum Anglorum*, ed. W. Stubbs (RS, I, 1887), 16.

34. William, however, did know one or more of the texts of the legend, which he summarized elsewhere (*ibid.*, I, 267).

35. *EH*, IV.12 and F. M. Stenton, 'The supremacy of the Mercian kings', *EHR*, XXXIII (1918), 437–8, reprinted in *Preparatory to Anglo-Saxon England*, ed. D. M. Stenton, 51–2. I am grateful to Patrick Wormald for suggesting the substance of this paragraph to me.

36. If so, it was admittedly long delayed for Egbert had died in 673, but the possibility that the killings had motivated this Mercian intervention must nevertheless form a shred of evidence in favour of their reality.

37. *SO*, II, 11; *HP*, 99; *Leechdoms*, III, 422; and *DHE*, 3 and 4 (sec. 9).

38. N. P. Brooks, 'The development of military obligations in eighth- and ninth-century England', in Clemoes and Hughes (eds.), *op. cit.*, 75, n. 1.

39. See below, p. 93, ll. 3–4 and p. 114, l. 21; *The Chronicle of Hugh Candidus*, ed. W. T. Mellows (1949), 57; Additional 34, 633, f. 207; and *PL*, CLV, cols. 99–100. The *Genealogia regum Cantuariorum* does not name Domne Eafe but names instead Æthelthryth as a daughter of Eormenred; see *Fl.Wig.*, I, 259. This probably represents an error made by the compiler. All these versions, except that in Hugh Candidus's chronicle, name an additional daughter with a name similar to Eormenburg. This too probably arose from confusion in the course of the legend's history.

## [4] *The Mildrith Legend and the Independent Kingdom of Kent*

1. See above, pp. 19–22.

2. *SO*, II, 12.

3. *Ibid.*, 3 and 13, and *EH*, II.5.

4. See below, p. 94, l. 5.

5. *Fl.Wig.*, II, 248 and 258–60. These items appear together in the manuscripts.

6. *DHE*, 3 (secs. 8 and 9).

7. *SO*, II, 4.

8. *PL*, CLV, col. 99.

9. *The Chronicle of Hugh Candidus*, ed. W. T. Mellows (1949), 58.

10. Monumenta Germaniae Historica, Auctores Antiquissimi, *Chronica Minora*, III, ed. T. Mommsen (Berlin, 1888), 203, and D. Dumville, 'The Anglian collection of royal genealogies and regnal lists', *ASE*, v (1976), 31.

11. *Ibid.*, 23–50, and K. Sisam, 'Anglo-Saxon royal genealogies', *Procs. British Academy*, XXXIX (1953), 287–348.

12. *ASC* (A), s.a. 855.

13. Printed by J. O. Halliwell and T. Wright, *Reliquiae Antiquae, Scraps from Ancient Manuscripts illustrating chiefly Early English Literature and the English Language*, I (1841), 172–3.
14. *Les généalogies* (Typologie des sources du moyen âge occidental, XV, Turnhout, 1975), 13 and 23.
15. *DHE*, 9–19. D. W. Rollason, 'Lists of saints' resting-places in Anglo-Saxon England', *ASE*, VII (1978), 73–4, discusses the conjoining of the two texts and argues that the Mildrith Legend's compilers may have had access to a text resembling the *Secgan* in form. *Þa halgan* is there misleadingly referred to as the 'Kentish Royal Legend'.
16. *EH*, IV.19, II.9, and II.3.
17. *CS* 42, on which, see K. Harrison, *The Framework of Anglo-Saxon History to A.D. 900* (1978), 142.
18. *SO*, II, 11, and Additional 34, 633, f. 208v.
19. Reference should be made to Appendix A.
20. The Mildrith Legend is itself the evidence for the royal foundation of all of these except St Augustine's Abbey, on which see *EH*, I.33.
21. *EH*, I.33.
22. *ASC*, s.a. 669.
23. N. P. Brooks, *The Early History of the Church in Canterbury* (forthcoming).
24. *CS* 22 and *CS* 89; *ASC* s.a. (I am grateful to Dr Nicholas Brooks for this reference); and G. Ward, 'The forgotten Saxon nunnery of Saint Werburg at Hoo', *Arch. Cant.*, XLVII (1935), 117–25, which must be used with caution.
25. *Textus Roffensis, Rochester Cathedral Library Manuscript A.3.5.*, ed. P. H. Sawyer, Early English Manuscripts in Facsimile, XI (Copenhagen, 1962), f. 221r.
26. *SO*, II, 4–5 and 10.
27. See above, pp. 45–6.
28. See above, p. 35.
29. *CS* 97, 98, 148, 160, 289 and 411.
30. *CS* 36, 67, 73, 90, 190 and 191; and W. Levison, *England and the Continent in the Eighth Century* (1946), 346, where references are given.
31. *CS* 45, 176 and 243.
32. Levison, *op. cit.* 252.
33. H. M. Chadwick, *Studies on Anglo-Saxon Institutions* (1905), 249–62, and J. E. A. Jolliffe, *Pre-Feudal England: The Jutes* (1933), 41.
34. I owe this information to Mr Kenneth P. Witney who has generously allowed me to use the results of his researches which are to be published in his forthcoming book, *The Kingdom of Kent*. They supersede some of his previous conclusions in his *The Jutish Forest* (1976), 45–7, and also those of J. E. A. Jolliffe, 'The hidation of Kent', *EHR*, XLIV (1929), 614, and, in corrected form, *Pre-Feudal England*, 44, n. 7.
35. E. Ekwall, *The Concise Oxford Dictionary of English Place-Names* (4th edn, 1960), 309 and 158.
36. Chadwick, *op. cit.*, 249–50, and Witney, *Jutish Forest*, 42.
37. *Anglo-Saxon Charters*, ed. A. J. Robertson (2nd edn, 1956), no. 52.
38. Jolliffe, *Pre-Feudal England*, 45.
39. *Ibid.*

40. Ekwall, *op. cit.*, 158; *CS* 318 (cf. *CS* 380) and Jolliffe, *Pre-Feudal England*, 44–5. See also S. C. Hawkes, 'Eastry in Anglo-Saxon Kent: Its importance and a newly found grave', *Anglo-Saxon Studies in Archaeology and History*, I, ed. S. C. Hawkes, D. Brown and J. Campbell (BAR 72, 1979), 94–7.

41. They are *S. Mildryð* and *þa halgan*; see *Leechdoms*, III, 426, and *DHE*, 3 (sec. 12). The Gotha Text also gives this figure; see *HP*, 99. Those versions which give a figure other than 80 are noted below, pp. 66, 76 and 78.

42. *Domesday Book*, I (1783), 12.

43. Jolliffe, 'The hidation of kent', 612–18, and *Pre-Feudal England*, 44–6.

44. G. W. O. Addleshaw, *The Beginnings of the Parochial System* (St Anthony's Hall Publications, III, 3rd edn, 1970), 11–15; M. Deanesly, 'Early English and Gallic minsters', *TRHS*, 4th ser., XXIII (1941), 25–69; and F. M. Stenton, 'St Frideswide and her times', *Oxoniensia*, I (1936), 110–12, reprinted in *Preparatory to Anglo-Saxon England, Being the Collected Papers of Frank Merry Stenton*, ed. D. M. Stenton (1970), 231–2.

45. *The Domesday Monachorum of Christ Church, Canterbury*, ed. D. C. Douglas (1944), 9–11 and 78–9; and G. Ward, 'The list of Saxon churches in the *Domesday Monachorum* and the White Book of St Augustine's', *Arch. Cant.*, XLV (1933), 68–74, 76–7 and 84–8.

46. H. Mayr-Harting, *The Coming of Christianity to Anglo-Saxon England* (1972), 244–6.

47. M. Bateson, 'The origin and early history of double monasteries', *TRHS*, new ser., XIII (1899), 168–83.

48. See above, pp. 25–6.

49. See, for example, *The Laws of the Earliest English Kings*, ed. F. L. Attenborough (1922), 18.

50. On the Frankish church's attitude to feud, see J. M. Wallace-Hadrill, *The Long-Haired Kings and Other Studies in Frankish History* (1962), 126–7.

51. *Councils and Ecclesiastical Documents relating to Great Britain and Ireland*, ed. A. W. Haddan and W. Stubbs, III (1871), 180.

52. *EH*, IV.21.

53. *Leechdoms*, III, 426; *DHE*, 3 and 4 (sec. 12); and below, p. 96, l. 29 and p. 117, l. 34.

54. For assessments in coinage in the laws of King Æthelberht I, see Attenborough (ed.), *op. cit.*, 8. Assessments connected with oaths could be made in hides; see Chadwick, *op. cit.*, 134–9.

55. W. Stubbs, *The Constitutional History of England*, I (1875), 157, n. 2.

56. *Die Gesetze der Angelsachsen*, ed. F. Liebermann, II (1906), 513–14; cf. Paul Vinogradoff, 'Sulung and hide', *EHR*, XIX (1904), 282–6.

57. *Liber Eliensis*, ed. E. O. Blake (Camden 3rd ser., XCII, 1962), 66–7 and 79–80.

58. See above, p. 49, n. 9.

59. *EH*, III. 14 and III. 24; and Mayr-Harting, *op. cit.*, 106.

60. *Beowulf and the Fight at Finnsburg*, ed. F. Klaeber (3rd edn, Boston, 1950), ll. 102–9. I owe this comparison to Professor P. A. M. Clemoes, who has generously allowed me to use his paper delivered to the conference on the dating of *Beowulf*, held at the University of Toronto in April 1980. This paper will be published as part of that conference's proceedings.

61. *Leechdoms*, III, 424.

[5] *The Mildrith Legend in Tenth- and Eleventh-Century England*

1. F. M. Stenton, *Anglo-Saxon England* (3rd edn, 1971), 206–8 and 231.
2. *SO*, II, 143; *Historiae Anglicanae Scriptores X*, ed. R. Twysden (1652), col. 1908; and *ASC* (E), s.a. 1011 (which names the abbess Leofwine and does not name her abbey).
3. *TT* c.5.
4. See above, p. 46.
5. N. P. Brooks, *The Early History of the Church at Canterbury* (forthcoming), and W. Page (ed.) *The Victoria History of the County of Kent*, II (1926), 113–14, 126–8.
6. J. E. A. Jolliffe, 'The origin of the hundred in Kent', in *Historical Essays in Honour of James Tait*, ed. J. G. Edwards, V. H. Galbraith and E. F. Jacob (1933), 155–68.
7. *Alcuini Epistolae*, ed. Ernst Dümmler, Monumenta Germaniae Historica, Epistolae 4 (Berlin, 1895), no. 3; also printed (though not from the manuscript) in *Councils and Ecclesiastical Documents*, ed. A. W. Haddan and W. Stubbs (3 vols., 1869–71), III, 447–62, esp. 453–4. For what follows, I am indebted to J. L. Nelson, 'Royal saints and early medieval kingship', in *Sanctity and Secularity: The Church and the World*, ed. D. Baker, *Studies in Church History*, x (1973), 39–44.
8. *SO*, II, 52. On the reliability of these annals, see P. H. Blair, 'Some observations on the *Historia Regum* attributed to Symeon of Durham', in *Celt and Saxon: Studies in the Early British Border*, ed. N. K. Chadwick (1963), 86–99.
9. *SO*, II, 52, and, for Alcuin's letter, Dümmler (ed.), *op. cit.* in n. 7, 155. On Eardwulf's alleged resting-place, see D. W. Rollason, 'Lists of saints' resting-places in Anglo-Saxon England', *ASE*, VII (1978), 71.
10. *SO*, II, 63; and *DHE*, 11 (sec. 11). Ealhmund's history has been confused by the existence of the *Vita sancti Aelkmundi regis* in Gotha I.81 (printed in P. Grosjean, 'De codice hagiographico Gothano', *AB*, LVIII (1940), 178–83). This text, which represents Ealhmund as having been killed at the Battle of Kempsford, seems to be based on a confused reading of *Fl.Wig*, I, 64 (s.a. 800).
11. *ASC*, s.a. 792; M. R. James, 'Two lives of St Ethelbert, king and martyr', *EHR*, XXXII (1917), 214–44; and C. E. Wright, *The Cultivation of Saga in Anglo-Saxon England* (1939), 95–106.
12. T. D. Hardy, *Descriptive Catalogue of Materials Relating to Great Britain and Ireland to the End of the Reign of Henry VII* (RS, I, pt ii, 1862), no. 1069, is the fullest version of his *passio*. An abbreviated version is to be found in *NLA*, II, 110–13. See also E. S. Hartland, 'The legend of St Kenelm', *Trans. Bristol and Glos. Archaeol. Soc.*, XXXIX (1916), 13–65, and W. Levison, *England and the Continent in the Eighth Century* (1946), 249–51.
13. On Wigstan and other saints of the same type, see D. W. Rollason, *The Search for St Wigstan, Prince-Martyr of the Kingdom of Mercia* (1981), and *idem*, 'The cults of murdered royal saints in Anglo-Saxon England', *ASE*, XI (1982), forthcoming.
14. Levison, *op. cit.*, 249–50; and D. Knowles, *The Monastic Order in England* (2nd edn, 1966), 51.
15. *Chronicon Abbatiae de Evesham ad Annum 1418*, ed. W. D. Macray (RS, 1863), 83 and 325–6; and, on Evesham, Knowles, *op. cit.*, 52, and M. Lapidge, 'The medieval hagiography of St Ecgwine', *Vale of Evesham Hist. Soc. Research Papers*, VI (1977), 77–9.

16. Stenton, *op. cit.*, 372–3. S. Keynes, *The Diplomas of King Æthelred 'the Unready'* *978–1016* (1980), 233 and n. 7, argues in favour of the date 978 for the murder.

17. For the law, see *Die Gesetze der Angelsachsen*, ed. F. Liebermann, I (1898), 253; on the grounds for assigning it to Cnut's reign rather than Æthelred's, see P. Wormald, 'Æthelred the Lawmaker', *Ethelred the Unready: Papers from the Millenary Conference*, ed. D. Hill (BAR 59, 1978), 53–4. For a survey of the early development of the cult which is critical by implication of Wormald's argument, see Keynes, *op. cit.*, 169–71.

18. Printed in *Historians of the Church of York and its Archbishops*, ed. J. Raine (RS, I, 1879), 449–52; on the date, see *English Historical Documents, I, c. 500–1042*, ed. D. Whitelock (2nd edn, 1979), 911–12.

19. C. E. Fell, *Edward King and Martyr* (1971), xix–xx and 1–16.

20. See above, p. 17. For the attribution of the *Vita Oswaldi* to Byrhtferth, see M. Lapidge, 'The hermeneutic style in tenth-century Anglo-Latin literature', *ASE*, IV (1975), 91–4; and *idem*, 'Byrhtferth and the *Vita S. Ecgwini*', *Mediaeval Studies*, XLI (1979), 331–53.

21. See above, pp. 49–51.

22. D. J. V. Fisher. 'The anti-monastic reaction in the reign of Edward the Martyr', *Cambridge Hist. J.*, X (1950–2), 268–9. Keynes, *op. cit.*, 169–74, disputes this interpretation, suggesting that the translation of Edward's remains was not regarded as an attempt at expiation for his murder and that Ælfhere was not implicated in that crime. Keynes does not seem to attach any importance to the juxtaposition in the *Vita Oswaldi* of an account of Ælfhere's part in Edward's translation and an analysis of the attitude and fate of those guilty of Edward's death (*Historians of the Church of York*, ed. Raine, I, 450–1).

23. Stenton, *op. cit.*, 408–9. Stenton believed that an 'atmosphere of suspicion' surrounded Æthelred as a result of Edward's murder (*ibid.*, 373). Keynes, *op. cit.*, 163–74, argues that Æthelred was not involved in the murder and that contemporaries did not suspect him of complicity in it. The vagueness of the early sources makes possible divergent interpretations of these matters and Keynes's position is undoubtedly tenable. But his arguments are not decisive and the weight of probability seems to be in favour of Stenton's view. It is hard to believe that many contemporaries did not suspect Æthelred or his mother of involvement in a crime from which they benefited so directly.

24. Fisher, *op. cit.*, 255, and P. Stafford, 'The reign of Æthelred II: A study in the limitations on royal policy and action', in Hill (ed.), *op. cit.*, 21.

25. Knowles, *op. cit.*, 51, and below, pp. 102–3.

26. *ASC*, s.a. 983.

27. Fisher, *op. cit.*, 254.

28. See above, p. 28.

29. Rollason, *op. cit.* in n. 9, 73 and 82–3.

30. *Anglo-Saxon England* (3rd edn, 1971), 396.

31. F. E. Harmer (ed.), *Anglo-Saxon Writs* (1952), 191.

32. Monumenta Germaniae Historica, Legum Sectio III, *Concilia Aeri Karolini*, Ii, ed. A. Werminghoff (Hanover, 1906), 272.

33. *Chronicon de Evesham*, ed. Macray, 325–6.

34. See above, p. 19.

35. See above, pp. 20–2.

36. *The Life of St Anselm, Archbishop of Canterbury, by Eadmer*, ed. and trans. R. W. Southern (1962), 51.

37. *Chronicon de Evesham*, ed. Macray, 323 and 335–7.
38. *Life of Anselm*, ed. Southern, 51, and E. Bishop and F. Gasquet, *The Bosworth Psalter* (1908), 33, n. 1.
39. P. M. Korhammer, 'The origin of the Bosworth Psalter', *ASE*, II (1973), 173–87, esp. 179; for a different view, see Bishop and Gasquet, *op. cit.*, 27–34.
40. *Life of Anselm*, ed. Southern, 53–4. See also R. W. Southern, *St Anselm and his Biographer* (1963), 249.
41. See above, pp. 20–1, n. 33.
42. 'Raginald von Canterbury', ed. F. Liebermann, *Neues Archiv der Gesellschaft für ältere deutsche Geschichtskunde*, XIII (1888), 542–6, esp. 543, 1.55. See also, *ibid.*, 544–6.
43. William of Malmesbury, *De Gestis Regum Anglorum*, ed. W. Stubbs (RS, II, 1889), 389.
44. See below, p. 109, ll. 13–15.
45. *SO*, II, 9, and *Leechdoms*, III, 426; see below, Appendix A.
46. See below, pp. 75–9.
47. Lapidge, *op. cit.* in n. 20, 67–111, discusses this style.
48. See below, p. 109, ll. 5–6.
49. See below, p. 93, ll. 5–12.
50. See below, p. 114, l. 23–p. 115, l. 13.
51. For example, see below, pp. 13–14.
52. *TT*, on which see above, pp. 20–1.
53. *TT*, c. 17; cf. *HP*, 84.
54. *TT*, c. 4 and c. 30.
55. See above, pp. 21–2.
56. *HP*, 70–3.
57. See above, pp. 24–5.
58. *HP*, 107.
59. *Ibid.*, 78–83.
60. *Ibid.*, 73–5.
61. *Ibid.*, 84–5.
62. *Ibid.*, 88.
63. *Ibid.*, 75–7; and *TT*, c. 24–5, 18, 19 and 20.
64. *HP*, 85–7, 89–91 and 92–6.
65. See below, pp. 105–6.
66. Knowles, *op. cit.*, 539–42.
67. *HP*, 86, and Knowles, *op. cit.*, 103–4.
68. *ASC*, I, 287–92; and Knowles, *op. cit.*, 115–16, who pointed out (116, n. 1) the incorrectness of the assertion that Wido was a monk of St Augustine's Abbey.
69. See also M. Gibson, *Lanfranc of Bec* (1978), 189.
70. See above, p. 20. Cf. Southern, *Anselm and his Biographer*, 267, for the view that the disposition of native saints at Christ Church represented 'the final union of the Anglo-Saxon past and the Norman present'.
71. *HP*, 70.
72. *TT*, c. 23 and 18.
73. *Ibid.*, c. 13.
74. *Ibid.*, c. 17, 20 and 27.
75. *HP*, 70.
76. *TT*, c. 6–12; see also Harmer (ed.), *op. cit.*, no. 37.

77. *DHE*, 4 (sec. 12), and above, p. 48, n. 42.
78. See above, p. 21.
79. D. W. Rollason, 'The date of the parish-boundary of Minster-in-Thanet', *Arch. Cant.*, XCV (1979), 7–17.
80. C. Platt, *The Monastic Grange in Medieval England* (1969), 217–19.
81. *TT*, c. 14.
82. *TT*, c. 19 and 20–37.
83. *Ibid.*, c. 19.
84. See below, pp. 132–3.
85. *HP*, 70.

## Conclusion

1. T. D. Hardy, *Descriptive Catalogue of Materials Relating to Great Britain and Ireland to the End of the Reign of Henry VII* (RS, I, 1862), nos. 753–4, 714–25, 1098–1117 and 920–32.
2. Since charters may often have been fabricated in the same *scriptoria* where hagiographies were written, charter studies might benefit from such examinations of hagiography. See for example, W. Levison, *England and the Continent in the Eighth Century* (1946), 199–200.
3. See above, pp. 6–7.
4. P. Brown, 'The rise and function of the holy man in Late Antiquity', *J. Roman Studies*, LXI (1971), 80–101; and H. Mayr-Harting, 'Functions of a twelfth-century recluse: Wulfric of Haselbury', *History*, LX (1975), 337–52.
5. R. M. Clay, *Hermits and Anchorites of England* (1914).

## APPENDIX B: *Introduction*

1. A much abbreviated version occurs in *NLA*, I, 429–31.
2. *Chronicon Abbatiae Ramesiensis*, ed. W. D. Macray (RS, 1886), 107, 114 and 339, and T. D. Hardy, *Descriptive Catalogue of Materials Relating to Great Britain and Ireland to the End of the Reign of Henry VII* (RS, I, 1862), nos. 516–19. It should be noted, however, that f. 83v contains, after an account of Kenelm's life and miracles, the text of a hymn to Kenelm which might suggest that the manuscript was associated with Winchcombe, of which house Kenelm was patron.

## APPENDIX B: *Bodley 285 Text*

1. Pope Gregory I (590–604). The influence of *EH*, I, 23–7, is clear in the passage which follows.
2. Æthelberht I, king of Kent (d. 616).
3. Canterbury (Kent).

4. Bede says he died on 24 February (*EH*, II.5).
5. Eadbald (616–40), whose apostasy and reconversion is described by Bede in *EH*, II. 5 and 6.
6. Æthelburg, on whose nickname see *EH*, II, 9.
7. Edwin, king of Northumbria (616–32). On this marriage, see *ibid.*
8. Rochester (Kent).
9. For Bede's account of Paulinus, see *EH*, II. 9 and following; and *EH*, II, 20, which has verbal similarities to this passage.
10. This person is named Eanswith in other versions of this material (see above, pp. 9, 80, 81, 82, 83, 85, 86.
11. Folkestone (Kent).
12. 640–64.
13. Æthelthryth and Seaxburg were daughters of Anna, king of the East Angles (see Bede, *EH*, III, 8).
14. Egbert I (664–73).
15. Much Wenlock (Shropshire).
16. Isle of Thanet (Kent).
17. St Augustine's Abbey, Canterbury.
18. Eastry (Kent).
19. Compare Matthew 10.26 and Luke 12.2.
20. Theodore, archbishop of Canterbury (668–90).
21. Chelles (near Paris).
22. Daniel 3.
23. Ebbsfleet (Kent).
24. Æthelred (978/9–1016).
25. Æthelwine, ealdorman of East Anglia (d. 992).
26. Ramsey (Huntingdonshire), founded c. 969 by a grant to Oswald, archbishop of York (972–92).
27. Æscwig, bishop of Dorchester (975 × 9–1002).
28. Cf. *SO*, II, 10.
29. Great or Little Wakering (Essex).
30. There is an entry for the princes under this date in a thirteenth-century kalendar from St Augustine's Abbey, Canterbury (*English Benedictine Kalendars after A.D. 1100*, ed. F. Wormald, I [Henry Bradshaw Society, LXXVII, 1939], 60.) However, the only pre-1100 kalendar to record their feast is that in Cambridge, Corpus Christi College MS 9, which assigns it to 14 October rather than 17 October (*English Kalendars before A.D. 1100*, ed. F. Wormald [Henry Bradshaw Society, LXXII, 1934], 235 and vii, where the kalendar is printed and its provenance discussed).

APPENDIX C: *Introduction*

1. T. D. Hardy, *Descriptive Catalogue of Materials Relating to Great Britain and Ireland to the End of the Reign of Henry VII* (RS, I, 1862), no. 888, states that a *Vita sanctae Mildrethae* is extant in Rome, Bibliotheca Apostolica Vaticana, MS Reginensis 587; but this is erroneous. I am grateful to the Prefect of the Vatican Library for his help in this matter.

2. J. Planta, *A Catalogue of Manuscripts in the Cottonian Library Deposited in the British Museum* (1802), 442; *New Palaeographical Society*, 1st ser., II, pt 1 (1903–12), pl. 85; C. R. Dodwell, *The Canterbury School of Illumination, 1066–1200* (1954), 123; and N. R. Ker, *English Manuscripts in the Century after the Norman Conquest* (1960), 27 and 29 and pl. 11.

3. This view of the relationship of A and B is supported by Dodwell, *op. cit.*, 28, 52 and 123.

4. *A Catalogue of the Harleian Manuscripts in the British Museum*, I (1808), 31, and Dodwell, *op. cit.*, 123.

5. A. G. Watson, *The Library of Sir Simonds d'Ewes* (1966), 116–17, pl. 4 and frontispiece; and C. E. Wright, *Fontes Harleiani: A Study of the Sources of the Harleian Collection of Manuscripts Preserved in the Department of Manuscripts in the British Museum* (1972), 373.

6. *Historiae Anglicanae Scriptores X*, ed. R. Twysden (1652), col. 1912.

7. *Catalogue of Harleian Manuscripts*, III (1808), 95; Ker, *op. cit.*, 30, and Wright, *op. cit.*, 437.

8. *Catalogus Codicum Manuscriptorum Bibliothecae Bodleianae, Partis Quintae, Fasciculus Secundus*, ed. W. D. Macray (1878), cols. 224–5, and C. E. Fell, *Edward, King and Martyr* (1971), viii.

9. N. R. Ker, *Medieval Libraries of Great Britain* (2nd edn, 1964), 197.

10. P. Grosjean, 'Catalogus codicum hagiographicorum latinorum bibliothecarum Dubliniensium', *AB*, XLVI (1928), 86–8, and T. K. Abbot, *Catalogue of the Manuscripts in the Library of Trinity College, Dublin* (Dublin and London, 1900), no. 72.

11. P. Grosjean, 'De codice hagiographico Gothano', *AB*, LVIII (1940), 90–103 and 177–204, and Fell, *op. cit.*, vi–vii.

12. For its former contents, see T. Smith, *Catalogus Librorum Manuscriptorum Bibliothecae Cottonianae* (1696), 66–7.

13. David Yerkes, 'The earliest fragments of Goscelin's writings on St Mildred' (forthcoming). I am extremely grateful to Mr Yerkes for drawing my attention to this manuscript and for allowing me access to his paper before publication.

14. Yerkes, *op. cit.*

## APPENDIX C: *Vita Mildrethae*

1. This is a reference to Jerome's second preface to the Book of Job, *Biblia Sacra Vulgatae Editionis* (Paris, 1837), xiv, which is also reflected in *Quocirca, O karissimi mei*. I owe this reference to Mr B. S. Benedikz.

2. C. H. Talbot considered such openings to be characteristic of Goscelin's style and cited parallel examples from works attributed to him in 'The *Liber Confortatorius* of Goscelin of St Bertin', Analecta Monastica, 3rd ser., *Studia Anselmiana*, XXXVII (1955), 15.

3. Æthelbert I, king of Kent (d. 616).

4. Augustine, archbishop of Canterbury (597–604).

5. Pope Gregory I (590–604).

6. River Humber.

7. *EH*, II. 5; *Die Gesetze der Angelsachsen*, ed. F. Liebermann (1898), I, 3–8.

8. Eadbald, king of Kent (616–40). The following account of his apostasy and reconversion is based on Bede, *EH*, II. 5 and 6.

9. All manuscripts except E and F err in naming this king as Sigeberht. This error occurs in Æthelweard and in several manuscripts of Bede's *Ecclesiastical History*, see *Venerabilis Bedae Opera Historica*, ed. C. Plummer (2 vols., 1896), I, 353, n. 7, and II, 79. As regards Sæberht's sons, Bede makes it clear that they had always been pagan (*EH*, II. 5).

10. Mellitus, bishop of London (601 × 4–24), Justus, bishop of Rochester (604–24) and Laurence, archbishop of Canterbury (604–19).

11. The meaning seems to be: 'You have not resisted until your blood is shed, and you flee'.

12. John 10.11.

13. Folkestone (Kent). The corresponding personal name forms are: Ymme, Eormenred, Eorcenberht and Eanswith.

14. Song of Songs 3.10.

15. I have been unable to trace this reference.

16. Much Wenlock (Shropshire).

17. On Mildrith's translation from Minster-in-Thanet to St Augustine's Abbey, Canterbury, in 1035, see above, p. 19.

18. Merewalh, king of the Magonsætan.

19. *EH*, V. 24.

20. Wulfhere, king of the Mercians (657–74), on whom see *EH*, III, 24 and 30, and IV. 3 and 13; and *Fl.Wig.*, I, 32.

21. Æthelred, king of the Mercians (674–704), on whom see *EH*, V. 19.

22. For a possible source for the following account, see *NLA*, II, 130–2.

23. Peterborough (Northamptonshire).

24. Castor (Northamptonshire).

25. This sentence, which has an over-complex construction, seems to mean: 'Cineswith, who was married to Offa, king of the West Angles, wrested the palm of perpetual virginity and, impetuous as she was, seized the Kingdom of Heaven from Mary, mistress of the world, who appeared to her in splendour, saying "I come watered with your tears"'. Cineswith's husband was presumably Offa, king of the East Saxons, who was a contemporary of Æthelred of Mercia and who abdicated in 709, not Offa of Mercia (757–96) as Goscelin here states.

26. *EH*, III. 8.

27. Seaxburg.

28. Anna, king of the East Angles (d. 654).

29. Æthelthryth.

30. Egbert, king of Kent (664–73).

31. Eorcengota (on whom, *see EH*, III. 8) and Eormenhild.

32. Werburg.

33. Hanbury (Staffordshire).

34. This phrase is obscure and the text is probably corrupt. The meaning is presumably that the princes were twin stars and the lights of their father's life.

35. Eorcenberht, king of Kent (640–64).

36. Archbishop of Canterbury (655–64).

37. *EH*, IV. 1.

38. This unusual phrase seems to mean 'night having fallen'.

39. Eastry (Kent).

40. Theodore, archbishop of Canterbury (668–90).
41. Adrian, abbot of St Augustine's Abbey, Canterbury.
42. *EH*, IV. 1.
43. A charming valley in Thessaly, whence applied to beautiful valleys in general.
44. St Augustine's Abbey, Canterbury.
45. Dathan and Abiron were the sons of Eliab who rebelled against Moses and were swallowed by the earth (Numbers 16).
46. The meaning seems to be: 'of the very religious crowd of virgins, which she the first foundress of the church first assembled and instituted, she was the first abbess.'
47. *EH*, IV. 2.
48. *EH*, III. 8.
49. Psalms 44. 11–12.
50. Chelles (near Paris).
51. Les Andelys (Seine-Maritime). See *EH*, III. 8.
52. Psalms 76. 20.
53. Psalms 118. 1–2 and 5.
54. In his introduction to the *Vita Bertilae abbatissae Calensis*, in Monumenta Germaniae Historica, *Scriptores Rerum Merovingicarum*, VI, ed. B. Krusch and W. Levison (Hanover, 1913), 95–109, W. Levison points out that Bertila is said to have ruled the abbey for 46 years and she died between 703 and 713, probably after 710. Since Mildrith was already abbess of Minster-in-Thanet in 696 (*CS* 88), the abbess who received her at Chelles would have been Bertila and not Wilcoma. Despite this and Levison's rejection of Goscelin's reference as '*omnino fabulosa*', there may have been a tradition at Chelles to the effect that Bertila was succeeded first by an abbess called Sigissa and then by Wilcoma, the former having died in 708 (*Gallia Christiana* [Paris, 1744], VII, cols. 558–60, citing William Thorne and a catalogue of abbesses drawn up from the charters of Chelles). The chronology remains problematic but the question may merit further investigation.
55. Compare *Venerabilis Bedae Opera Historica*, ed. Plummer, II, 219.
56. Isaiah 14. 13–14.
57. The infinitives *cedere* and *relinquere* seem to be dependent on *impatiens*. For this construction, see B. H. Kennedy, *Revised Latin Primer*, ed. and futher rev. J. Mountford (1962), sec. 373.
58. There is a possibility that the vestal virgin Amata is being alluded to here.
59. I Corinthians 7. 9.
60. I Timothy 5. 14.
61. The meaning of this sentence seems to be: 'These and similar words guarded the wholly protesting girl from the inflamed and perverted (*transversa*) tyrant'.
62. Matthew 23. 3.
63. I Peter 2. 18; compare the Rule of St Benedict, Chapter 4, Section 60.
64. The meaning seems to be 'idolater'. This medieval rendering of *idololatres* or *idololatris* is noted in *Revised Medieval Latin Word-List from British and Irish Sources*, ed. R. E. Latham (1965), s.v. *idolum*.
65. Acts 5. 29.
66. II Corinthians 3. 6.
67. II Corinthians 3. 17.
68. Psalms 123. 2 and 3.

69. Lucia was a virgin martyr at Syracuse under Diocletian. On her passion, see *BHL* 4992 and A. Beaugrand, *Sainte Lucie* (Paris, 1882).
70. Daniel 3.
71. Agnes, virgin martyr at Rome.
72. The meaning of this phrase seems to be: 'as they were unbolting it'.
73. Psalms 16. 3.
74. The meaning seems to be: 'and she began to blush more for the palm acquired by the virgin than for her own tyranny'.
75. Tisiphone was one of the Furies.
76. The meaning seems to be: 'For greatly did the elegance of Christ inform and teach the transmarine world in her, making known what gold, what gems Christ himself possessed in England'. The grammar appears to be defective.
77. The meaning seems to be: 'She wished to set forth herself for the liberation of her daughter, but there was insufficient reason in this piety, both because the constant illness, which was preparing her for heaven, forbade her, and because she might be despised as a stranger'.
78. For this alternative spelling of *derivat*, see *Revised Medieval Latin Word-List*, ed. Latham, s.v. *derivatio*.
79. Virgil, *Aeneid*, II. 120–1.
80. Exodus 14. 15.
81. Exodus 6. 1.
82. I have been unable to trace this reference.
83. 'Gilded'. See *Revised Medieval Latin Word-List*, ed. Latham, s.v. *inauratio*.
84. Psalms 16. 6.
85. Psalms 118.
86. Compare Virgil, *Aeneid*, IV, 581–3.
87. II Corinthians 1. 3.
88. II Corinthians 2. 14.
89. Ebbsfleet (Kent).
90. The motif of footprints miraculously imprinting themselves on rocks is common both in hagiography and in secular legend. See, for example, S. Reinach, 'Les Monuments de pierre brute dans le langage et les croyances populaires', *Revue Archéologique*, 3rd ser., XXI (1893), 223–6. For the survival of this tradition about Mildrith in the eighteenth century, see J. Lewis, *The History and Antiquities as well Ecclesiastical as Civil of the Isle of Tenet in Kent* (2nd edn, 1736), 88.
91. Genesis 28. 22 and Psalms 117. 22.
92. Isaiah, 49. 23 and 60. 14.
93. Song of Songs 3. 6.
94. Genesis 46. 30.
95. This word, which appears to be a neologism, seems to mean 'relations by marriage', possibly 'daughters-in-law'.
96. The meaning of this sentence seems to be: 'But, so that nothing should be lacking to her by any grace, she should be consecrated a third time, so that what she was in mind, body and life, she should be also in habit, profession and religion, that is holy in the faith, hope and charity of the Holy Trinity'.
97. Song of Songs 6. 8.
98. Compare Exodus 33. 17 and Isaiah 62. 2.
99. *Ibid*. 2. 14.
100. *Ibid*. 4. 3.

101. *Ibid.* 1. 9.
102. *Ibid.* 2. 16.
103. *Ibid.* 3. 4.
104. Psalms 44. 5.
105. *Ibid.* 44. 3.
106. *Ibid.* 44. 15.
107. Numbers 11. 12.
108. Cf. Psalms 67. 26.
109. A queen of the Amazons who fought against the Greeks at Troy and was killed by Achilles (see e.g., Virgil, *Aeneid*, I, 491).
110. I have been unable to trace the source of this allusion.
111. The women of Lemnos killed all their husbands in one night.
112. Datianus was a governor in Spain under Diocletian. He was responsible for persecuting Christians, including Vincent of Saragossa (d. 304) who is mentioned here. See, for example, the *Acta S. Vincentii martyris, ASS, Ian.,* II, 393–8.
113. This appears to be a neologism, perhaps meaning 'war-monger'.
114. Song of Songs 5. 2.
115. Psalms 16.8 and 56.2.
116. Agnes was a virgin martyr in Rome in the third or fourth century. A passion of hers, which includes the sentence quoted here, is printed in *PL,* XVII, cols. 735–42 (*BHL* 156).
117. Song of Songs 7. 4.
118. Job 31. 35.
119. Psalms 119. 5–6.
120. *Ibid.* 9. 1.
121. *Ibid.* 12. 1.
122. *Ibid.* 34. 17.
123. *Ibid.* 41. 3.
124. Song of Songs 5. 6.
125. *Ibid.* 3. 1.
126. *Ibid.* 5. 6 and 8.
127. *Ibid.* 3. 4.
128. *Ibid.* 2. 10–12.
129. *Ibid.* 4. 8.
130. 13 July.
131. On Eadburg, abbess of Minster-in-Thanet, see above, pp. 13, 16, 21–4, 35–6.
132. Goscelin appears to be referring to the work of Pope Gregory I. I have however, been unable to trace the quotations in that author's best-known work, the *Cura Pastoralis,* or in the indexes to the edition of his works in *PL,* LXXV–LXXIX.
133. Cuthbert, archbishop of Canterbury (740–60).
134. A reference to Goscelin's *TT.*

# Index